The Artificial Language Movement

THE LANGUAGE LIBRARY

EDITED BY DAVID CRYSTAL

The Artificial Language Movement

ANDREW LARGE

Basil Blackwell
in association with
André Deutsch

© Andrew Large 1985

First published 1985

Basil Blackwell Ltd
108 Cowley Road, Oxford OX4 1JF, UK

Basil Blackwell Inc.
432 Park Avenue South, Suite 1505,
New York, NY 10016, USA

in association with André Deutsch Limited
105 Great Russell Street, London WC1B 3LJ, England

British Library Cataloguing in Publication Data

Large, Andrew
  The artificial language movement. — (The
  Language library)
  1. Languages, Artificial
  I. Title
  499'.99   PM8008

ISBN 0-631-14497-8

Library of Congress Cataloging in Publication Data

Large, Andrew.
  The artificial language movement.
  (The Language library)
  Bibliography: p.
  Includes index.
  1. Languages, Artificial.   I. Title.   II. Series.
PM8008.L28   1985   499'.99   85—6206
ISBN 0-631-14497-8

Typeset by Pioneer, East Sussex.
Printed in Great Britain by
Page Bros (Norwich) Ltd.

Contents

Introduction

Since the early seventeenth century, several hundred artificial language schemes have been constructed in the hope that a universal medium for international communication can be adopted. Unlike any natural language, which already possesses a group of native speakers, an artificial language would represent, it is argued, a neutral tongue acceptable to all. Furthermore, it has variously been posited that artificial languages facilitate logical thought, eliminate ambiguity of expression, and foster the brotherhood of mankind. Whether or not such claims can be substantiated, a significant number of men and women over the last four centuries have been prepared to devote their energies to the construction and active support of artificial languages. In some cases these language schemes have been intended to act as a universal language in place of all existing languages: one language for the world. More usually, however, the language constructors have shouldered less ambitious aims; to create an international auxiliary language which would function for international communication alongside its parochial natural cousins.

No attempt has been made in this study to catalogue each of the numerous artificial language schemes devised by human ingenuity. Rather, a sample of the more interesting or more significant has been selected in order to chart the development of the artificial language movement against its historical background and to assess its current status and future prospects. Not all artificial languages have been devised to facilitate human communication. Languages such as Fortran and Pascal are artificial constructions possessing syntax and vocabulary, but they are written to act as a medium through which instructions can be passed from a human to a computer. Such computer languages fall outside the remit of this work.

Part I traces the historical development of artificial languages from the seventeenth century until the outbreak of the First World War. The starting point is relatively easy to justify. Although the idea of constructing an artificial language had been voiced in earlier times, the first real flowering of interest in this line of activity bloomed in the age of Descartes and Leibniz. Some of the greatest minds in Europe were directed towards this linguistic puzzle during the seventeenth century, and the philosophical language schemes which emerged remain a fascinating reminder of the intellectual richness and diversity of that period. The conclusion of this historical section is perhaps more controversial, yet the outbreak of war in 1914, in retrospect, marked the end of the period of hope for the artificial language movement. From the middle of the nineteenth century the popularity of constructed language schemes had grown, partly at least in answer to the expansion of international contacts in politics, trade, science and the arts. With the emergence of Volapük and then Esperanto, artificial languages having the power to attract a mass following now promised ultimate success after so many failures. The tide of nationalism, alas, proved more endurable than the ripple of internationalism; the forward march of Esperanto was brought to a bloody halt with the Sarajevan assassination, never really to be fully resumed thereafter.

Part II abandons the chronological for a thematic approach. The Esperanto language and movement is examined in some detail, not because of any predilection on the author's part for this language but because of its undoubted dominance in recent decades, whether such dominance is measured in terms of active support or passive acquaintanceship. In order to restore some balance, however, the major rivals of Esperanto are then examined in order to ascertain whether any one of them holds the seeds of success. Finally, the present condition and future prospects of the artificial language movement are considered. Is the world likely to find itself the proud possessor of an international language and be rid of the curse dealt to mankind at faraway Babel? Can human ingenuity now compensate for that earlier human frailty?

Throughout this work the terms 'artificial' and 'constructed' are interchangeably linked with 'language' despite the objections frequently expressed by the committed against the former. Julius Balbin, for example, remarked of one language, Esperanto:

It is regrettable that after more than three generations of the uninterrupted growth, evolution, worldwide diffusion of Esperanto and a large body of literary achievement in the language . . . one still has to 'defend' Esperanto against linguists who refuse to see its reality as a fully developed language and who call it 'artificial', if they choose to notice it at all. We are not unaware of the perjorative connotations that this adjective carries. In most people's minds the word evokes such synonyms as colorless, dead, pale, unable to grow, develop and evolve, or lifeless.[1]

In using 'artificial' there has been no intention to imply that languages devised by men and women are necessarily any less workable as languages than those which have evolved over the millenia, nor that 'natural' languages (or ethnic languages as Balbin would have them called) are free from conscious and unconscious manipulation by social and individual forces.

Some studies are intended to break new ground, to mine a rich vein of archive material in order to corroborate or even overturn existing theories and perceptions. Others plough a more modest furrow, satisfied if they are able to synthesise existing scholarship into a coherent, even a lucid, pattern, through which ideas and events can the better be understood. It is to the latter tradition that this book most certainly belongs. Neither specialised 'in-depth' linguistic analyses nor important new documentary sources will be unearthed here. Rather, the task will have been accomplished if the causes and effects, the successess and failures of the artificial language movement against its historical and social back-cloth, are realised.

An author writing in a field so bedevilled by partisanship and intolerance must declare his own standpoint. No attempt has consciously been made to present the case for one language scheme at the expense of the others. That elusive quarry, objectivity, has been pursued, if not always caught. As Leszek Kolakowski observed at the outset of his investigation into the *Main currents of Marxism,* an area equally plagued by controversy:

Naturally an author's opinions and preferences are bound to be reflected in his presentation of the material, his selection of themes, and the relative importance he attaches to different ideas, events, writings and individuals. But it would be impossible to compile a historical manual of any kind — whether of political history, the history of ideas, or the history of art — if we were to suppose that every presentation of the facts is equally distorted by the author's personal views and is in fact a more or less arbitrary construction, so that there is no such thing as a historical account but only a series of historical assessments.[2]

I should like to express my thanks to the various artificial language societies which have kindly supplied me with information on their activities, and hope they will forgive me if I have not always interpreted it quite as they would themselves. I am also obliged for the assistance rendered by the staffs of the National Library of Wales and the Library at the College of Librarianship Wales. Mrs Wendy Reynolds has gallantly battled with my handwriting to type a considerable part of the text, and her skill and perseverance in this task is much appreciated. Above all, however, my gratitude is expressed to my family — Valerie, Amanda and now also Kirsty — who have once again accepted my absences and excused my domestic failings during the preparation of this book; to them it is dedicated.

Andrew Large
Comins Coch
Aberystwyth

PART I

Artificial Languages in Historical Perspective

1

Origins

Men and women in all probability have dreamed of a common language since first they found it impossible to talk with neighbouring peoples speaking strange and incomprehensible tongues. Mime and gesture are but poor substitutes for the flexibility and precision of language, 'without a doubt, the most momentous and at the same time the most mysterious product of the human mind'.[1] The theme of a universal language as an essential element in any vision of utopia is shared by many diverse cultures. In the Judaic tradition, the Book of Genesis looks back to a golden past when 'the whole earth was of one language, and of one speech'. The Manichaean religion of Persia, on the other hand, looked forward to the reign of the fair Ohrmazd who would replace his evil twin, Ahriman, as king over the second half of the world's course, when men would live happily with one law, one government and one language for all.

A belief that such a vision can become reality has caught the imagination of many individuals over the centuries. According to Mario Pei, Diodorus Siculus, a Greek historian in the first century BC and the Graeco-Roman physician, Galen ($c.130-200$), were both interested in the idea of a universal language.[2] St Hildegarde, a twelfth-century Abbess of Rupertsberg in the diocese of Mainz is reputed actually to have constructed a language composed of 900 words with an alphabet of 23 letters.[3] It was in the seventeenth century, however, that the idea of constructing a universal language really became a serious proposition, engaging the attention of the leading thinkers of the day.

THE SCIENTIFIC REVOLUTION

In many respects, the seventeenth century was not a happy one for the peoples of Europe. Cooler and wetter summers reduced the crop growing season, causing poor harvests and famine for a population almost entirely dependent on vegetables and cereals. Epidemics — plague, typhus and smallpox — swept the continent wreaking, especially on the overcrowded cities, a havoc unchecked by the medical profession. The plague was often spread by armies which ate and burned their way across Europe in a century when states became more efficient organisations for fighting wars: Central Europe in particular was devastated by the Thirty Years' War which raged from 1618 until 1648. Rebellion and revolution also flared in many localities, and in England a civil war was fought, a king beheaded and a Lord Protector briefly installed.

Despite these calamities, the arts flourished: Racine, Molière, Donne, Shakespeare, Rembrandt, Rubens, Van Dyck, Vermeer and many others were at work in the seventeenth century. In the realm of political thought, Hobbes, Locke and Spinoza propounded their philosophies while such artists as Bernini, Wren and Inigo Jones wrought their ideas in stone. But above all, this century is remembered for its men of science. Galileo, Kepler and Descartes; Boyle, Leibniz and Newton, to name just a few: the list is long and distinguished. It is not so much their individual contributions, however, as their approach to scientific research which has justified the term 'scientific revolution' to describe this period. The older habits of speculation in natural philosophy, based upon Aristotelian principles, were being replaced by systematic research and experimentation. As *The new Cambridge modern history* sums up, 'the distinctive new move made in scientific research was to look for the intelligibility of nature not in immediate observation but in an underlying mathematical and mechanical structure, and to seek by systematic and quantitative theoretical analysis and experimentation to discover the one actual structure of this real world.'[4] The most systematic critic of the Aristotelian approach to science and the man whose name is now most closely linked to the new developments in scientific thinking was Francis Bacon, described by Paolo Rossi as 'the first modern philosopher, a typical product of Renaissance culture, the theorist and father of empiricism, a rationalist, the philosopher of industrial science, a man who was saturated in magic and alchemy, the demolisher of scholastic tradition, a medieval philosopher haunted by a modern dream'.[5] And it is Bacon who forges our link with universal language schemes in the seventeenth century. In his influential writing Bacon drew attention to the possibility of representing things instead of sounds by 'real characters' rather than letters, characters which could be understood regardless of language. His ideas had been triggered by Chinese which he thought offered a form of communication to solve the problem of language diversity. By his writings, Bacon suggested a line of enquiry which was to be pursued by some of Europe's leading minds in the following decades.

A fascination with language in the seventeenth century, in fact, extended beyond a small group of learned 'amateurs and scientists', as they have been described, to much broader strata of society. A leading scholar of the period has described it as one in which 'educated men, from merchant to bishop, thought, spoke and wrote about language as never before, and possibly as never since.'[6] Enthusiasts disputed the origin of language, debated the best methods of language teaching, constructed shorthand systems, delved into the art of cryptography, sought means of communicating with the deaf and dumb and, as Thomas Sprat wrote of the Royal Society, 'made a constant Resolution, to reject all the amplifications, digressions, and swellings of style: to return back to the primitive purity, and shortness, when men deliver'd so many *things*, almost in an equal number of *words*'.[7] Above all, however, the challenge of constructing a language which should serve as a universal means of communication seized the imagination. In this way would the curse of Babel be overcome.

THE ROLE OF LATIN

It may seem perverse that universal language schemes should attract so much attention when one language had for centuries successfully played an international role, at least in the case of Western civilisation. Latin had initially been spread by the might of Imperial Rome, and then later by the no less effective spiritual influence of the Church. Throughout the feudal era the language of the educated was almost uniformly Latin:

On the one hand there was the immense majority of uneducated people, each one imprisoned in his regional dialect, limited, so far as literary culture was concerned, to a few secular poems transmitted almost exclusively by word of mouth, and to those pious cantilenas which well-meaning clerics composed in the vulgar tongue for the benefit of simple folk and which they sometimes committed to parchment. On the other hand, there was the little handful of educated people who, constantly alternating between the local everyday speech and the universal language of learning, were in the true sense bilingual.[8]

Latin was not only the medium of instruction in schools but it was the only language taught. It reigned supreme as the language of learned discourse in Europe at the outset of the sixteenth century. Yet by the end of the following century its role, though by no means at an end, was undoubtedly greatly diminished. The universal language movement anticipated this decline in Latin as an effective means of international communication, but also played its own part in hastening the eclipse. Why should men who were passionately committed to establishing a universal language turn their backs on the one natural language which at that time still seemed capable of fulfilling this role? What factors persuaded them to renounce attempts to revive the flagging fortunes of Latin and instead to invest their considerable talents in a different solution?

So long as international intercourse was largely confined to Europe, and was mainly the prerogative of a scholastic elite, it did not greatly matter that the vast majority of the population was ignorant of Latin. But the growing need of merchants and traders for an effective means of communicating with clients on the other side of the continent was not so easily met by the Roman language. Furthermore, the establishment of commercial and religious relations with the Far East, India, the West Indies and the Americas in the sixteenth century highlighted the obvious weakness of Latin as a universal rather than a pan-European language. The work of converting the heathen was handicapped for want of a common language in which missionaries could instruct their new brethren. As one of the early universal language projectors, Cave Beck, expressed it, a universal character 'would much advantage mankind in their civil commerce, and be a singular means of propagating all sorts of Learning and true Religion in the world'.[9]

A consequence of increasing scientific activity was a need and desire on the part of Europe's scientists to exchange ideas and research findings. In France, for example, the friar, Marin Mersenne, made his convent cell a meeting place for scientific discussions and experiments, and from 1620 to 1648 the centre of a vast and systematic scientific correspondence by which he maintained a flow of information between most of the leading scientists of the day. In 1666 the Académie royale des Sciences was founded in Paris and a few years earlier, in 1662, the Royal Society in London received its charter from Charles II. Its first secretary, Henry Oldenberg, like Mersenne, conducted a voluminous correspondence with scientists at home and abroad, acting as a sort of clearing bank for ideas. It was assumed that every scientist would be able to read Latin and many scientific works did continue to be written in that language; in 1687, for example, Isaac Newton chose to publish his *Principia mathematica* in Latin. Nevertheless, the European vernacular languages were beginning to challenge the supremacy of Latin, especially when the author wished to reach a wider local audience: the gentry in the countryside and the artisans and craftsmen in the town. By 1704, when Newton published his *Opticks,* he had decided to switch from Latin to English. From the second half of the seventeenth century, it could no longer be assumed that all important works would be published in Latin.

As well as keeping abreast of scientific publications, scientists travelled to foreign libraries and attended meetings abroad. Like merchants, they needed to communicate orally, but for this purpose Latin was becoming increasingly unsuitable. Despite efforts to re-establish the purity of classical Latin, the language, especially in its oral form, was showing signs of breaking down into dialects. The pronunciation of Latin by English speakers was especially difficult for others to understand, and for a growing number of foreigners the answer increasingly became to learn English, a task which they found by no means easy.

This debasement of medieval Latin had concerned Renaissance scholars, who argued for a return to the pure Latin such as Cicero or any other educated Roman would have spoken. They appreciated that 'if corrupted, the language forthwith ceases to be a unity, portions of the country one by one will have its own corruptions of dialect Latin' and people would not understand one another.[10] Yet their attempts to re-establish Latin only seemed to emphasise its unsuitability for modern needs. Medieval Latin might have been debased, but at least it was a living language in which people could carouse and swear as well as engage in scholarly discourse. The attempt to re-classicalise the language only served to emphasise its exclusiveness at a time when social, cultural, economic and political participation was becoming more democratic.

Educational considerations also played a part in condemning the role of Latin as an everyday language. A growing body of opinion already believed that too much school time was wasted by students struggling with the intricacies of Latin grammar; if classical purity was the only acceptable objective then even less time would be left for other scholastic pursuits. Some critics argued for better ways of teaching classical languages. Joseph Webbe, for example, believed that languages are not learnt by means of rules but by reading and unconsciously assimilating sentence-patterns. He also asserted that literal translation from English to Latin and *vice versa* is totally impossible because of their different structures. He proposed that Latin should be taught by the structural analysis of Latin and English into 'pieces' which were to be learnt by children as entities without further analysis.[11] The Czech scholar, Comenius (Jan Amos Komensky), was especially interested in educational matters, and met with instant and phenomenal success with his *Janua linguarum reserata* ('The gate of language unlocked'), published in 1631. This original work provided some 8,000 words arranged in sentences which were divided into sections dealing with various classes of phenomena.

Comenius was concerned to associate a word with the thing it represented, and also to ensure that Latin was studied as a means of acquiring knowledge about the world rather than an arid exercise in rote learning: 'The study of languages, especially in youth, should be joined to that of objects, that our acquaintance with the objective world and with language, that is to say, our knowledge of facts and our power to express them, may progress side by side.'[12] Later, in his very influential *Orbis sensualium pictus* (The world of sense objects pictured) Comenius provided illustrations to help the student in learning Latin. (It is interesting that Comenius, in fact, remained sceptical about teaching Latin and was an important proponent of the universal language ideal, especially in his *Via lucis* (The way of light), published in 1642.) Other critics of Latin teaching in schools proposed a more drastic reform. John Webster's attacks were particularly scathing:

Now for a Carpenter to spend seven years time about the sharpning and preparing of his instruments, and then had no further skill how to imploy them, were ridiculous and wearisome; so for Schollars to spend divers years for some small scantling and smattering in the tongues, having for the most part got no further knowledge, but like Parrats to babble and prattle, that whereby the intellect is in no way inriched, is but toylsome, and almost lost labour.[13]

Instead, Webster urged:

That care may be had of improving, and advancing our own language, and that arts and sciences may be taught in it, that thereby a more easie and short way may be had to the attaining of all sorts of knowledge: and that thereby after the example of the *Romans* we may labour to propogate it amongst other nations, that they may rather be induced to learn ours, than we theirs, which would be of vast advantage to the Commonwealth.[14]

Such criticisms of Latin were not confined to Englishmen; Descartes, for example, declared that 'There is no more sense in studying Latin and Greek than old Breton or Swiss German.'[15]

THE RISE OF THE VERNACULAR

Dissatisfaction with Latin as an international language must be seen against the growing influence of the West European vernaculars. Although rates of progress differed, by the seventeenth century these languages were becoming efficient instruments of literary, religious and scientific communication. As late as the previous century, the literary qualities of English, for example, had been distrusted; it was considered ineloquent and was most frequently described by the adjectives rude, gross, barbarous, base and vile. Despite strong opposition to its use, however, it succeeded in becoming acceptable as a medium of written communication in a relatively short time. According to Richard Foster Jones, the turning point was not earlier than 1575 and not later than 1580.[16]

The reasons for the success of the vernaculars at the expense of Latin cannot be fully explored here. Undoubtedly, though, printing played a considerable part. The shift from hand-written script to print allowed copies to be produced much more cheaply and quickly, and in far greater numbers. The market for the product of the presses could only be expanded, however, if books were to be sold to those unfamiliar with the classical languages.

This economic pressure to develop the book trade coincided with a growing feeling that 'the people' should be educated as a duty and even a necessity. Many artisans had a need for printed information but were unable to read Latin, at least with ease. Nicholas Culpepper, a translator from Latin into English whose audience was the ordinary householder, claimed in 1648 that the medical profession deliberately used Latin to hide medical truths from its patients:

Time was when all physitians wrote in their mother tongues, time was when they thought it their glory to instruct others in matters belonging to their own health . . . time was when he would have been considered a monster and unfit to live in a Commonwealth that should have attempted such a thing as to hide the Rules of Physick from the Vulgar in an unknown tongue.[17]

John Wilkins, the leading English universal language projector, and a writer on a variety of scientific and religious topics, used English in order to disperse scientific knowledge as widely as possible. In England, especially, a growing and strong prejudice against Latin was fuelled by the Puritans, who associated the language with the Catholic Church. Scientists held other objections: Latin was the language in which the Ancients had propounded their ideas on nature which were now at odds with new ways of thinking. A break with Aristotelian philosophy would be assisted by the abandonment of its classical language of expression.

As German became the language of the Hapsburg Empire, and French, Italian, Spanish, English, etc., were gradually substituted for Latin amongst their native speakers, the printed word became accessible to wider social classes within these countries. At the same time, of course, the linguistic unity of Western civilisation was crumbling with the assault of these vernaculars upon Latin, and international communication became more difficult for those unprepared or unable to learn the numerous languages now in common use. Such a linguistic facility was not easily acquired as educational practice in Europe was firmly geared to the teaching of the classical languages only. In any case, the vernacular languages themselves, like Latin, were open to criticism. Apart from irregularities in grammar and anomalies between orthography and pronunciation, they lacked precision and wallowed in ambiguity. Furthermore, they did not possess the specialised vocabulary necessary for scientific writing. A carefully constructed language universal to all mankind seemed the solution to the shortcomings inherent in all national languages, ancient and modern.

THE LANGUAGE OF ADAM

It was widely believed in the seventeenth century that the original language spoken by Adam in the Garden of Eden had been the universal language of mankind until the confusion consequent upon the building of the tower at Babel. The discovery of ever more languages in the East and in the Americas only served to emphasise the magnitude of the curse imposed. Furthermore, the language of Adam had not merely been a universal medium of communication but a language which expressed precisely the nature of things; words mirrored reality. The quest to find the first language was therefore fuelled not only by curiosity, but by the belief that in discovering the original language of God and Man, something of God's divine plan would be revealed. Until the sixteenth century, most Western thinkers assumed that this *Lingua humana* was Hebrew. Other challengers, however, were forthcoming. In the mid-sixteenth century a Dutch linguist, Goropius Becanus, found Dutch equivalents for all the proper names in Genesis, although his hypothesis was not received very seriously. Claims were also made for such languages as Latin, German and even Chinese.[18]

Although James Knowlson argues that 'The majority of the seventeenth-century universal language planners had, in my own view, little sympathy for the mystic overtones of those scholars who sought to rediscover the language of Adam', he does agree that the idea of a language in which names had conveyed the essence of the things signified probably influenced some of them far more than they recognised.[19] Certainly, most of the universal language projects refer to the confusion of tongues and their remedy for it. John Wilkins, for example, believed of his scheme that 'supposing such a thing as is here proposed, could be well established, it would be the surest remedy that could be against the Curse of the Confusion, by rendring all other *Languages* and *Characters* useless.'[20]

A REAL CHARACTER

The earliest attempts to construct a means of international communication concentrated on the design of a universal character rather than a universal language. Such a 'real character', or universal writing system, would represent concepts (not sounds) by characters which would continue to have different spoken forms according to the natural language of the user. Analogies were found in musical notes, Arabic numerals, Chinese ideograms and Egyptian hieroglyphics, all of which it was believed provided a representation of concepts which could be understood regardless of language.

The first scholar to examine in some detail the idea of a universal character, Francis Bacon, believed that words imperfectly expressed things: 'In short, language does not impart to the mind a true or accurate picture of material reality, but fills it with more or less fantastic ideas of nature.'[21] An interest in the transmission of knowledge led Bacon to consider the possibility of expressing notions not by letters and words (which are only the images of things) but by symbols, without the intervention of words. He believed (wrongly) that Egyptian hieroglyphics were congruent with the objects they represented, and Chinese characters (again wrongly) represented objects in purely conventional symbols. These conventional symbols he termed real characters: 'it is the use of China and the kingdoms of the high Levant to write in Characters Real, which express neither letters nor words in gross, but Things or Notions; insomuch as countries and provinces, which understand not one another's language, can nevertheless read one another's writings because the characters are accepted more generally than the languages do extend.'[22]

Intriguing details of China were beginning to percolate to Western Europe in the late sixteenth century from returning missionaries and travellers. According to these accounts, the Chinese language represented not sounds, but ideas. In the influential diary of an Italian missionary, Father Ricci, who worked in China for nearly 30 years, it was pointed out that not only did Chinese offer a common written language to many nations which had no contact through the spoken vernacular but it offered an additional bonus: 'This method of writing by drawing symbols instead of forming letters gives rise to a distinct mode of expression by which one is able, not only with a few phrases but with a few words, to set forth ideas with great clearness, which in our writing would have to be expressed in roundabout circumlocutions and perhaps with far less clarity.'[23] Chinese characters in fact represent morphemes (a morpheme is a minimal grammatical unit beyond which no further grammatical analysis can produce smaller units) not concepts, although it is true that the characters can be given different pronunciations by speakers of mutually unintelligible languages. This lack of knowledge of Chinese characters handicapped the proponents of a universal language, but nevertheless the ideographic nature of Chinese script did stimulate widespread discussion of an artificial language which could directly represent things by its characters, and suggested the feasibility of such an approach. Despite the attractions of Chinese, however, few argued that it should be adopted as a universal character. In his *Historia natural y moral de las Indians* (1590), José de Acosta had pointed out that the Chinese spent their time mastering the intricate language and that this prevented them attaining 'high knowledge' either in religious or secular thought. Again, although John Wilkins cites the Chinese character in his list of reasons why he believes that a real character is possible, he adds later in his *Essay*:

As for the *China* Character and Language so much talked of in the world, if it be rightly represented by those that have lived in that Country, and pretend to understand the Language, there are many considerable faults in it, which make it come far short of the advantages which may be in such a Philosophical Language as is here designed.

He emphasises the multitude of characters which must be learnt, the difficulty of pronunciation and the absence of analogy 'betwixt the shape of the Characters, and the things represented by them'.[24] For Wilkins, interested in designing a philosophical language including just such a relationship between the characters and the order of reality, this latter objection was particularly telling.

Of lesser importance in the language debate were Egyptian hieroglyphs, which had first attracted scholarly curiosity in the fifteenth century. Italian scholars were aware of hieroglyphs from the obelisks which had been transported from Egypt to Rome, but in the sixteenth and seventeenth centuries their nature was misunderstood. They were thought to be pictures having some kind of mystical symbolism and which held a natural relationship to the objects they denoted. The most famous Coptic scholar of the seventeenth century, Athanasius Kircher, even tried to forge a link between hieroglyphs and Chinese characters. In 1652 he published a work which attempted to show that the early Chinese were instructed by priests who had fled from Egypt, bringing their knowledge of hieroglyphic script.[25] Understanding of hieroglyphs was so limited and contradictory, therefore, that it was difficult to base precise language structures upon them (they were only deciphered in the early nineteenth century after the discovery of the Rosetta Stone, a fragmentary decree of one of the Ptolemies). Hieroglyphs, like the Mayan inscriptions which had been uncovered in Mexico, did offer yet more examples, however, of characters which were thought to represent notions directly rather than through sounds.

A drawback soon associated with the attempt to create a universal character was the difficulty of memorising the large number of unrelated, and possibly strange-looking, symbols which would be required to express even a basic vocabulary. Indeed, this problem had been identified in relation to Chinese ideographs. Seventeenth-century scholars were still much concerned with the 'art of memory', the technique of memorising by impressing images upon the memory, invented by the Greeks and transmitted to the European tradition by way of Rome.[26] Before the invention of printing a trained memory was crucial, but even after the 'Gutenberg revolution' the role played by memory remained important. Bacon, for example, had a very full knowledge of the art of memory. The universal language projectors, such as Dalgarno, Wilkins and Leibniz, came from that tradition which looked for signs and symbols as an aid to memory. Of particular significance in this respect was the work of the thirteenth-century Spanish monk, Raymond Lully, who invented a system of logic depending upon an alphabetical notation and a set of elementary notions. Lully's emphasis on classification and memory influenced the seventeenth-century language projectors and led Wilkins, for example, to adopt mnemonic logic in the classification tables which lie at the heart of his scheme. Wilkins chose to adopt such a classification despite its conflict with natural logic as revealed by contemporary scientific taxonomic work. The botanist, John Ray, who advised Wilkins on the natural history table, was wont to complain that 'I was constrained in arranging the Tables not to follow the lead of nature, but to accommodate the plants to the author's prescribed system'[27] In such a manner was even a forward-looking scientist such as Wilkins hide-bound by medieval concepts.

A PHILOSOPHICAL LANGUAGE

Merchants, missionaries and scientists needed a language in which they could communicate with foreigners, but this motive alone might not have been sufficient to stimulate such eminent figures as Descartes, Leibniz and Wilkins to devote considerable effort to universal language schemes. An additional impetus was provided by the desire to create a language which would accurately reflect 'nature' as it was revealed by seventeenth-century science. The goal was to construct a rational, philosophical language in which a logical relationship would exist between ideas and the words used to express them (much as in the language believed to have been spoken by Adam). The philosophical language would be free of irregularities, idiosyncracies and ambiguities; instead it would enable ideas to be expressed concisely and clearly, with no room for misinterpretation. It would also be easier to learn, remember and use than any natural language.

Vivian Salmon identifies two very different views of philosophical languages taken by seventeenth-century scholars.[28] Some sought to provide accurate and unambiguous names for phenomena which would extend human knowledge and prevent confusion in argument. Wilkins, for example, was primarily interested in the classification of concepts and the assignment to them of a notation, much as in a modern library classification scheme. Every concept would have its logical place in the classification, and would be tied to that place and linked to related concepts by the notation:

But what ever may be the issue of this attempt, as to the establishing of a real Character, and the bringing of it into Common use, amongst several Nations of the World (of which I have but very slender expectations;) yet this I shall assert with greater confidence, That the reducing of all things and notions, to such kind of Tables, as are here proposed . . . would prove the shortest and plainest way for the attainment of real Knowledge, that hath been yet offered to the World.[29]

Other scholars regarded the use of a universal language as a logical instrument to be of more importance: an instrument to enable men to think more precisely and clearly. These scholars were therefore primarily concerned with the combination of concepts rather than with individual concepts.

In Margaret Slaughter's view, 'for the most part the motivation of the language projectors was more scientific than linguistic; their concern was more with nature than with language'.[30] Although the language schemes started out with the utilitarian purpose of providing a simple universal writing, they developed into a complex analysis of things themselves: that is, into taxonomic schemes. At the same time, a different impetus was provided by a desire to ameliorate the religious conflicts in Europe between Catholic and Protestant and also between the rival Protestant sects. Many believed that these conflicts were exacerbated by misunderstandings resultant upon a lack of precision in language. Wilkins, himself a bishop and writer on ecclesiastical matters, considered that his project would 'contribute much to the clearing of some of our Modern differences in Religion, by unmasking many wild errors, that shelter themselves under the disguise of affected phrases'.[31]

CRYPTOGRAPHIC AND SHORTHAND SYSTEMS

Work on universal language schemes was influenced by developments in the related areas of cryptography and shorthand, and indeed some of the leading universal language projectors also made contributions in these areas. Cryptography has a long history dating back to classical times, but interest was rekindled in the sixteenth century, to be further stimulated in the following century by war and civil disturbance. In England the Civil War engendered a particular fascination with secret codes. The close relationship between secret codes and universal language schemes is illustrated in the work of the Jesuit scholar, Athanasius Kircher. On the suggestion of the Emperor Ferdinand, Kircher attempted to design a universal language based upon the cryptographic system which had been developed a century earlier by Johannes Trithemius, Abbot of Spanheim in the diocese of Mainz. Trithemius, also renowned for his pioneering work in the field of bibliography, had written a treatise on cryptography, although *Polygraphia* was only published in 1518, two years after his death. At the time, he had himself appreciated the possibilities of the *Polygraphia* as a universal character, and his system was much cited by seventeenth-century writers. Kircher's *Polygraphia nova et universalis* was itself published in 1663, and although a failure in terms of international communication, proved to be a valuable contribution to the science of cryptography.[32] John Wilkins was also interested in secret codes, and some years before his *Essay* he had dealt with this topic in *Mercury, or the secret and swift messenger: shewing, how a man may with privacy and speed communicate his thoughts to a friend at any distance,* a book published in 1641. He also considered the problems of communicating at a distance using signs which could be interpreted in any language. Such signs were especially useful in time of war when the need might arise to communicate from and to a besieged fortress or town. The codes used in cryptography supplied the universal language projectors with ideas about the various signs which might be adopted as characters instead of letters or numbers. They also showed that one sign might stand for a word or even a sentence, that is, a concept.

The need to make a rapid written report of the spoken word also engaged the attention of language projects, at least in England. The Scottish teacher, George Dalgarno (who also had an interest in teaching the deaf and dumb to communicate) and the Dutch merchant, Francis Lodwick (both living in England) were interested in shorthand and commented upon its relationship with universal language projects. The former, in fact, claimed that it was an attempt to improve shorthand which had led him to his universal language scheme. A form of shorthand had been used in classical times but had fallen into disuse in the Middle Ages. Salmon notes that after its revival in England towards the end of the sixteenth century, shorthand took nearly 100 years to find general acceptance elsewhere in Europe. In England it was even studied at school, and Salmon believes its popularity was due to the English love of preaching; sermons were commonly taken down in shorthand to be read at home at family prayers.[33]

As with cryptographies, shorthand systems also provided examples of single letters representing whole words and even special signs standing for words. It is only one step further to imagine a system of signs in which *all* the symbols used would represent *ideas* rather than words, so as to be universally intelligible.

ARTIFICIAL LANGUAGES IN SEVENTEENTH-CENTURY LITERATURE

The imaginary voyages in seventeenth-century literature to little-known parts of the world, or even further afield to the planets and stars, often included encounters with natives speaking imaginary languages and are yet one more indication of the general interest in language at that time. Real voyages were discovering new peoples with strange customs and languages, and it is not too surprising that writers of imaginary voyages should also wish to populate their novels with inhabitants who used exotic words in which to communicate with each other and with the newly-arrived travellers from Europe. Yet in some cases the author's fascination with language went much further than this.

Of the many examples which could be cited, Francis Godwin's *The man in the moon: or a discourse of a voyage thither by Domingo Gonsales, the speedy messenger* (which incidentally marks the beginning of English science fiction), can be chosen. Published after its author's death, in 1638, it recounts how its Spanish hero, Domingo Gonsales, after several amazing adventures, was carried after twelve days' flight on a craft towed by birds to the moon. Life on the moon resembles in several respects Chinese society and was based on contemporary accounts of that distant land. In particular, the universal language of the Lunarians is influenced by Godwin's ideas about the Chinese language: 'it consisteth not so much of words, and letters, as of tunes and uncouth sounds, that no letters can express.' Gonsales later returns to Earth but lands by mistake in China where he discovers that each province has it own language but that the language of the Mandarins was common throughout the land and, like that of the Lunarians, 'did consist much of Tunes'.[34] The idea that a language might be formed of musical notes was later discussed at some length by Wilkins in *Mercury*.

The many accounts of imaginary languages in seventeenth- and eighteenth-century literature are further evidence of the fascination which language exerted over our ancestors; such stories contributed to the intellectual environment from which the universal language projects emerged. In the next chapter these projects will be examined in more detail to reveal the extent to which they really offered a solution to the twin needs for a means of international communication and a more precise and logical philosophical language.

2

Seventeenth-century Language Projects

The idea of constructing a universal language engaged the attention of a surprising number of men in the seventeenth century, especially in Germany, France and England. In some cases the idea did not develop beyond initial statements of intent or preliminary plans. In one case, at least, the proposal of the eccentric Scot, Sir Thomas Urquhart (now best remembered for his outstanding translation of Rabelais), may even have included a satirical element. His 'Introduction to the Universal Language' was published in 1652 in a miscellany of materials entitled *Ekskubalauron, or the Discovery of A most exquisite Jewel, more precious then Diamonds inchased in Gold, the like where-of was never seen in any age; found in the kennel of Worcester-Streets, the day after the fight, and six after the Autumnal Equinox, anno 1651. Serving in this place, to frontal a VINDICATION of the honour of SCOTLAND, from the Infamy, where into the Rigid Presbyterian party of that Nation, out of that Covetousness and ambition, most disembledly hath involved it* (Ekskubalauron is supposed to be an abbreviated Greek phrase meaning gold from a dung hill). This lengthy and unusual title was prompted by the fact that most of Urquhart's papers had been lost in the Civil War the previous autumn when he was captured on the Royalist side at the Battle of Worcester and briefly imprisoned in the Tower of London. The unfortunate author's manuscripts, scattered over the field of conflict, were used for 'packeting up of raisins, figs, dates, almonds, caraway and other such-like dry confections' and to kindle pipes, as well as being deemed 'necessary for inferior employments and posterior uses'. Out of 642 quinternions (gatherings of five sheets of paper) only two quinternions were found by a Mr Braughton of Worcester 'together with two other loose sheets more, by virtue of a drizelling rain, which had made it stick fast to the ground, where there was a heap of seven and twenty dead men, lying upon one another'. These papers formed part of a preface for a planned 'Grammar and Lexicon of an Universal Language' which Urquhart never actually completed. He did set forward 66 advantages for his proposed language, however, including such seemingly strange ones as having 11 cases and 11 genders 'wherein it . . . exceedeth all other languages'. Urquhart believed that he was exercising considerable restraint in confining himself to this number of advantages: 'I might have couched thrice as many more of no less consideration than the aforesaid, but that these same will suffice to sharpen the longing of the generous Reader, after the intrinsecal and most researched secrets of the new grammar and lexicon which I am to evulge.' This unusual language projector died in 1660, reputedly of an uncontrollable laughing fit on hearing of the Restoration of Charles II.[1] Not all schemes met such an unpromising fate as Urquhart's, however, and a number were published, arousing considerable interest and widespread discussion.

There is no intention in this chapter to enumerate the many schemes designed; such a listing can be found elsewhere.[2] Nor will individual schemes be discussed in any detail, an enterprise beyond the scope of this volume. Rather, a selection of the more interesting or influential projects will be briefly examined to provide some flavour of seventeenth-century *a priori* artificial languages.

UNIVERSAL CHARACTERS AND PHILOSOPHICAL LANGUAGES

Reference was made in the previous chapter to universal real characters and philosophical languages. The distinction between them is important. Early interest in the idea of constructing a universal language centred upon the design of a character — a set of symbols — which would act as a sort of pivot or intermediary language into and from which natural languages could be converted. An analogy was drawn with arabic numerals, a set of symbols which could be combined according to a conventional system to represent numbers. These numbers could be read and understood equally well in any language, even though their written and spoken equivalents were different in each language.

The major problems encountered in the construction of such a universal character were three-fold. In the first place, it does not follow that all concepts are as unambiguously defined as, say, numerals. The number '2' always means the same thing regardless of the language in which it is expressed. Many concepts, however, do not have exact semantic equivalents in all languages. To take a well-known example, the colours of the spectrum are not divided in exactly the same way in, say, English and Welsh. Any translator knows the problems inherent in using uncritically the precise translation equivalents located in a bilingual dictionary. A universal character would work a little like a huge multilingual dictionary in which words from the various languages are given their equivalent in the character. The lack of equivalence between words led the language projectors to begin a search for the basic, underlying concepts from which complex ideas are formed.

Second, and related to this first problem, was that of memorising the vast number of characters which would be necessary to express all the concepts likely to be needed in a universal language. This is no great problem in an alphabetical language where the letters represent sounds. In a universal character, however, the symbols could not represent sounds (as each word would have its own pronunciation according to the natural language of the reader); they must represent things. Again, one way of minimising this mnemonic problem was to reduce the number of individual words in the character by identifying the relatively small number of simple concepts from which all words could be constructed.

Third, a set of symbols had to be devised which could be written and read with relative ease and which, if necessary, would show the relationship between a complex concept expressed in the character and the simple concepts from which it was assembled. In some projects existing symbols, such as arabic numerals or alphabetical letters were used; in other cases special symbols were designed.

These problems inherent in universal characters, together with a desire to systematise the universal language in order to provide a logical and unambiguous medium of communication superior to the haphazard and imprecise natural languages, led in the 1650s to philosophical language projects. Knowledge was organised in classification tables according to 'philosophical' or scientific principles. In this way relationships between things in the real world could be expressed by the language itself, and the structure of a word (or its sound, as the philosophical languages were normally designed as oral as well as written languages) revealed the nature of the thing it represented.

LODWICK AND BECK

The first universal language scheme to be published, *A common writing: whereby two, although not understanding one the others language, yet by the helpe thereof, may communicate their minds one to another,* appeared in 1647. Its author, Francis Lodwick, the son of a Flemish father and a French Huguenot mother, was brought up in the Protestant refugee community in the City of London and, like his father, was a merchant by profession.[3] His family and professional backgrounds therefore both served to emphasise the advantages which a universal medium of communication would offer. Typical for his times, his range of interests was wide, including a preoccupation with plans for rebuilding the City after the Great Fire of 1666 which destroyed his house located very close to Pudding Lane, the source of the conflagration. Lodwick's linguistic interests included shorthand, the origin of language and Chinese characters as well as universal language, and he is now best remembered for his phonetic alphabet which appeared in the Royal Society *Philosophical transactions* in 1686.

In the introduction to his universal character, Lodwick informed the reader that the character was 'common to all Languages, that is, that one skilled in the same, shall have no need, for what is written with this writing, to learne any other language then his mother Tongue, which he already hath; although the writing were written by one, who understood not the readers Language, and writ the said writing according to his owne Language'.[4] The character itself was 'rather a kind of hieroglyphical representation of words', as shown in figure 2.1. Lodwick tackled the problem of learning a multitude of characters by selecting a limited number of radical words which were broken down into words of 'action' and words of 'no action'. This latter group was further subdivided into nouns; pronouns; adjectives; and adverbs, prepositions, interjections and conjunctions. Each radical was allocated a character, and words related to the radical were formed from this basic character by the addition of specific marks. This system did partially alleviate the problem of remembering the characters, but the challenge posed to the memory was still daunting. In Knowlson's words, 'simply learning all the radicals would prove to be an impossible task, requiring an entire lifetime . . . and references would constantly need to be made to the two parts of what would have to be a vast lexicon'.[5] Lodwick did intend to compile a lexicon

(23)

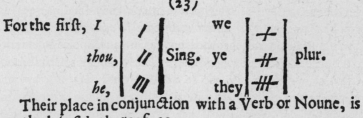

Their place in conjunction with a Verb or Noune, is on the left side thereof, as

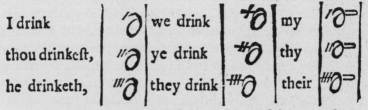

But joyned with either Advers, Prepositions, or Conjunctions, their place is on the right hand, as

<table>
<tr><td>٦٧</td><td>from me,</td></tr>
<tr><td>٦٧//</td><td>from thee,</td></tr>
<tr><td>٦٧#</td><td>from them.</td></tr>
</table>

The demonstrative Characters are these,

| | this, | | these, |
| | that, | | those. |

Their place joyned before either Verb or Noune, is on the left hand, but with the other undeclined parts, is on the right hand, as

| | this | | | | from this |
| | that | } drink. | | | from that |

The Relative character is (8) *who or which.*

D 3

Figure 2.1   The universal character of Francis Lodwick
Source: Vivian Salmon, *The works of Francis Lodwick.*
London: Longman, 1972, p. 192.

to facilitate conversion between the character and English, but it was never accomplished. The character was hardly universal in structure as it accepted English as its norm and catered for basic English words rather than trying to identify universal concepts. Furthermore, its grammar was mainly based upon English. The special symbols devised by Lodwick for the character, and the system of adding marks to these sysmbols to distinguish words of related meaning, meant that writing and reading mistakes were easily made.

Lodwick was himself aware of the shortcomings in *A common writing* and in 1652 he published a second project: *The ground-work, or foundation laid, (or so intended) for the framing of a new perfect language: an universall or common writing.* Although some of his earlier ideas were repeated, the overall scheme was simpler. Presaging the later philosophical languages of Dalgarno and Wilkins, Lodwick emphasised that 'The proper names of things to give them signification is the work, we suppose, of a sound philosopher, who from the knowledge of things and their order in nature, should give them names accordingly, describing that in them by their name, by which in the naming they may be known.'[6]

Several universal characters were published which basically used arabic numerals as their symbols. Words were listed alphabetically in an index with the corresponding number in the character. The semantically equivalent words in other languages could then be given the same number. An example published in English and French was constructed by Cave Beck, an Ipswich schoolmaster.[7] The project appeared in 1657 under the comprehensively descriptive title, *The universal character: by which all the nations in the world may understand one anothers conceptions, reading out of one common writing their own mother tongues. An invention of general use, the practice whereof may be attained in two hours space, observing the grammatical directions. Which character is so contrived, that it may be spoken as well as written.* Beck thought that by using numbers rather than inventing new symbols for his character he 'will fright no Eye with an unusual shape'. The numerals from 0 to 9 are combined to represent words, and a letter or syllable before or after each word signifies the part of speech, case, number, gender, person, tense, etc. (see figure 2.2). Unlike Lodwick, Beck based his scheme largely on the grammar of the classical languages rather than English. Most of his published scheme is taken up with a lexicon of about 4,000 English words, and their equivalents in the character (see figure 2.3). Although

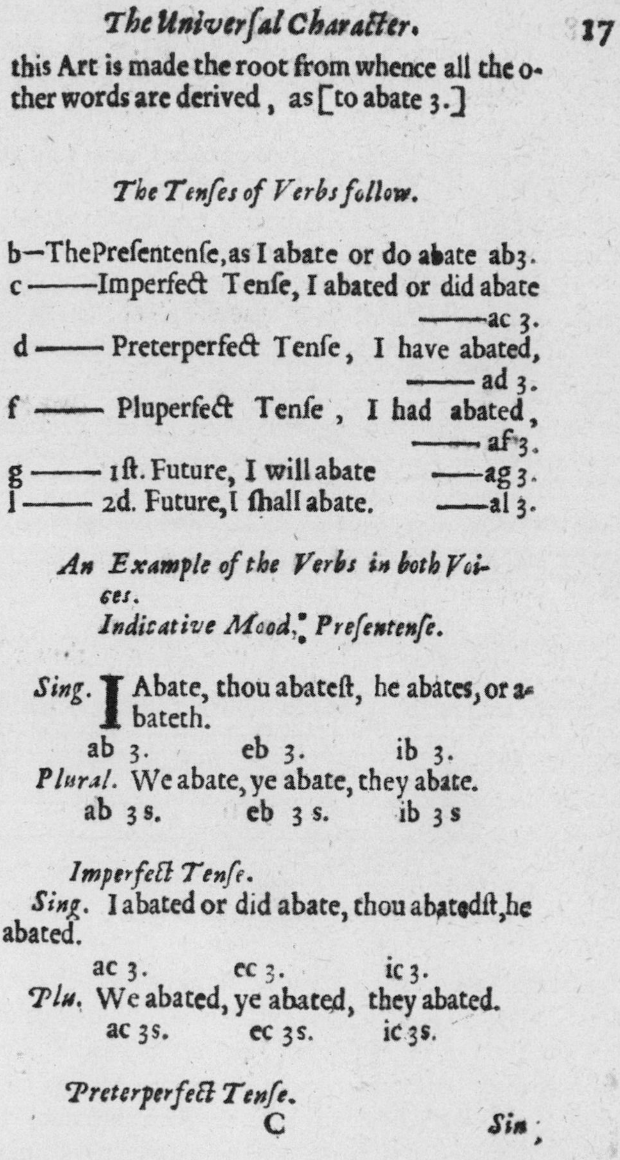

The Universal Character. 17

this Art is made the root from whence all the o-
ther words are derived , as [to abate 3.]

The Tenses of Verbs follow.

b—ThePresentense, as I abate or do abate ab3.
c ———Imperfect Tense, I abated or did abate
——————ac 3.
d ———— Preterperfect Tense , I have abated,
——— ad 3.
f ———— Pluperfect Tense , I had abated ,
——— af 3.
g ———— 1st. Future, I will abate ——ag 3.
l ———— 2d. Future, I shall abate. ——al 3.

*An Example of the Verbs in both Voi-
ces.*
Indicative Mood, Presentense.

Sing. **I** Abate, thou abatest, he abates, or a-
bateth.
ab 3. eb 3. ib 3.
Plural. We abate, ye abate, they abate.
ab 3 s. eb 3 s. ib 3 s

Imperfect Tense.
Sing. I abated or did abate, thou abatedst, he
abated.
ac 3. ec 3. ic 3.
Plu. We abated, ye abated, they abated.
ac 3 s. ec 3 s. ic 3 s.

Preterperfect Tense.
C
Sin

Figure 2.2 Cave Beck's universal character
Source: Cave Beck, *The universal character.* London: Maxey, 1657, p. 17.

A before B.		A before C.	
To Abandon	1	to abfolve	21
to Abafe ⁴¹²		to abftaine	22
to Abafh	2	an abftract ɾ⁶	
to Abate	3	abftrufe	q 23
an Abbot	p 4	abfurd	q 24
to Abette	5	to abufe	tel 25
to Abbreviate	nu 6		
to Abut or border	7	An Academy	26
an Abecedary	p 8	to accent	27
to Abhor	9	to accept	28
to Abide or ftay	10	acceffe, or admiffion	r 29
to Abide or bear	11	acceffory	q 30
an Abyffe	r 12	an accedent	r 31
to Abjure	u 13	to accomodate	32
Able	q 14	to accomplifh	33
to Abolifh	15	to accompany	34
Abortive	16	to account	35
Above	Supra	to accord	36
to Abound	17	accoutrement	r 37
About	Circa	according to	Iuxta
Abroad	ur 18	to accumulate	38
to Abrogate ¹⁵		to accufe	39
to be Abrupt	19	to accuftom	40
Abfent	q 20	D 3	to

Figure 2.3   Extract from index to Beck's *The universal character*
Source: Cave Beck, *The universal character*. London: Maxey, 1657.

Beck intended that his character should be pronounceable by applying approximations of the English sounds for the arabic numerals used (for example, the number 1 is pronounced 'on', 3 is 'tre' and 5 'fi'), it is improbable that he thought of it primarily as an effective language of oral communication, and his scheme is best considered as a character rather than a language. Beck's objective was the relatively modest one of creating a written notation which could be read in any language rather than a language based upon a philosophical classification of concepts; nevertheless Salmon has described his *Character* as representing 'the summit of achievement in this direction in the 17th Century in England'.[8]

The undoubted ingenuity of Lodwick's and Beck's characters, and a number of others similarly constructed, could not conceal their impracticality as media of international communication. They were difficult to memorise, clumsy to write and tied closely to one or another natural language. Furthermore, they offered nothing to those who were bent upon designing a language better suited to reflect real concepts, a philosophical language based upon a logical classification of phenomena.

JOHN WILKINS

Of the many universal language projects contemplated or actually constructed in the seventeenth century, John Wilkins's *An essay towards a real character and a philosophical language,* published in London in 1668, is probably the most interesting and most fully developed. In many respects, Wilkins was a typical scholar of that century, exhibiting a breadth of scientific interest which is astounding to those who have matured in our century of specialisation. By profession a clergyman, Wilkins interested himself in astronomy, mathematics, anatomy, agriculture, mechanics and biology, as well as language. Although not amongst the leading scientific minds of his time, Wilkins's scientific works 'are informed by a desire to spread scientific information to those who would not ordinarily come upon it or who were themselves incapable of dealing directly with scientific discourse due to a lack of education or the failure of their education to provide the proper mathematical, technical, and linguistic tools'.[9] Not that Wilkins was a rural cleric remote from the hurly-burly of scientific activity. In fact he was one of the leaders of the group of thinkers who founded the Royal Society, acting as chairman of the meeting at which it was projected, one of its presidents in the months before it was chartered, its first secretary and a member of its council until his death. Earlier, he had been a member of a group of London gentlemen who regularly met to discuss the latest scientific developments (later termed by Robert Boyle the 'Invisible College'), and while at Oxford his home became the centre of English scientific discussion. By all accounts, his was an engaging and stimulating mind, extending even to such distractions as the construction of 'waterworks . . . whereby, of but few gallons of *water* forced through a narrow *fissure,* he could raise a *mist* in his *Garden,* wherein a person placed at a due distance between the *Sun* and the *mist,* might see an exquisite *Rainbow* in all its proper *colours'.*[10] In *Brief lives,* Aubrey described Wilkins thus: 'He was no great read man; but one of much and deepe thinking, and of a working head; and a prudent man as well as ingeniose . . . He was a lustie, strong growne, well sett, broad shouldered person, cheerfull, and hospitable.'[11]

John Wilkins was born in 1614 in Northamptonshire, the son of a goldsmith. After coming down from Oxford he became a tutor at Magdalen Hall before succeeding his grandfather as vicar of Fawsley in his native county. There followed a succession of chaplaincies before his appointment as Warden of Wadham College, Oxford, in 1648, a post he held until his advancement to the Mastership of Trinity College, Cambridge, in 1659. Wilkins had supported Cromwell during these troubled political times; indeed in 1656 he married Robina French, widow of an Oxford colleague and youngest sister of Oliver Cromwell. With the restoration of Charles II to the English throne, however, Wilkins was removed from his Cambridge post in favour of a Royalist. He returned to London on taking up the position of Dean at Ripon, and his final appointment as Bishop of Chester was confirmed in 1668, a post he held until his death in 1672.

The earlier writings of Wilkins dealt with lunar inhabitants and inter-planetary travel. When still only 24, he had published the *Discovery of a new world, or a discourse tending to prove that it is probable that there may be another habitable world in the moon,* followed two years later by *A discourse concerning a new planet.* According to his biographer, Wilkins's work on these subjects had a greater influence on literature than science, but he did make an original, though not the first, contribution to speculation about human flight.[12] Of more relevance to his later philosophical language was *Mercury: or the secret and swift messenger,* first published in 1641.

Mercury was thought by the Ancient Egyptians to have been the inventor of the alphabet, and in his treatise John Wilkins dealt with the ways in which information could be communicated secretly. The relationship between cryptography and universal language schemes was discussed in the previous chapter, and Wilkins's book is a good example of such a link in seventeenth-century thinking. Its major part is concerned with cyphers of various types, but he also considers the problem resulting from the curse of language inflicted upon Mankind after the Fall. The best that could be offered to combat this curse was Latin and the other learned languages:

But now if there were such an universal character to express things and notions, as might be legible to all People and Countries, so that men of several Nations might with the same ease both write and read it, this invention would be a far greater advantage in this particular, and mightily conduce to the spreading and promoting of all Arts and Science: Because that great part of our time which is now required to the Learning of words, might then be imployed in the study of things.[13]

He noted that the same concepts were expressed by men using the various languages, only the words differed. Around 8,000 symbols were needed to express adequately all things, he estimated, and these should be no more difficult to learn than a conventional language. Wilkins interestingly raised the idea of representing each letter of the alphabet by a simple sound, and goes on to suggest: 'but now if these inarticulate sounds be contrived for the expression, not of *words* and *letters,* but of *things* and *notions,* then might there be such a general Language, as should be equally speakable by all People and Nations.'[14] Two hundred years later a Frenchman, Sudre, was to construct a language which actually used musical notation (see chapter 3).

By the 1650s, Wilkins's ideas on a universal language had progressed very considerably. A sizeable literature has developed on the reasons for Wilkins's new insight into a philosophical language. The Czech educational reformer, Comenius (see chapter 1), the Silesian educational theorist, Cyprian Kinner, the merchant and scientific 'go-between', Samuel Hartlib, and the Scot, George Dalgarno, are some of the influences proposed by one or another scholar. The important point is that Wilkins began seriously to consider how a universal language might be constructed according to philosophical (that is, scientific) principles. His earlier interest in creating a relatively simple 'pivot' language into which existing languages could be converted was replaced by the more ambitious goal of constructing a language better suited to the communication of philosophical truth.

WARD, DESCARTES AND DALGARNO

Wilkins himself traced his work on a philosophical language back to his friend Seth Ward, Professor of astronomy at Oxford (and later to become Bishop of Salisbury). Ward in turn traced his belief in the plausibility of a philosophical language to the earlier writings of the French philosopher, René Descartes. In a letter to Mersenne (see chapter 1) in 1629, Descartes had expressed a critical opinion of a language project by an unknown author which Mersenne had sent him (Mersenne himself considered a universal language project in his *Harmonie universelle* published in 1636). Descartes thought the language impractical, particularly because of the prodigious memory which would be required of the user unless constant resort was to be had to a dictionary. He believed that this fault could be overcome, however, by constructing a universal language according to philosophical principles. It was necessary to impose order over thoughts much as an order is naturally established between numbers. The resulting universal language would be constructed from simple elements, identified by rational analysis based upon a 'true philosophy'. These elements could then be combined according to precise rules in order to express the complex ideas conveyed by language (rather as a faceted library classification scheme enables complex subject descriptions to be assembled from a combination of simple concepts). Such a language, Descartes believed, would be easy to learn. Furthermore, it would help rather than hinder clear, logical thought and sound judgement: 'I maintain that this language is possible and that the science on which it depends can be discovered, and through it the common man will be better able to judge the truth of things than philosophers do now.'[15] Nevertheless, Descartes had remained sceptical about the general acceptability of such a philosophical language; he did not develop his proposal further and never supplied any actual examples.

In *Vindiciae academiarum* (the preface of which was written by Wilkins) published in 1654, Ward set out his general ideas about how a philosophical language might be constructed:

But it did presently occurre to me, that by the helpe of Logicke and Mathematicks this might soon receive a mighty advantage, for all Discourses being resolved in sentences, those into words, words signifying either simple notions or being resolvable into simple notions it is manifest, that if all the sorts of simple notions be found out, and have Symboles assigned to them those will be extremely few in respect of the other, (which are indeed Characters of words . . .) the reason of their composition easily known and the compounded ones at once will be comprehended, and yet will represent to the very eye all the elements of the composition.

Ward further believed that such a language should be capable of spoken as well as written expression.[16]

Wilkins became seriously involved in the task of constructing a philosophical language when he began to help George Dalgarno draw up certain classification tables for his project. Dalgarno, born in Aberdeen, published his project, *Ars signorum,* in 1661. He had originally set out to improve an existing system of shorthand, but he later realised the need for some kind of conceptual classification upon which his language could be constructed. The completed project was based upon a classification of 'simple notions' into 17 abstract classes, subdivided in Aristotelian fashion into species and differentiae. In such a way, Dalgarno believed that the actual words in this language would reveal relationships between concepts existing in the real world. Complex concepts could then be expressed by combining these simple notions. For example, the concept expressed in English by the word 'palace' symbolises 'a house belonging to a king'. The word for 'palace' in Dalgarno's language, therefore, must be formed by combining the primitive notions 'house', 'king' and 'belonging to'.[17] The symbols chosen for the language are the letters of the alphabet. Dalgarno wanted his language to be spoken as well as written, an objective facilitated by the choice of letters, and he also pointed out that it was easier than inventing entirely new symbols. The language itself used a vocabulary based upon Latin and English.

Although Dalgarno's project received support from King Charles, who recommended it especially to clergymen as an asset in the propagation of the Gospel, it revealed a number of shortcomings. His classification tables, for example, remained incomplete, as he acknowledged (the tables prepared by Wilkins were not used by Dalgarno as he disapproved of Wilkins's method). Margaret Slaughter points out that the herbalist Baukin had classified 6,000 plants, whereas Dalgarno only included 32 kinds. She also draws attention to the ambiguity latent in any formation of complex notions from the simple elements in the tables. A complex notion can only be formed by determining its proper genus and its appropriate characteristics, so enabling the correct simple elements to be joined. But appropriate characteristics for one person may not be the same for anyone else: 'The name is self-defining relative to the speaker's individual taxonomy, but the taxonomy and the defining are left to the individual.'[18]

The grammarian and friend of Wilkins, John Wallis, made a criticism to be directed many times at universal language projects over the following centuries: such a project

was certainly feasible in Nature . . . but that [he] did not think it likely to obtain in Practice. Because this Universal Character, must be in the nature of a New Language . . . So that, For all Persons, to Learn his Character, and have all Books written in it; is the same thing as to Translate all Books into one Language, and to have this language learned by all. Which if it cannot be hoped, of any of the languages now in being . . . much less is it to be hoped for, in a New Language, now to be contrived.[19]

Nevertheless, *Ars signorum* was the first project for a universal philosophical language to be realised, and Salmon judiciously assesses it thus: 'however useless his work proved, from a practical point of view, it revealed an astonishing insight into language and stimulated others to similar investigation.'[20]

AN ESSAY TOWARDS A REAL CHARACTER

Following Dalgarno's refusal to use the tables drawn up by Wilkins, the latter continued to work independently on a philosophical language, but undoubtedly there is a firm connection between *Ars signorum* and *An essay towards a real character,* which Wilkins eventually published in 1668. Writing of the former book, Vivian Salmon comments that 'The genesis of this work is so closely linked to that of the *Essay* . . . that it is impossible to know whether Dalgarno's grammatical theory is derived from Wilkins's or vice-versa.'[21] Despite the publication of *Ars signorum* in 1661, Wilkins continued with his own project, evidently not entirely satisfied with Dalgarno's efforts. The *Essay* was ready for publication in January 1666 but the Great Fire then destroyed most of the manuscript and all but two copies of the portion of the work that had already been printed. Wilkins, undaunted, immediately set out to improve his project and asked two naturalists, Francis Willoughby and John Ray, if they would help in making the 'regular enumeration and defining of all the families of plants and animals', as he wrote to Willoughby.[22] (It is interesting to note that Samuel Pepys also helped Wilkins, in this case with the nautical tables.) After a great deal of work, the final revisions were carried out in the spring of 1668 and the *Essay* was finally licensed by the Council of the Royal Society on Monday 13 April. In his statement to the President, Council and Fellows of the Society printed at the beginning of the *Essay,* Wilkins assures them that:

I am not so vain as to think that I have here completely finished this great undertaking, with all the advantages of which such a design is capable. Nor on the other hand, am I so diffident of this *Essay,* as not to believe it sufficient for the business to which it pretends, namely the distinct expression of all things and notions that fall under discourse.[23]

At the heart of Wilkins's language lay the 'Universal Philosophy', as he called it: 'the great foundation of the thing here designed, namely a regular *enumeration* and *description* of all those things and notions, to which marks or names ought to be assigned according to their respective natures, which may be styled the *scientifical* Part' of the project.[24] Relying largely upon the Aristotelian distinction between genus and difference, as had Dalgarno before him, Wilkins attempted to allocate all 'things and notions' into 40 genera (see figure 2.4). In this way he intended to group related objects in some kind of meaningful order. An 'alphabetical dictionary' then provided an index to the tables. Wilkins believed that his tables served two crucial purposes. First, they established 'real' relationships between things themselves, revealing something about their nature by their juxtaposition: 'the reducing of all things and notions, to such kind of Tables, as are here proposed . . . would prove the shortest and plainest way for the attainment of real knowledge, that hath been yet offered to the World.' Second, they served as a mnemonic device, thereby countering a major criticism of the earlier universal character projects that they required prodigious feats of memory: 'Now in the way here proposed, the words necessary for communication are not three thousand, and those so ordered by the help of natural method, that they may be more easily learned and remembered than a thousand words otherwise disposed of.' As Wilkins summed up:

if the *Names* of things could be so ordered, as to contain such a kind of

All kinds of things and notions, to which names are to be affigned, may be diftributed into fuch as are either more

General; namely thofe Univerfal notions, whether belonging more properly to

Things; called TRANSCENDENTAL
{ GENERAL. I
{ RELATION MIXED. II
{ RELATION OF ACTION. III

Words; DISCOURSE. IV

Special; denoting either

CREATOR. V

Creature; namely fuch things as were either *created* or *concreated* by God, not excluding feveral of thofe notions, which are framed by the minds of men, confidered either

Collectively; WORLD. VI

Diftributively; according to the feveral kinds of Beings. whether fuch as do
                 (belong to

Substance;

Inanimate; ELEMENT. VII

Animate; confidered according to their feveral

Species; whether

Vegetative

Imperfect; as *Minerals*,
{ STONE. VIII
{ METAL. IX

HERB confid. accord. to the
{ LEAF. X
{ FLOWER. XI
{ SEED-VESSEL. XII

Perfect; as *Plant*,
{ SHRUB. XIII
{ TREE. XIV

Senfitive;
{ EXANGUIOUS. XV

Sanguineous;
{ FISH. XVI
{ BIRD. XVII
{ BEAST. XVIII

Parts;
PECULIAR. XIX
GENERAL. XX

Accident;

Quantity;
{ MAGNITUDE. XXI
{ SPACE. XXII
{ MEASURE. XXIII

Quality; whether
{ NATURAL POWER. XXIV
{ HABIT. XXV
{ MANNERS. XXVI
{ SENSIBLE QUALITY. XXVII
{ SICKNESS. XXVIII

Action
{ SPIRITUAL. XXIX
{ CORPOREAL. XXX
{ MOTION. XXXI
{ OPERATION. XXXII

Relation; whether more

Private.
{ OECONOMICAL. XXXIII
{ POSSESSIONS. XXXIV
{ PROVISIONS. XXXV

Publick.
{ CIVIL. XXXVI.
{ JUDICIAL. XXXVII
{ MILITARY. XXXVIII
{ NAVAL. XXXIX
{ ECCLESIASTICAL. XL.

Figure 2.4 The forty genera in Wilkins's *An essay*
Source: John Wilkins, *An essay towards a real character.*
London: Gellibrand, 1668, p. 23.

affinity or *opposition* in their letters and sounds, as might be some way answerable to the nature of the things which they signified; This would yet be a farther advantage superadded: by which, besides the best way of helping the *Memory* by natural Method, the *Understanding* likewise would be highly improved; and we should, by learning the *Character* and the *Names* of things, be instructed likewise in their *Natures*, the knowledg of both which ought to be conjoyned.[25]

Slaughter draws an interesting comparison between the different uses of the term 'philosophical' by Dalgarno and Wilkins. For Dalgarno the term meant 'logical' whereas for Wilkins it meant 'scientific' or 'biological'. In a biological model, a species is a 'simple notion', so that, for example, even though blueberry and white water lily contain a 'simple notion' from a logical or linguistic point of view (genus berry, water lily) there is no reality to this 'simple notion' of genus in the world of nature. A complex notion in logic is not of the same order as a species in biology, as a species is not divisible.[26]

Although the philosophical tables produced by Wilkins were quite detailed, and certainly the most fully developed of his time, they vary in quality. The most impressive sections are reckoned to be those dealing with botany and zoology provided by John Ray (an excerpt from which is shown in figure 2.5). Yet Ray himself was far from happy with his work. As he confided to a friend:

In arranging the tables I was not allowed to follow the lead of nature, but was required to fit the plants to the author's own system. I had to divide herbs into three squadrons of kinds as nearly equal as possible; I had to divide each squadron into nine lesser kinds of 'differences' . . . seeing to it that the plants ordered under each 'difference' did not exceed a certain fixed number; and finally I had to join plants in pairs or otherwise couple them. How could anyone ever hope that a method of this sort would be satisfactory, and not transparently absurd and imperfect?

As Benjamin De Mott points out, Ray's chief target was the mnemonic aspect of Wilkins's scheme; he rejected the idea that the symbols of a language could be arranged both to suit the memory and still to follow the lead of nature.[27] Knowledge, alas, seldom fits perfectly into even the best constructed of classification schemes.

Once Wilkins had produced his tables, it was necessary to provide grammatical rules by which simple concepts could be assembled into complex ideas and then into continuous prose or speech. Each genus was

Of Fiſh.

§. III. FISH may be diſtributed into ſuch as are

⎰ *Viviparous* ; and ſkinned ; whoſe figure is either
⎰ ⎰ OBLONG and roundiſh. I.
⎰ ⎰ FLAT or thick. II.
⎱ *Oviparous* ; whether ſuch as do generally belong to
 ⎰ *Salt water* ; to be further diſtinguiſhed by their
 ⎮ ⎰ *Finns on the back* ; whether ſuch, the *rays* of whoſe *finns* are
 ⎮ ⎮ ⎰ *Wholly ſoft* and flexile. III.
 ⎮ ⎮ ⎱ *Partly ſoft,* and partly *ſpinous* ; having
 ⎮ ⎮   ⎰ TWO FINNS on the back. IV.
 ⎮ ⎮   ⎱ But ONE FINN. V.
 ⎮ ⎮ *Figure* ; whether
 ⎮ ⎮   ⎰ OBLONG. VI.
 ⎮ ⎮   ⎱ FLAT. VII.
 ⎮ ⎮ CRUSTACEOUS COVERING. VIII.
 ⎱ *Freſh water* ; being ſcaly. IX.

1. VIVIPA-
ROUS OB- I. VIVIPAROUS OBLONG FISH, may be diſtributed into ſuch as
LONG FISH. are

 ⎰ *Cetaceous* ; *breeding* their young within them, having *lungs* and no *gills,*
 ⎮ and but *one pair of finns* ; ‖ either the *greateſt of all living Creatures,* of
 ⎮ which there are ſeveral *ſpecies* , one without *teeth* or a *tube* to caſt
 ⎮ *water,* another with *teeth* and ſuch a *tube,* and another with a large
 ⎮ long *horn :* or that other *Fiſh* of a *leſs magnitude,* which is *gregarious,*
 ⎮ often *appearing above water.*
Balæna. ⎮ ⎰ WHALE.
Delphinus. ⎮ 1. ⎱ PORPOIS, *Dolphin.*
 ⎱ *Cartilagineous* ; ſaid to *hatch* their young ones within their *bellies,* whoſe
   mouths are placed under their *noſes* ; whether ſuch as are more
   ⎰ *Proper to the Sea* ; having generally a double *Penis, wide mouths,* and
   ⎮ five *apertures* on each ſide inſtead of *Gills* ; to be further diſtin-
   ⎮ guiſhed by their having
   ⎮ ⎰ *Long ſnouts* or *prominencies* ; ‖ either in the faſhion of a *Saw :* or
   ⎮ ⎮ in the figure of a *Sword,* being without thoſe apertures on the
   ⎮ ⎮ ſide, common to the reſt.
Priſtis. ⎮ ⎮ ⎰ SAW-FISH.
Xiphias. ⎮ ⎮ 2. ⎱ SWORD-FISH.
   ⎮ *Rows of very ſharp teeth* ; ‖ the *Greater :* or the *Leſſer.*
Canis carcha- ⎮ ⎰ SHARKE.
rias. ⎮ 3. ⎱ GLAUCUS.
Glaucus. ⎮
   ⎮ *Lips rough like a File,* but *without teeth* ; ‖ the *Greater :* or the *Leſſen.*
Muſtelus levis. ⎮ ⎰ HOUND-FISH.
Aſterias. ⎮ 4. ⎱ SPOTTED HOUND-FISH.
   ⎮ *Thorns on their backs* ; ‖ either *joyning to* the former part of the
   ⎮ *Finns :* or *obliquely croſſing the rays of the finn.*
Galeus ſpinax. ⎮ ⎰ THORNBACK DOG.
Centrina. ⎮ 5. ⎱ HOG-FISH.

Figure 2.5 Excerpt from Wilkins's philosophical tables
Source: John Wilkins, *An essay towards a real character.*
London: Gellibrand, 1668 p. 132.

assigned a particular consonant and vowel (for spoken use) and a corresponding written sign. Differences are next expressed by an additional consonant and species by a further vowel or dipthong. In the written character, difference is indicated by a stroke on the left-hand side of the character and species by a stroke on the right-hand side. Further hooks and loops denote active and passive voice, plural, and so on. An example of the written character and its phonetic representation can be seen in figure 2.6, the opening of the Lord's Prayer. The arabic numerals are not from Wilkins's scheme but were included by him as reference numbers pointing to explanations (appended at the end of his book) of the writing and speech systems.

Although Wilkins asserted that 'a man of an ordinary capacity may more easily learn to express himself this way [using the Real Character] in one Month, than he can by the Latin in forty Months', in dedicating the *Essay* to the Royal Society he admitted that he had 'but very slender expectations' of it entering into common use.[28] Robert Hooke, the scientist, wrote a short description of his invention for pocket watches in the Real Character *(Descriptions of helioscopes and some other instruments,* 1676), and described it as a 'Language perfectly free from all manner of ambiguity, and yet the most copious, expressive and significative of any thing or Notion imaginable, and, which recommends it most to common use, the most easie to be understood and learnt in the World'.[29] Yet the language failed to rouse much support even within the Royal Society, under whose auspices it had been printed. The Society did appoint a committee, including Boyle, Wren, Hooke and Ward, to report on the *Essay,* but there is no evidence that any report was ever produced, Wilkins himself never considered that the *Essay* was finished, and he was working on a new edition, to be published in Latin in order to gain a wider circulation than the English edition could achieve, at the time of his death in November 1672 (a French edition was later also planned but never printed). John Ray had been persuaded to work on altering and amending his natural history tables which he had already completed and sent to Wilkins. A few years later, in 1678, a Somerset clergyman by the name of Andrew Paschall devised a scheme to popularise some of Ray's tables by casting them in a more convenient form and hanging them like maps in garden houses. The brass tables were never produced, however, as Paschall was unable to find time for the fundamental revision of Wilkins's structure which he came to believe was a necessary adjunct to any successful popularisation.[30]

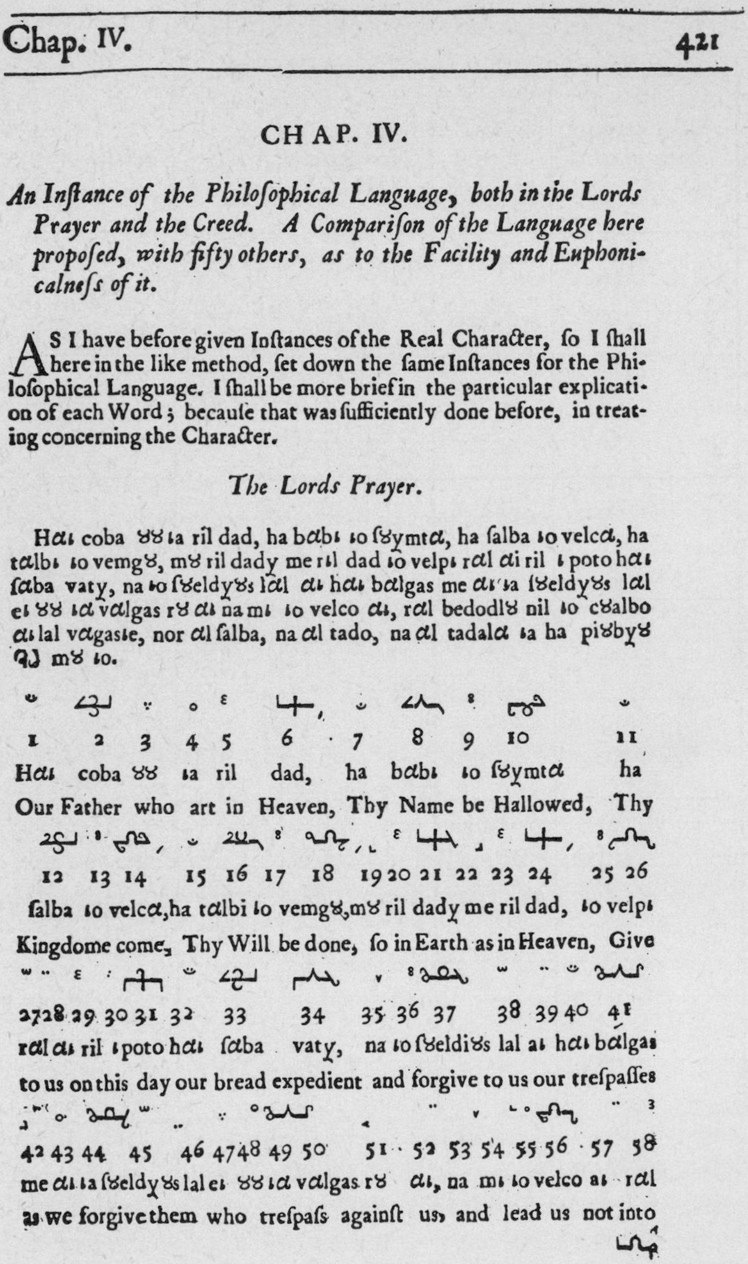

Chap. IV.   421

CHAP. IV.

An Instance of the Philosophical Language, both in the Lords Prayer and the Creed. A Comparison of the Language here proposed, with fifty others, as to the Facility and Euphonicalness of it.

AS I have before given Instances of the Real Character, so I shall here in the like method, set down the same Instances for the Philosophical Language. I shall be more brief in the particular explication of each Word; because that was sufficiently done before, in treating concerning the Character.

The Lords Prayer.

Hai coba ᵼᵼ ia ril dad, ha babi io ſʸymta, ha ſalba io velca, ha talbi io vemgᵼ, mᵼ ril dady me rii dad io velpi ral ai ril ı poto hai ſaba vaty, na io ſʸeldyᵼi lal ai hai balgas me ai ia ſʸeldyᵼi lal ei ᵼᵼ ia valgas rᵼ ai na mi io velco ai, ral bedodlᵼ nil io cᵼalbo ai lal vagasie, nor ai ſalba, na ai tado, na ai tadala ia ha piᵼbyᵼ ꝙ mᵼ io.

Hai coba ᵼᵼ ia ril dad, ha babi io ſʸymta ha
Our Father who art in Heaven, Thy Name be Hallowed, Thy

ſalba io velca, ha talbi io vemgᵼ, mᵼ ril dady me ril dad, io velpi
Kingdome come, Thy Will be done, so in Earth as in Heaven, Give

ral ai ril ı poto hai ſaba vaty, na io ſʸeldiᵼi lal ai hai balgai
to us on this day our bread expedient and forgive to us our trespasses

me ai ia ſʸeldyᵼi lalei ᵼᵼ ia valgas rᵼ ai, na mi io velco ai ral
as we forgive them who trespass against us, and lead us not into

Figure 2.6   The written script and phonetic representation in *An essay*
Source: John Wilkins, *An essay towards a real character.*
London: Gellibrand, 1668, p. 421.

According to Aubrey's account of Wilkins in his *Brief lives,* the Real Character 'was his Darling, and nothing troubled him so much when he dyed, as that he had not completed it'.[31] After his death, the *Essay* continued to be discussed by a group including Robert Hooke, Seth Ward and Francis Lodwick, with a view to a possible revision of the scheme. These scholars were convinced of the importance of the project for the progress of learning and the benefit of mankind as a whole. Even John Ray conceded that 'it far excels any essay of that kind published before.' Seemingly, one suggestion included a children's game based on the scheme. Any plans for the *Essay* were undermined, however, by a growing feeling that substantial improvements were required in order for the project to be of practical value, and in particular that a revision of the tables was necessary.[32] If the language was ever to be successful, the tables would require constant revision to take account of new knowledge. For example, Wilkins classifies the whale as a fish. Once it is recognised as a mammal, its symbol in Wilkins's scheme, which deliberately and specifically identifies it is a fish, becomes misleading; it must be re-classified in accordance with the new state of knowledge. Although *An essay towards a real character* remains the most impressive monument to the language planners of the seventeenth century, Wilkins's language, alas, was not destined to offer the world a universal medium of communication.

LEIBNIZ

The German philosopher, Gottfried Wilhem von Leibniz, had considered the possibility of constructing a universal language earlier in the century. It should be simple to learn, he believed, and easy to remember, because it would have a logical basis. As he wrote in a letter of 1697, 'I had considered this matter before Mr. Wilkins' book, when I was just a young man of 19, in my little book, *De arte combinatoria*, and my opinion is that truly real and philosophical characters must answer to intellectual analysis.'[33] He reproached the schemes of Dalgarno and Wilkins for being insufficiently philosophical. Leibniz was anxious to construct a universal language suitable to express fundamental ideas as a part of his dream that all nations would cooperate in discovering the secrets of nature and use this knowledge to enable mankind to live peacefully and well. His language would be an 'instrument of reason' in which the words should be related to the ideas they express.[34] He believed that all complex ideas are the product of simple ideas just as all non-prime numbers are the products of prime numbers. It is therefore natural to represent simple ideas by prime numbers, and complex ideas formed from these simple ideas by the product of the corresponding prime numbers. Thus, if the number '2' represented 'animal' and '3' represented 'reasonable', then 'man' could be expressed by the combination of these two numbers, that is by '6' (man = animal × reasonable). As the suite of prime numbers is infinite, any number of simple ideas can be represented by such a notation. The language would therefore be able to accommodate new simple concepts as knowledge grew. To transform this 'logical calculus' into a language, it is only necessary to translate the numbers into pronounceable words, following a method analogous to that used by Dalgarno and Wilkins. The numbers 1 to 9 will be represented by the first nine consonants in the alphabet (b, c, d, f, g, h, l, m, n) and successive decimal units 1, 10, 100, 1,000, 10,000, etc, by the five vowels (a, e, i, o, u) and dipthongs formed from them. So the number 81, 374 is written and pronounced 'mubodilefa'. He thought that this notation had the advantage over Dalgarno's that the numerical value of the letters is independent of their position, enabling the syllables of a word to be inverted because each indicates by its vowel the correct order, so 'mubodilefa' can also be written 'bodifalemu' (1000 + 300 + 4 + 70 + 80,000 = 81,374). Such a permutation offered, Leibniz thought, marvellous resources to poetry and song. He even envisaged the possibility of converting this language into music.

In order to make a universal language, however, this framework required a vocabulary and a grammar. Leibniz spent much time in trying to analyse all human ideas as an initial step in reducing them to their simple elements, and attempting to compose a rational grammar by studying the grammars of natural languages. Alas, he never completed this daunting task and his philosophical language remained merely a theoretical project.

THE LEGACY

By the turn of the century, interest in *a priori* philosophical languages had largely evaporated. Slaughter accounts for this by developments in 'atomistic-mechanistic philosophy' which triumphed over Aristotelian physics: 'something had happened, something that vastly complicated the optimistic, and simple, world picture of the projectors; something which made the projects for the universal language look like child's play'. Since the taxonomic method employed in constructing the classification tables of schemes such as Wilkins's was based upon Aristotelian philosophy, the latter's demise proved fatal. The new atomistic philosophy suggested that there were limits to what could be obtained through observation: the certainty needed to construct tables of knowledge was eroded. Following the publication of Newton's *Principia mathematica* in 1687, 'classification could no longer be seen as a means of explaining and representing the nature of nature. Taxonomy was supplanted by mathematics as the method and the language of science.'[35]

Interest had also declined in universal languages because, fascinating and imaginative as they might be, they palpably were incapable of playing the role for which they had been designed. No-one could seriously believe that any of the schemes constructed in the seventeenth century would be adopted as the universal language, not because people could not be persuaded to use them (though this would have proved the case) but because they were unsuited to the role. They were too complicated, too incomplete and too rigid. They provided a focus for the intellectual interest in language so prevalent at the time, but that was their weakness as well as their strength. Shapiro argues that 'If Wilkins and his associates had continued with their original plan for an international non-philosophical language, based on the smallest number of radicals, their work might have had more practical effect.'[36] But the incentive to continue with their work lay precisely in the challenge to devise a language based upon philosophical principles rather than merely a practical, working international medium of communication. However, the seventeenth-century language experiments did leave their mark. Wilkins's own work, for example, played an important role in the standardisation of scientific nomenclature as well as inspiring Roget during his compilation of the *Thesaurus*. As Roget, like Wilkins two centuries before him Secretary to the Royal Society, wrote in the Introduction to the first edition published in 1852:

Such analysis [of ideas] alone can determine the principles on which a strictly *Philosophical Language* might be constructed. The probable result of the construction of such a language would be its eventual adoption by every civilised nation; thus realising that splendid aspiration of philanthropists — the establishment of a Universal Language. However utopian such a project may appear to the present generation, and however abortive may have been the former endeavours of Bishop Wilkins and others to realise it, its accomplishment is surely not beset with greater difficulties than have impeded the progress to many other beneficial objects, which in former times appeared to be no less visionary, and which yet were successfully achieved, in later ages, by the continued and persevering exertions of the human intellect.[37]

The universal language schemes were but one element in the far-reaching concern with language matters in seventeenth-century Europe, a concern which touched many of the leading thinkers. The current revival of interest in language universals has re-kindled a concern for the work of Wilkins and his contemporaries, even though we may no longer share their faith in a perfect universal language as the answer to the problems of the world. The tendency in the eighteenth century was to ridicule these earlier schemes. Horace Walpole, for example, claimed a connection between Wilkins's aeronautical interests and his universal language, 'the latter of which he no doubt calculated to prevent the want of an interpreter when he would arrive at the moon'.[38] Commentators now are more generous. As Salmon has expressed it, 'even if we now have nothing more to learn from the *Essay* we can regard it with sympathy and interest as an attempt to solve a problem which is still with us — the international dissemination of scientific knowledge.'[39]

3

The Enlightenment and After

In the opening decades of the eighteenth century the enthusiasm for universal language projects, which had been apparent in the preceding century, languished. Such a flagging of ardour cannot only be explained by the impracticality of schemes such as those produced by Dalgarno or Wilkins. A new language of international discourse was emerging to replace Latin and to answer the needs of European society. The rise of French as the language of educated Europeans inevitably lessened interest in a constructed language which could act as a medium of international communication.

At the outset of the eighteenth century France was the dominant power in Western Europe. By the standards of the age it had a huge population of over twenty million (one-sixth of the total population of the continent), armies larger than any other state and a talented diplomatic corps. It was also from France above all that the ideas now associated with the Enlightenment emanated: 'what historians have generally agreed to regard as the central strand in the Enlightenment, its critical, rationalistic, intellectually liberating element, suspicious of tradition and received ideas, scornful of what were seen as the destructive follies of the past, was predominantly French.'[1] Ideas spread from Paris, where they appeared in their most concentrated form, to the rest of the continent. Many of the leading thinkers of the time — Montesquieu, Voltaire, Rousseau and Diderot — were Frenchmen, and, for example, the English historian, Edward Gibbon, wrote several works in French 'because I think in French and, strange as it may seem, I can say, with some shame but no affectation that it would be a matter of difficulty to me to compose in my native language.'[2] (Gibbon did, of course, later in his career write at length in his own language, including the six quarto volumes of his most famous work, *The decline and fall of the Roman Empire.*) Anything published in French was immediately accessible to the educated classes throughout Europe, and what was not originally written in French was quickly translated into that international language. It was the diplomatic language of Europe, having replaced Latin by the end of the seventeenth century, and was spoken in most court circles. Many French schools were established all over the continent and an international press emerged which used French. The Royal Academy of Berlin, founded in 1700, adopted French as its official language, and later the Imperial Academy of St Petersburg and the Royal Academy of Turin used both French and Latin. Indeed in the Russian Empire of Peter the Great and his successors, French quickly gained such a hold on the aristocracy that a well-educated person felt ashamed to speak Russian except to the servants. Even Frederick William I, usually regarded as the embodiment of the Prussian spirit, a ruler never happier than when recruiting and drilling his army during his reign from 1713 to 1740, spoke better French than German. As a Sussex landowner wrote to his son, 'A man who understands French may travel all the World over without hesitation of making himself understood, and may make himself perfectly agreeable to all Good Company, which is not the case of any other Language whatever.'[3] In Eastern and Central Europe, French cultural influence was even stronger than in countries such as England and Spain which had well-established literatures of their own.

The dominance of the French language was precarious, however, challenged as it was by the growing strength of the vernaculars in other countries. Reading habits are notoriously hard to gauge, but there is little doubt that literacy did expand throughout the eighteenth century, and especially in the vernacular. At the same time the decline of Latin continued. If early in the sixteenth century two out of every three books published in France were in Latin, by the 1780s these proportions were more than reversed; now only one book in twenty was published in Latin.[4] Even in Germany, by this date only one in eleven books was still published in Latin, although the supporters of the classical tongue had fought a strong rearguard action in the German states. Until nearly the beginning of the eighteenth century there were more books published annually in Germany in Latin than the vernacular, and Latin was still commonly used for university lectures in the second half of the century. In the preface to a translation of Einhard's *Life of Charlemagne* published in Germany in 1728, the writer voiced a not uncharacteristic lament that although the German language had many advantages over Latin its condition had steadily worsened and it was now almost in its last throes.[5] Yet by 1775

German had developed into a rich and subtle literary language, helped by the genius of Lessing and Goethe. In the generation following the Seven Years' War (1756—63) there was a general tendency for French influence to decline, and this was most marked in Germany.

THE REVIVAL OF INTEREST IN UNIVERSAL LANGUAGES

It is also from about 1760 that interest once again was renewed in the possibility of constructing a universal language. The preceding 60 years were not devoid of schemes, but Knowlson lists only four projects published during the period, two in France, one in London and one in Berlin, and none of any significance.[6] This revived enthusiasm can be explained by several factors. One was the publication of a number of previously unpublished writings by Leibniz, who had seriously considered the construction of a universal language in the previous century (see chapter 2). Several scholars in the 1760s and 1770s attempted to develop Leibniz's suggestion that simple ideas could be combined to form complex ideas in much the same way that prime numbers can be combined to produce non-prime numbers. Jean Henri Lambert, for example, attempted to apply mathematical analysis and symbolisation to logic in his *Neues Organon,* published in 1764, while the scheme designed by the Hungarian, Georgius Kalmar, published in three versions in Berlin (1772), Rome (1773) and Vienna (1774), was explicitly linked with Leibniz's ideas for a universal language.[7]

The work carried out by the French Jesuit, Dieudonné Thiébault, shows not only the influence of Leibniz's thinking but also that of contemporary investigations into the nature of the primitive language from which it was believed all languages had developed.[8] Thiébault suggested that a few hundred root-words should be selected, each possessing a single, constant meaning, from which all other terms could be derived. It would then only be necessary to learn by heart these radical root-words and the system for deriving complex terms in order to understand the entire language without difficulty. He believed that all languages could, indeed, be reduced to a very small number of mostly monosyllabic common root-words of one, two or three letters from which they had originally been formed, and which lay at the centre of all our ideas. The consonants in these words represented their important part, while the vowels merely facilitated pronunciation. Once identified, these words would form the vocabulary of his new language. As regards its grammar, Thiébault thought it should be very simple and regular, with, for example, only one declension for nouns, one for adjectives, and one conjunction for verbs. In this he reflected another influence on the universal language projectors of the late eighteenth century: the growing general grammar movement which attempted to discover the universal principles of human thought that lie behind the apparent profusion of existing grammatical forms. The obvious differences between the grammatical principles in existing languages suggested to many grammarians that they should look towards a new, ideal language in which the grammar could reflect the true relations between ideas.

Dieudonné Thiébault's 'Observations générales sur la grammaire et les langues' was published in the *Noveaux mémoires de l'académie royale des sciences et belles-lettres de Berlin* in 1776 (after the expulsion of the Jesuit Order from France in 1764 Thiébault had worked at the Ecole militaire in Berlin). Interest in the idea of a universal language grew more intense, however, in the 1790s, and especially in Republican France. At a time when education, law and administration were all being rationalised it is perhaps not surprising that language should also be selected for consideration. Furthermore, it was hoped by some that a new universal language would help to bind citizens of different nations into a single brotherhood of man. One of the best-known universal language projects of this era, Jean Delormel's *Projet d'une langue universelle présenté à la convention nationale* (1795), expressed it thus: 'if the Government embarks on the teaching of this language, within six months without needing to use it every day at length, it will already be useful for communication, appropriate for disseminating the principles of equality and will bring honour throughout the world to the Republic'.[9]

Delormel had designed a language not unlike those constructed more than 100 years earlier by Dalgarno and Wilkins. In his search for a logical and regular language Delormel based his *Projet* upon a logical classification of ideas into genera and species. He also constituted his language from ten vowels and twenty consonants to conform with the decimal system. The nouns, from which are derived verbs, adverbs and adjectives, are divided into classes, each characterised by one vowel or consonant. Thus 'a' represented grammar, 'f' geography, 'p' astronomy, 'g' religion, and so on. To take a few examples,[10]

ava = grammar
ave = letter
avi = syllable
avo = accent
avau = word

Delormel believed that such a regular system would be extremely simple to learn and use. In practice, however, his project had no more lasting influence than the similar attempts made in the previous century.

A rather different scheme which aroused considerable interest was published in 1797 in French and German editions under the title *Pasigraphie.* [11] Its author, Joseph de Maimieux, originally announced the scheme in 1795, and between that date and publication he claimed to have received almost 6,000 letters from scholars, teachers and businessmen in all parts of Europe expressing hopes that the work would be successfully concluded. One critic praised the project as being of as great importance to humanity as the invention of printing, and Napoleon is said to have admired it. The language was demonstrated in public and even taught in a few schools in France and Germany.

Although de Maimieux later provided a spoken version, the language was primarily a means of written communication. It used only 12 characters and had just 12 general rules to which there were no exceptions. The 12 characters could be combined to form three types of words: three-character words for 'connective and expletive particles of frequent recurrence'; four-character words for 'objects and ideas daily noticed in society'; and five-character words for 'terms of art, science, and recondite inquiry'. Since the number of basic characters was so limited, the method of combining them was of crucial importance. Like Dalgarno and Wilkins, de Maimieux compiled tables, and each character of a word served as a guide to the location of a word and therefore its meaning in the tables. For example, in a three-character word, the first character indicates the column in which the word can be found, the second character indicates the sub-division of the column and the third character the line. Gender and number were indicated by dots and signs. Unfortunately, the characters were sufficiently alike to cause confusion and the language in general was very difficult to learn and use. Furthermore, the classification tables were even less satisfactory than those created in the seventeenth century by John Wilkins.

THE IDEOLOGUES

Another reason for the upsurge of interest in universal language projects in the 1790s was the preoccupation of the French Idéologues with the relationship between language and ideas. The Idéologues — whom Baker calls the true heirs of the Enlightenment — regarded *ideology,* the philosophy of signs, as the only means of reducing the moral and political sciences to positive truths as certain as those in the physical sciences.[12] If, as they believed, the entire thought process depended upon language, then language must be extremely accurate to ensure that truths are attained. There was a general feeling that existing languages were lacking this accuracy and were therefore inadequate vehicles for ideas. One solution to this problem was the development of a universal language which would avoid the shortcomings found in its natural counterparts. The Abbé Condillac, for example, extended John Locke's thesis on the importance of a clear, well-defined language for the combination and comunication of ideas. For Condillac, there was no thought independent of language. He believed that every science could be reduced to simple truths for which signs could be created, and advocated a universal language for each individual science. Condillac's arguments were enthusiastically adopted by the 'father of modern chemistry', Antoine-Laurent Lavoisier. In his *Méthode de nomenclature chimique* (1787) he wrote:

A well made language adapted to the natural and successive order of ideas will bring in its train a necessary and immediate revolution in the method of teaching, and will not allow teachers of chemistry to deviate from the course of nature; either they must reject the nomenclature or they must irresistably follow the course marked out by it. The logic of the sciences is thus essentially dependent on their language.[13]

The French philosopher and mathematician, the Marquis de Condorcet, also pictured a universal language for all men, or rather, for all learned men. Although he could see drawbacks in the kind of classification of knowledge into tables as advocated by Condillac, he thought it was impossible to manage without artificial methods of classifying data: 'If there is little philosophy in mistaking these methodological arrangements for science itself, there is still less in despising them.'[14] In his *Eléments du calcul des probabilités,* Condorcet developed a classification system which has similarities with a modern faceted library classification scheme (but not, as Baker asserts, with the Decimal Classification scheme developed in the nineteenth century by Melvil Dewey).[15] Condorcet's classification scheme consisted of five categories (or facets) with ten terms in each, according to which concepts could be organised. The first category concerns the nature of things, the second methods, the third points of view from which the concepts are considered, the fourth the use and utility of the information, and the fifth the way in which the information was acquired. In each category the divisions are numbered from 0 to 9. To take the first category as an example:

0   Man as an animal
1   Man as a thinking being
2   Society
3   Quantity, size, position
4   Properties common to bodies and general phenomena
5   System of the world and knowledge of the earth
6   Animals
7   Vegetables
8   Minerals
9   Physical technologies and their products

Condorcet claimed that with five categories and ten divisions of each, 100,000 combinations of numbers would be available (10^5).

Knowledge, for Condorcet, was essentially understanding the relationship between things; a classification reducing complex phenomena to a system of signs would enable these phenomena to be ordered in the way that mathematics had ordered phenomena in the physical sciences. His aim was to unite mathematics and classification so as to create in the empirical sciences the abstract relations already achieved in the mathematical sciences. Condorcet's ideas were similar to those of Leibniz, and he thought that the decimal figures he envisaged would not only designate the object concerned but also contain a precise description of its characteristics. He also began to formulate a symbolic logic which would enable terms from his scheme to be combined. His 'Essai d'une langue universelle' was never finished, and Condorcet was aware of the significant differences between the natural sciences and the moral sciences; in the latter, 'it is first of all a question of making known the very objects of the science. It is even necessary to find and to form these first combinations of ideas and to seek to designate them.' The moral sciences were obscure precisely because their terminology was vague and imprecise.[16]

Condorcet was not simply involved with the philosophical and mathematical abstractions of language construction, but envisaged real human gains from the adoption of a universal language. He argued that the invention of printing had helped hasten the decline of Latin as an international scientific language in favour of the vernaculars. As a consequence, knowledge became more accessible to the less enlightened in each country, but at the expense of becoming less accessible internationally to the elite in each country. This in turn had the benefit, however, of saving scientists from becoming a closed caste with an esoteric language, stifling progress and condemning the masses to superstition and ignorance. A universal language would now be a further instrument in the diffusion of knowledge. Condorcet also anticipated a more bizarre benefit from a universal language. In his 'Essai', drafted in France in the 1790s, he expressed fears of a revolution which might destroy cities and scatter nations: 'Is it not possible that a global cataclysm, while not annihilating the human species completely, swallowing them in the eternal abyss with the monuments they have raised, might nevertheless destroy the arts and sciences, their fragile repositories, and even the languages now known?' In case of such a calamity, Condorcet urged the need for an encyclopedic ordering of all knowledge to be translated into an immediately intelligible universal language and then to be kept in a fire-proof vault.[17] Happily, this catastrophe has not yet materialised, but Condorcet's own fate was not so fortunate; having sided with the Revolution, he was then arrested as a member of the Girondist Group on the ascendency of the Jacobins and died in prison in 1794.

Other Idéologues were less confident of the benefits which a universal language might offer the world, fearing that an analytical language suited to the needs of science and philosophy might further widen the gap between a scholarly minority and the rest of the population. Instead of advancing knowledge, such a language might retard it. As Destutt de Tracy wrote,

I believe that the usefulness of a purely learned universal language is more than compensated for by its drawbacks, everywhere where it is not the usual language; and that its inevitable effect, supposing that it does not slow down the progress of luminaries is to concentrate them and reduce them to a single centre of learning which is another way to bring harm to them.[18]

Furthermore, many Idéologues like Destutt de Tracy even questioned the feasibility of constructing a perfect philosophical language. He believed that the major difficulty did not lie with the invention of a written character or spoken syllables, but with the classification of ideas, the problem that had engaged Dalgarno, Wilkins and Leibniz. Scholars would never agree about how simple ideas should be ordered in tables nor how they should be combined to form complex ideas. In any case, he argued, our ideas are imperfect and cannot be expressed precisely like mathematical statements. Languages are inherently flawed. Such arguments undermined the very foundations of *a priori* schemes. As Knowlson concludes:

Although the *a priori* constructed language did not entirely disappear from the scene in the nineteenth century, largely as a result of the criticisms levelled at such schemes by the idéologues it became increasingly difficult to regard such artificial ideal languages as capable of supplying both an international auxiliary language and an improved instrument of thought. And so those who were seeking to construct a language for international usage tended to turn increasingly to the non-philosophical, *a posteriori* method of language building.[19]

A POSTERIORI LANGUAGES

While an *a priori* language is composed entirely of invented elements not to be found in any existing language, and is usually based on a logical classification of ideas, an *a posteriori* language is based on elements of grammar, vocabulary and syntax drawn from one or more natural languages. Although in practice most universal language projects have included a mixture of the two approaches, it is usually possible and helpful to place any particular scheme into one or the other of these general types.

A very early proposal based upon *a posteriori* principles appeared in 1765 in volume nine of that famous symbol of the French Enlightenment, the *Encyclopédie: ou dictionnaire raisonné des sciences, des arts et des métiers,* published in Paris in 35 volumes between 1751 and 1780. The *Encyclopédie,* for which that eminent French man of letters, Diderot, was mainly responsible, had enormous success and influence. It was the largest single publishing venture of the period, attempting to summarise the whole of human knowledge and to disseminate and popularise the ideas of the Enlightenment. The universal language scheme entitled 'Langue nouvelle' by its author, Joachim Faiguet de Villeneuve, was little more than an outline of a regular and simplified grammar, taking up only four pages of the *Encyclopédie,* and he never completed the vocabulary. Nevertheless, he believed that he had found a system which incorporated both natural and easy features. Although the grammar included *a priori* aspects, the vocabulary was derived from French roots, but without articles, genders or variable adjectives. Cases were replaced by prepositions, and nouns formed their plural by adding the letter 's'. Verbs were invariable in person and number, and tenses were indicated by their endings (see Figure 3.1). Numerals, however, were *a priori;* the numbers 1 to 10 were written as follows:

ba, co, de, ga, ji, lu, ma, ni, pa, vu

Eleven was 'vuba', 12 'vuco', etc., to 20, then 'covu', 21 'covuba', and so on. It is interesting to note that some of the tense endings for verbs are the same as those found in Esperanto:

present tense	-as
past tense	-is
future tense	-os

Faiguet himself made it clear that: 'My aim is not to form a universal language for use by the various nations. Such an enterprise will only be suitable for the learned academies which we have in Europe, on the assumption that they will work in cooperation and under Government auspices.'[20] It is not very probable that such a cooperative effort would have been forthcoming, but it was never put to the test as Faiguet, Treasurer at the Department of Finance and author of several works on economics, did not complete his scheme. Nevertheless, 'Langue nouvelle' had broken away from the philosophical underpinnings of the *a priori* projects and set an example which many later universal language schemes were to follow.

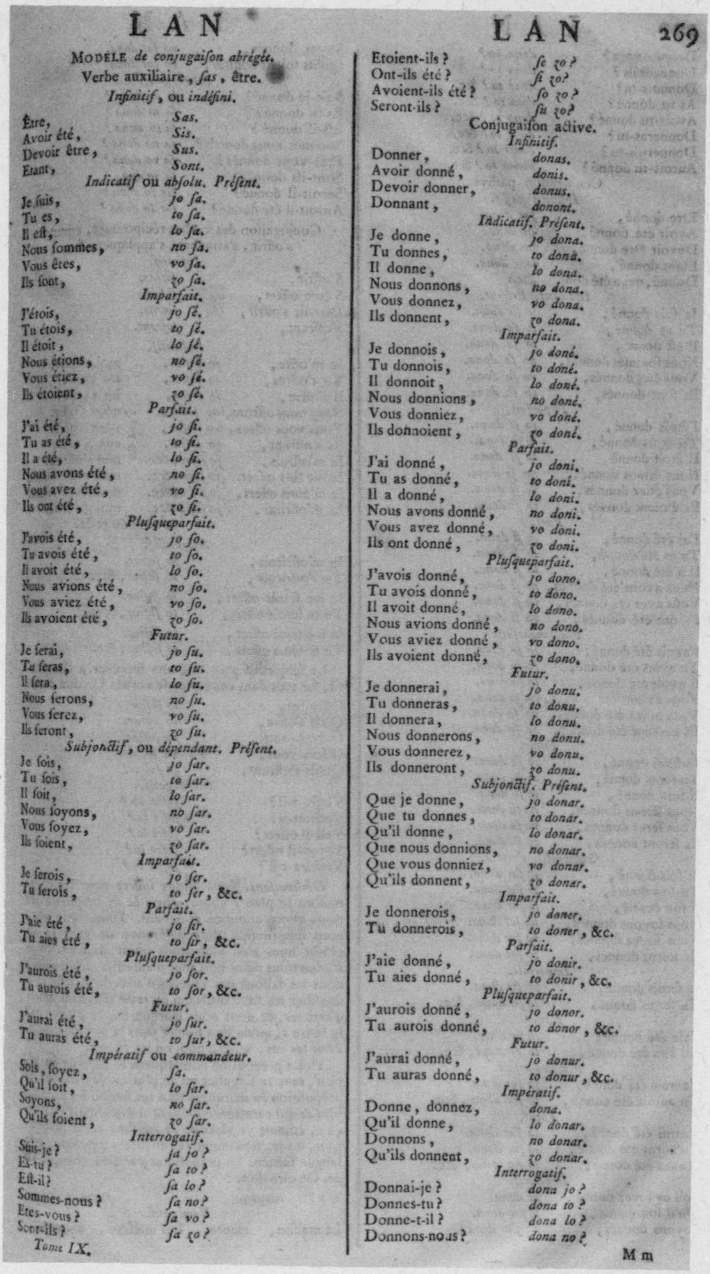

MODELE *de conjugaison abrégée.*
Verbe auxiliaire, *sas*, être.

Infinitif, ou *indéfini.*

Être,	*Sas.*
Avoir été,	*Sis.*
Devoir être,	*Sus.*
Etant,	*Sont.*
Indicatif ou *absolu. Présent.*	
Je suis,	*jo sa.*
Tu es,	*to sa.*
Il est,	*lo sa.*
Nous sommes,	*no sa.*
Vous êtes,	*vo sa.*
Ils sont,	*zo sa.*
Imparfait.	
J'étois,	*jo sé.*
Tu étois,	*to sé.*
Il étoit,	*lo sé.*
Nous étions,	*no sé.*
Vous étiez,	*vo sé.*
Ils étoient,	*zo sé.*
Parfait.	
J'ai été,	*jo si.*
Tu as été,	*to si.*
Il a été,	*lo si.*
Nous avons été,	*no si.*
Vous avez été,	*vo si.*
Ils ont été,	*zo si.*
Plusqueparfait.	
J'avois été,	*jo so.*
Tu avois été,	*to so.*
Il avoit été,	*lo so.*
Nous avions été,	*no so.*
Vous aviez été,	*vo so.*
Ils avoient été,	*zo so.*
Futur.	
Je serai,	*jo su.*
Tu seras,	*to su.*
Il sera,	*lo su.*
Nous serons,	*no su.*
Vous serez,	*vo su.*
Ils seront,	*zo su.*
Subjonctif, ou *dépendant. Présent.*	
Je sois,	*jo sar.*
Tu sois,	*to sar.*
Il soit,	*lo sar.*
Nous soyons,	*no sar.*
Vous soyez,	*vo sar.*
Ils soient,	*zo sar.*
Imparfait.	
Je serois,	*jo ser.*
Tu serois,	*to ser*, &c.
Parfait.	
J'aie été,	*jo sir.*
Tu aies été,	*to sir*, &c.
Plusqueparfait.	
J'aurois été,	*jo sor.*
Tu aurois été,	*to sor*, &c.
Futur.	
J'aurai été,	*jo sur.*
Tu auras été,	*to sur*, &c.
Impératif ou *commandeur.*	
Sois, soyez,	*sa.*
Qu'il soit,	*lo sar.*
Soyons,	*no sar.*
Qu'ils soient,	*zo sar.*
Interrogatif.	
Suis-je?	*sa jo?*
Es-tu?	*sa to?*
Est-il?	*sa lo?*
Sommes-nous?	*sa no?*
Etes-vous?	*sa vo?*
Sont-ils?	*sa zo?*

Tome IX.

Etoient-ils?	*se zo?*
Ont-ils été?	*si zo?*
Avoient-ils été?	*so zo?*
Seront-ils?	*su zo?*

Conjugaison active.

Infinitif.	
Donner,	*donas.*
Avoir donné,	*donis.*
Devoir donner,	*donus.*
Donnant,	*donont.*
Indicatif. Présent.	
Je donne,	*jo dona.*
Tu donnes,	*to dona.*
Il donne,	*lo dona.*
Nous donnons,	*no dona.*
Vous donnez,	*vo dona.*
Ils donnent,	*zo dona.*
Imparfait.	
Je donnois,	*jo doné.*
Tu donnois,	*to doné.*
Il donnoit,	*lo doné.*
Nous donnions,	*no doné.*
Vous donniez,	*vo doné.*
Ils donnoient,	*zo doné.*
Parfait.	
J'ai donné,	*jo doni.*
Tu as donné,	*to doni.*
Il a donné,	*lo doni.*
Nous avons donné,	*no doni.*
Vous avez donné,	*vo doni.*
Ils ont donné,	*zo doni.*
Plusqueparfait.	
J'avois donné,	*jo dono.*
Tu avois donné,	*to dono.*
Il avoit donné,	*lo dono.*
Nous avions donné,	*no dono.*
Vous aviez donné,	*vo dono.*
Ils avoient donné,	*zo dono.*
Futur.	
Je donnerai,	*jo donu.*
Tu donneras,	*to donu.*
Il donnera,	*lo donu.*
Nous donnerons,	*no donu.*
Vous donnerez,	*vo donu.*
Ils donneront,	*zo donu.*
Subjonctif. Présent.	
Que je donne,	*jo donar.*
Que tu donnes,	*to donar.*
Qu'il donne,	*lo donar.*
Que nous donnions,	*no donar.*
Que vous donniez,	*vo donar.*
Qu'ils donnent,	*zo donar.*
Imparfait.	
Je donnerois,	*jo doner.*
Tu donnerois,	*to doner*, &c.
Parfait.	
J'aie donné,	*jo donir.*
Tu aies donné,	*to donir*, &c.
Plusqueparfait.	
J'aurois donné,	*jo donor.*
Tu aurois donné,	*to donor*, &c.
Futur.	
J'aurai donné,	*jo donur.*
Tu auras donné,	*to donur*, &c.
Impératif.	
Donne, donnez,	*dona.*
Qu'il donne,	*lo donar.*
Donnons,	*no donar.*
Qu'ils donnent,	*zo donar.*
Interrogatif.	
Donnai-je?	*dona jo?*
Donnes-tu?	*dona to?*
Donne-t-il?	*dona lo?*
Donnons-nous?	*dona no?*

Mm

Figure 3.1 Excerpt from Faiguet's 'Langue nouvelle' showing verbal tenses
Source: Encyclopédie, vol. 9. Paris: A. Neufchastel, 1765, p. 269.

GESTURE AS A UNIVERSAL LANGUAGE

The human species, like its anthropoid cousins, must have used gesture as a means of communication since primordial times. In the seventeenth and eighteenth centuries, however, gesture received particular attention as a way of communicating with the deaf. George Dalgarno, for example, claimed that his universal character

shall be a ready way, and a singular means, to convey Knowledge to deaf and dumb people (which is a secret of learning heretofore not discovered) and it is conceived upon good ground that a deaf man might be taught to communicate in this Character, in the sixth part of the time that any other man could learn a foreign language.[21]

Indeed, in 1680 a work by Dalgarno was published which was devoted to this topic, but it was in the following century that individual enthusiasts in England and France really turned to the systematic education of the deaf.[22]

Emphasis in the two countries, however, was different. In England, the education of the deaf was marked by an ignorance of the psychology of deafness and an unwillingness to apply the new psychological and philosophical concepts which were being developed in France. This can largely be explained by the pre-eminent role of charities manned by evangelical reformers in the education of the deaf in England. The main goal of such evangelists was to lead the deaf to the sacred Biblical text. In France the situation was quite different; there was an evident desire to develop systematic methods for studying the problems of communication which involved an investigation of the sign language used by the deaf themselves.

The idea that gesture could provide a universal language had first been inspired by the use of gestures in Renaissance rhetoric. This was explicitly stated in a later manual of rhetoric published in 1644 by the English physician, John Bulwer. In *Chirologia: or the Naturall Language of the Hand,* Bulwer pointed out that the hand 'Speakes all languages, and as *universall character of Reason* is generally understood and knowne by all Nations, among the formal differences of their Tongue'. He thought that signs were superior to spoken words because they are more striking, speedier to use and more natural; they could therefore be universally understood without being learned or translated. Bulwer in fact believed gesture to have been the language of Adam and all mankind until the famous event at Babel.

Although the deaf and dumb had been observed to use signs, there was still a strongly-held feeling that gesture was only suitable for primitive communication. The Scottish judge and linguist, Lord Monboddo, for example, grouped the deaf with children and savages as representing the first stages in the 'progress of the human mind'. Furthermore, the discovery at the beginning of the seventeenth century that deaf mutes could be taught to understand conventional written characters or to lip read diverted attention from sign language until the late eighteenth century. Renewed interest in sign language was largely the result of work by the Abbé de l'Epée, which marked a turning point in the education of the deaf. What is more, l'Epée linked his work on gesture with the idea of a universal language. His first book on teaching the deaf, published in 1776, had the title *Institution des sourds et muets, par la voie des signes méthodiques: ouvrage qui contient le projet d'une langue universelle, par l'entremise des signes naturels, assujettis à une méthode.* L'Epée wrote:

One has often desired a universal language, with the help of which men of all nations could understand each other. It seems to me that it has existed for a long time and that it is understood everywhere. This is not astonishing; it is a natural language. I am speaking of the language of signs. But hitherto it has not been of great use because it has always been retained in its crude state without perfecting it by introducing rules.[23]

L'Epée produced a language of signs consisting partly of gestures used spontaneously by the deaf, supplemented by others developed from these natural signs. Abstract ideas were difficult to cope with because if the signs were arbitrary the language would quickly become too complex to be easily learned or recalled. His solution was one already taken by many universal language projectors: to analyse all complex and abstract ideas into simpler and more concrete parts which could then be expressed by physical gesture. In this way, he argued, the language would possess the simplicity of arithmetical symbols rather than the complexity of Chinese characters. Such an analysis would offer the bonus of removing vagueness from the ideas themselves. Although l'Epée was probably unaware of the work by the earlier language projectors, his proposal resembles it (except that it was visual rather than written or spoken). But his reduction of complex ideas into simple constituents was a practical rather than a philosophical analysis with the aim of isolating ideas which could be represented by physical movements. Thus the phrase 'I believe' would be broken down into four elements, each with its own gesture:

> I say yes with my mind
> I say yes with my heart
> I say yes with my mouth
> I have not seen and I still cannot see with my eyes

Although the Abbé de l'Epée's sign language had tremendous success as a medium for instructing the deaf, it met with little support as a universal language. After his death the work was continued by his former pupil, the Abbé de Sicard, but the language was considered too complex for use as a vehicle of international communication. It also lacked a script and, finally, might not even have proved universal: a sign interpreted one way in one country may not be similarly interpreted in another country with different social habits.

DEVELOPMENTS IN ENGLAND

So far attention has been largely concentrated on developments in France, and with good reason. France was the pre-eminent country in eighteenth-century philosophy and linguistics. Nevertheless, all was not stagnant across the Channel. Scholarly interest in language remained, but with a changed emphasis. Alongside the growing interest in the English language, a view was increasingly expressed that a knowledge of the classical tongues was of little or no help in mastering the vernacular. Further, such topics as Egyptian hieroglyphs or Chinese ideograms, so dear to the hearts of linguists in the previous century, by the middle of the eighteenth century were considered irrelevant to general discussions on language. The great seventeenth-century language projectors were scarcely remembered at all. Following a fairly detailed account of John Wilkins's scheme in his book, *Of the origin and progress of language* (1774), James Burnet, Lord Monboddo, apologetically explained that 'I know many of my readers will think that I have given a fuller account . . . than was necessary or proper; but [the *Essay*] is little known.' Although Burnet added that 'I think it deserves to be very much known and admired', he could not resist poking fun at its author. Wilkins, he wrote, was

a man of a singular genius, aspiring to things great and extraordinary. Not contented with the possession of his native element the earth, nor with the power of making himself, if he pleased, an inhabitant of the water, as much as an otter, or any other amphibious animal, he wanted to vindicate to man the dominion of another element, I mean the air, by teaching him to fly. [A reference to Wilkins's astronautical ideas as expressed in his *The discovery of a new world in the moone: or a discourse tending to prove that 'tis probable there may be another habitable world in that planet.*] Of kin, I think, to this attempt, though not so romantic, was his scheme of an universal philosophical language, both written and vocal.[24]

Lord Monboddo was himself, it might be added, somewhat eccentric. He refused to travel in a carriage, for example, considering it an engine of effeminacy and idleness unused by his heroes, the Ancient Greeks. He thought the true position of a man was to be on a horse's back, not to be dragged behind its tail, as he expressed it, and he always rode on his journeys from Edinburgh to London.[25] As the *Dictionary of national biography* diplomatically comments, 'In his judicial capacity he showed himself to be both a profound lawyer and an upright judge, and his decisions were free from those paradoxes which so frequently appeared in his writings as well as in his conversation.'

Linguists were still interested in the origins of language and references to Babel continued to be made, but as the beginning of linguistics, not the end. Social and historical, rather than divine, explanations were sought for the origin of languages and their changes over time. As William Kenrick expressed it:

Speech, say the Divines, is the gift of God. It undoubtedly is so; as he hath given mankind the faculties and talents of attaining it: but a philosopher, employed in the investigation of second causes, who would trace the rise and progress of human attainments, should consider it is an art, which has gradually improved, from the rudest efforts of simple nature, to its present degree of artificial perfection.[26]

The diversity of languages was now seen as an asset to man rather than a handicap. Joseph Priestley, theologian and scientist, in his *A Course of Lectures on the Theory of Language, and Universal Grammar* (1762), ascribes moral virtues to the multiplicity of languages in use: 'The diversity of languages and diversity of government contribute to one another, the variations of speech have tended to check the propagation of vice and false religion.' The study of different languages frees the mind 'from many prejudices and errors' since people who only know one language 'are perpetually confounding the ideas of words with the idea of things; which the comparison of languages, and frequent rendering from one into another, helps to make us distinguish'.[27] This is far removed from the belief that a universal language alone can both unite mankind and help to overcome the divide between things and the words used to describe them. Linguistic differences now were not only objects of study but also sources of pride.

That is not to say that all interest in a universal language had perished in England. John Williams, a schoolmaster, sought to promote Latin as a universal language, especially for scientific works. He chose Latin not because of any inherent virtues but because it was the most widely known language. In the works of linguists like John Cleland (now better remembered for his novel, *Fanny Hill, or the Memoirs of a Woman of Pleasure*) and the Welshman, Rowland Jones (who in his books, *Hieroglyfic: or a Grammatical Introduction to An Universal Hieroglyfic Language* (1768) and *The Circles of Gomer* (1771) advocated English as a universal language) echoes of the seventeenth-century projects can be found. These works, however, lay outside the mainstream of English linguistic thought.

LANGUAGE AND NATIONALISM

Although a shared language may not always be a necessary condition for the formation of national consciousness (the Swiss, for example, are commonly cited as evidence of national unity despite linguistic diversity), there can be little doubt that language is usually a core element in any feeling of national unity and this was particularly true of nineteenth-century nationalism. Indeed, the eclipse of a supranational culture based upon training in the classical languages, and the growing emphasis on the vernaculars in Western civilisation, helped to foster national consciousness in Europe. In language resided the greatness of the past, the cultural history of the nation; 'the essence of a nationality is its spirit, its individuality, its soul' and 'this soul is not only reflected and protected by the mother tongue but, in a sense, the mother tongue is itself an aspect of the soul'.[28] This view was explicitly argued by the German romantic writer, Johann Gottfried von Herder (1744-1803). His first considerable work, *Fragmente über die neuere deutsche Literatur* (1767), was largely concerned with the origins of poetry and language, and set up the simple and spontaneous poetry of the people as the true model for the development of national genius. He emphasised the value of the individual contribution of each nation to the whole of history and the benefits of diversity in language and culture.

The growth of national particularism after the French Revolution and the romantic ideas of Herder and his like did not present a rich soil for the cultivation of universal language projects in the opening decades of the nineteenth century. Although the species did not wither completely, little of interest was produced. In 1855 the Société Internationale de Linguistique was set up in Paris to examine impartially different language schemes and to report on them. It began by formulating the theoretical premises of a universal language; it must have a scientific character and should also be clear, simple, easy, rational, logical, philosophical, rich, harmonious and flexible: no small order. Not surprisingly, none of the ancient or modern languages was felt to possess these attributes. The Society still held firmly to the belief that an artificial language should be purely philosophical. It therefore considered the ideas of such eminent scholars as Bacon, Descartes, Leibniz, Voltaire, Monboddo, Condillac and Condorcet, as well as studying the actual projects of Dalgarno and Wilkins, the 'ridiculous project' of Faiguet which was dismissed as 'a grotesque travesty of the French language', and the 'first serious project', that of Delormel, whose principles could serve as a basis for a universal language.[29]

The Society in fact selected two contemporary *a priori* schemes for special consideration, each of which it believed had great merits. The Abbé Bonifacio Sotos Ochando's *Proyecto y ensayo,* published in Madrid in 1851 or 1852 (and in French translation in 1855), arranged ideas into logical classes. The first letter of each word indicated the basic class of the concept, the second letter the first division of the general class, and so on. Thus inorganic matter was in class A, physical objects at Ab, simple elements at Aba, and oxygen at Ababa. The language, which was specifically designed for international scientific communication rather than general usage, was actually used in several works and a compendium was published as late as 1885. Nevertheless, as Couturat and Leau point out, it was a totally impractical language, if only because the lack of any correspondence between the words and the ideas they expressed made prodigious demands upon the memory.[30] The second project was somewhat similar in execution. Letellier's scheme, the result of 15 years' labour by a French inspector of schools, was completed in 1850 and published in four volumes between 1852 and 1855 under the title, *Course complet de langue universelle.* It was based upon an analysis of knowledge and its division into simple concepts.[31] Ideas are grouped into ten main categories, each divided into ten classes, with ten sub-classes, then genera and finally 100,000 species. So:

ege	=	father	$eg\bar{e}$	=	mother
egi	=	son	$eg\bar{i}$	=	daughter
ego	=	brother	$eg\bar{o}$	=	sister
egu	=	husband	$eg\bar{u}$	=	wife
egeg	=	grandfather	$eg\bar{e}g$	=	grandfather
		(father of the father)			(father of the mother)

The Société internationale de Linguistique thought Letellier's project to be theoretically excellent but too artificial and too complicated for use; it preferred Sotos Ochando's scheme, which although not perfect, provided a basis for a suitable language. Despite such a recommendation, neither project won any more popular support than the projects based upon similar philosophical principles which had been propounded in the previous two centuries.

One project, however, did generate considerable interest throughout much of the nineteenth century. Solresol (Langue Musicale Universelle) was an unusually eccentric language even by the standards of universal language projects, and this in all probability accounts for some of its undoubted popularity.[32] It was conceived shortly after the end of the Napoleonic Wars, and still had active supporters in the Société pour la propagation de la Langue universelle Solrésol at the outset of the First World War a century later. The inventor of Solresol, Jean François Sudre, was a music master who appreciated that not only was music an international medium but that the seven notes of the Solfrège or Sol-fa (now somewhat altered in the English forms of the Tonic Sol-fa), employed for teaching singing, had an internationally-recognised syllabic value: do, re, mi, fa, sol, la, si. He therefore set out to produce a language which would have a vocabulary constructed from these seven syllables alone.

Although Solresol was an *a priori* language, it was not a philosophical language based upon a logical classification of ideas. Combinations of one or two notes form the particles and pronouns:

si = yes	dore = I	redo = my
do = no	domi = you	remi = your
re = and	dofa = he	refa = his
mi = or		
sol = if		

Combinations of three notes are used for the most commonly encountered words:

doredo = time	doresol = month
doremi = day	dorela = year
dorefa = week	doresi = century

Combinations of four notes are divided into seven classes (called keys) according to the initial note. The key of 'do' includes the physical and moral aspects of man, 're' is used for the family, household and dress, 'la' for industry and commerce, and so on.

Combinations of five notes furnish the names of the three categories: animal, vegetable, and mineral. And finally, to accommodate proper names, geographical terms, etc., Sudre provided a transcription in notes of the letters of the alphabet. Altogether, Sudre planned to use seven words of one syllable, 49 of two sylables, 336 of three syllables, 2,268 of four syllables, and 9,072 of five syllables.

Grammatical categories may be distinguished by the position of an accent over the syllables as follows:

sirelasi	= to constitute	(verb)
sîrelasi	= constitution	(name of a thing)
sirêlasi	= constituent	(name of a person)
sirelâsi	= constitutional	(adjective)
sirelasî	= constitutionally	(adverb)

The opposite of an idea is often expressed by reversing the order of the syllables in a word, so:

misol	= good	solmi	= evil
domisol	= God	solmido	= Devil
sollasi	= to go up	silasol	= to go down

Based as it was on the musical scale, Solresol could not only be spoken but sung, whistled or played on a musical instrument. If each syllable was reduced to its first letter (which leaves no ambiguity) then a kind of shorthand is provided which could be written at speed. Solresol could also serve as a gesture language for the deaf and dumb. A point noted by the armed forces was that by using bells or horns, or designating a differently coloured flag for each syllable (and the rainbow is commonly broken into seven colours), Solresol could enable communication to take place over considerable distances. For this reason, the French Naval and War Ministries seriously considered it for military purposes.

Sudre conceived the idea of a musical language in 1817 and ten years later he presented his work to the Academy of Fine Arts in Paris. He continued perfecting his language until his death in 1862, but it was only in 1866 that Solresol was finally published. Yet it had already received widespread acclaim. At the Universal Exhibition in Paris in 1855 it was presented with an exceptional prize of 10,000 francs and at the London Exhibition in 1862 was awarded a medal of honour. The language was also endorsed by men of eminence including Victor Hugo, Lamartine and Napoleon III. Indeed, until Volapük and then Esperanto achieved mass popularity, Solresol was the artificial language which succeeded best in capturing the popular imagination. As such, it justly deserves its place in the history of the artificial language movement. As an artificial language, however, it suffered from grave weaknesses. In their famous study of universal languages, Couturat and Leau describe Solresol as 'the most artificial and the most impractical of all the *a priori* languages', and characterise it as 'possessing to an extreme degree, all the practical faults of philosophical languages [monotonous, difficult to learn, difficult to identify the individual words when used for oral communication as so few different syllables are used, etc.] without any of their theoretical advantages'.[33] As an aside, by the way, it is worth noting that two centuries earlier John Wilkins had also discussed the possibility of a

musical language in *Mercury, or the Secret and Swift Messenger* (1641),
a work devoted to cryptography, as had Francis Godwin in his imaginary
voyage, *The man in the moon* (see chapter 1).

Solresol by no means marked the final attempt to construct an artificial
language on *a priori* principles; indeed, such schemes continue to surface
today. Nevertheless, Sudre's scheme was one of the last to attract interest
from more than a handful of enthusiasts. Henceforward hopes for a
universal language were pinned firmly on projects based to varying extents
on *a posteriori* principles. The main highway of the artificial language
movement abandoned the philosophical abstractions of the seventeenth-
and eighteenth-century scholars; the goal now became above all the
construction of a language which would be accepted by the world as a
neutral and effective medium of international communication.

4

The Widening of Appeal

VOLAPÜK

Events in the last quarter of the nineteenth century finally seemed to be justifying the hopes and efforts of those who had striven during the previous 300 years to create a universal language. For the first time an artificial language had really caught the popular imagination; men and women in considerable numbers were embracing Volapük, the 'world language', as its name is translated into English. Was Volapük to succeed where all other schemes had failed; was it really to become a language of international communication for the peoples of the world rather than an obscure footnote to the history of ideas?

Volapük was the creation of a German parish priest, Monsignor Johann Martin Schleyer, a talented poet and musician from Litzelstetten on Lake Constance, who reputedly had some familiarity with more than 50 languages (according to one account, Schleyer even knew 'in one fashion or another' 83 languages).[1] As recounted by Schleyer himself, the invention of Volapük occurred as a result of sudden inspiration during a night of insomnia in 1879 when he was 47 years old, and was to be a contribution to the unity and fraternity of mankind, a grandiose work of peace. In fact, he had been troubled by the problems of international communication for some time. Indeed, the previous year had seen the unveiling of a universal alphabet, invented by Schleyer in order to transcribe foreign names. As the story goes, this work had been undertaken when he heard that a letter from a neighbour to his son had been returned by the postal authorities in America because the clumsy efforts of a German peasant to write an address in English had been undecipherable.[2]

Like many of the earlier language constructors, Schleyer believed that all natural languages had grave defects which the absolutely rational and regular grammar of a constructed language could avoid. It would be both capable of expressing thoughts with the greatest clarity and accuracy, and easy to learn by the greatest possible number of people. With this end in mind, towards the end of 1880 he presented his new language to the world for its judgement.

Volapük had an alphabet of eight vowels and twenty consonants, and was largely based upon English as the most widespread language of 'civilised peoples'.[3] Unlike English, however, it used four cases, a characteristic which was unlikely to appeal greatly to the Anglo-Saxons. Taking as an example the Volapük word for 'house', nouns were declined as follows:

	Singular	*Plural*
Nominitive:	dom	doms
Genitive:	doma	domas
Dative:	dome	domes
Accusative:	domi	domis

Feminine variations of masculine substantives were formed by adding the prefix 'ji'; thus 'blod' meant 'brother' and 'jiblod' was 'sister'. Adjectives were formed, on the other hand, by the suffix 'ik'; so 'gud' meant 'goodness' and 'gudik' meant 'good'.

Verbs have one regular conjugation, voice and tense being indicated by prefixes, person and personal pronouns by suffixes. The present tense of 'löfön', 'to love', is conjugated:

I love	löfob	We love	löfobs
You love	löfol	You love	löfols
He loves	löfom	They love (m)	löfoms
She loves	löfof	They love (f)	löfofs
It loves	löfos	They love (n)	löfon

Examples of other tenses of the indicative are:

I was loving	älöfob
I loved	elöfob
I had loved	ilöfob
I shall love	olöfob
I shall have loved	ulöfob

Moods are represented by suffixes:

la = subjunctive
öd = imperative
ön = infinitive

and the passive by the prefix 'p' or 'pa' with the active form ('palöfön', therefore, is 'to be loved').

Although the vocabulary of Volapük was largely based upon English, it also adopted words from German, French, Spanish and Italian. Many of these words, however, were quite radically transformed before entering Volapük, a cause of major criticism (see below). Schleyer totally excluded the letter 'h' from his language, and almost entirely eliminated 'r' in consideration of Chinese, old people and children, a disparate collection of individuals who supposedly had difficulty pronouncing the sound represented by this letter. Further, all radicals were to begin and end with a consonant and, as far as possible, use alternating consonant and vowel. The consequence of these rules in many instances was to generate a word in Volapük which was unrecognisable from its original source word. This point can easily be illustrated by taking a few Volapük words derived from English roots. Who would guess that 'mun', 'nol', 'pük', 'vol', 'tut' and 'flen' are derived respectively from 'moon', 'knowledge', 'speak', 'world', 'tooth' and 'friend'? Proper names were phonetically transcribed according to Schleyer's universal alphabet, following pronunciation in their national language, first names following surname. In such an unphonetical language as English, this method produces such completely unrecognisable monstrosities as 'Consn Cems' instead of 'James Johnson'.

The vocabulary of Volapük also tried to use logical word-building rules. The suffix 'av', for example, indicated a science; thus 'lit' was 'light' and 'litav' was 'optics'. Another suffix, 'äl', was used for spiritual or abstract concepts: 'kap' for 'head' and 'kapäl' for 'intelligence', 'men' is the Volapük for 'man' while menäl is used for 'humanity'. To demonstrate this schematic construction using a family of words, 'pük' (language) can be built into such related words as:

pükik	linguistic	möpüked	polyglot
pükatidel	teacher of languages	püköf	eloquence
pükön	to speak	püköfik	eloquent

motapük	mother tongue	okopükot	monologue
pükat	talk	lepükön	to assert
telapükat	dialogue	lepük	assertion
pükav	philology	nepük	silence
püked	sentence	sepük	pronunciation
pükedavod	proverb	tapük	contradiction

and so on. Composite words were normally formed from the genitive singular of the first word; so, Volapük itself means 'world language' ('vol' = 'world', 'pük' = 'speak') and 'ledamel' is 'Red Sea'.

The Volapük movement experienced a spectacular growth, spreading rapidly from Germany into Austria, France and the Low Countries, and thence to the far-flung corners of the globe. By 1889 there were some 283 societies or clubs scattered throughout the world as far away as Sydney and San Francisco, 1,600 holders of the Volapük diploma and an estimated one million Volapükists (at least according to their own estimates; one-fifth of this figure is a more realistic number).[4] Over 300 textbooks on the language had been published and 25 journals were devoted to Volapük, seven being entirely published in the language. The First Volapük International Congress, held in Friedrichshafen in August 1884, was conducted in German (most of the participants were from Germany), as was the Second Congress in Munich (1887), but the Third International Congress, held in Paris in 1889, was completed exclusively in Volapük. According to Albert Guérard, even the waiters and porters spoke Volapük.[5] This was a tremendous achievement for the young language, and seemed to consecrate its inevitable universal triumph. In the introduction to a *Handbook of Volapük* published in London in 1888, Charles Sprague confidently stated that 'Volapük has now become so widely diffused that it can no longer be treated as a mere project', and at last this comment on an artificial language seemed justified.[6] Yet the triumphant year of the Third Volapük International Congress also marked the zenith of the language: its decline, alas, was to be if anything even more dramatic than its ascent. What went wrong?

The answer to this question must be sought in both linguistic and personal issues. The initial successes of Volapük underline not only that a considerable number of people in a wide range of countries felt the need for an international medium of communication but also that there was a willingness to embrace an artificial language constructed for this purpose.

Yet Volapük exhibited several grave linguistic defects for a language
which was intended to be learnt by the masses rather than by just the few
for whom such projects exercise an intellectual attraction which may well
grow stronger as their complexity increases. This is not to argue that
linguistic merit will automatically ensure the universal adoption of a
constructed language: far from it. In the case of Volapük, however, its
perceived linguistic weaknesses contributed powerfully to the clash of
personalities which quickly destroyed it as an effective aspirant to the role
of international language.

Volapük can be categorised as a mixed language, exhibiting characteristics
of both *a priori* and *a posteriori* languages. Its grammar was complicated,
although regular, and included considerable *a priori* elements, such as its
inflections. One Volapükist boasted of the 505,440 different forms that a
verb might take in the language, but this very flexibility was seen by many
as a grave defect. Fine distinctions of meaning were purchased at the
expense of simplicity and memorability. The choice of vocabulary was
even more open to criticism, such as that levelled by Couturat and Leau in
their study of artificial languages.[7] First, they say, certain vowels such as
ä, ö and ü, are difficult to pronounce for many Europeans (they were
meant to be pronounced as the French è, eu and u respectively), while the
letter 'r', present in many of the words from which Volapük vocabulary
was derived, is largely excluded. And if 'r' is omitted for the benefit of the
Chinese, what about the letter 'l' which is troublesome for the Japanese?
Second, a preference for monosyllables led to convoluted word formation
if multiple meanings for words were to be avoided. To take one example,
the Volapük word for scissors, 'jim', is derived from the German 'Schere'.
A straight phonetic transcription would have given 'jer', but this is
unacceptable as it contains an 'r'. This letter might be swapped for an 'l' in
many cases, but in this particular example 'jel' was already in use as the
Volapük word for protection. Changing the vowel from 'e' to 'i' gives 'jil',
but again this word was already in use to mean 'female'. The final
transformation was therefore to change the last consonant as well as the
vowel; hence 'jim', which is no longer identifiable from 'Schere'. The
majority of Volapük radicals are difficult to recognise even by someone
with a knowledge of several European languages because they are not
based upon international roots. This makes them more difficult to learn.
Indeed, in some cases a seemingly international word turns out to mean
something quite different. The Volapük word for mountain, 'bel', would
evoke in Romance peoples the idea of beauty, while still being

unrecognisable to Germans, from whose language (berg) it was in fact derived. Similarly, 'fil' might suggest the idea of son, but it actually means fire. As Couturat and Leau plaintively ask, what is the point of using English radicals such as 'father', 'mother' and 'prince' if they become unrecognisable even to the English as 'fat', 'mot' and 'plin'? Even when English words were taken directly into Volapük, the tendency to prefer the phonetic rather than the graphemic method of transfer effectively disguised their origin; 'stajen', for example, is no longer easily recognisable as the English 'station'. Overall, Volapük was undoubtedly difficult to learn and to use, although, it must be said, easier by far than its predecessors like Solresol.

These linguistic shortcomings quickly became the focus of a heated conflict within the Volapük movement. Schleyer himself considered his language capable of the most complex nuances, but this very richness became increasingly an irritant to others who wanted a simple and practical language for everyday international communication. Attempts to simplify Volapük centred upon its leading French exponent, Auguste Kerckhoffs, Professor of modern languages at the Ecole des hautes études commerciales in Paris. Whilst respecting the principles of Volapük, Kerckhoffs tried to simplify certain features. He argued, for example, that the transcription of proper names into the universal alphabet should be abandoned: each name would be written and pronounced as in its language of origin. The genitive and dative case endings ought to be replaced, he thought, by prepositions, and four of the six conditional tenses scrapped. These corrections were approved by many Volapükists, but Schleyer and the majority of his German supporters opposed any changes. The Second International Congress had founded the Universal Association of Volapükists and set up an International Academy of Volapük charged with overseeing the regular development of the language and preserving its unity. The election of Schleyer as its Grand Master and Kerckhoffs as its Director did not bode well, however, for such a unity within the movement. In particular, a clash occurred over Schleyer's insistence that as its father figure he should have a right of veto over any changes to the language. Kerckhoffs was prepared to give Schleyer three votes (there were 17 members on the Grand Council) but refused a right of veto. The Academy continued to vote on reforms and decided to seek ratification for them at the Third Congress in 1889. Kerckhoffs was elected President of the Academy, which now became the sole authority on all linguistic questions, but tension between Schleyer and himself continued to increase, and he resigned two years later. Despite continued pressure for linguistic reforms, Schleyer refused to accept changes, and eventually he refused to accept the Academy at all. Volapük was finished as a serious contender for international language. Schleyer did form a new Academy consisting only of those prepared to accept his authority, but this failed to reverse the fortunes of Volapük. Its supporters rapidly melted away and by the time of Schleyer's death in 1912 its speakers were far outnumbered by a new challenger which had entered the arena and to which many Volapükists transferred their allegiance (although, amazingly, one Volapük journal survived until 1960).

The Danish linguist and artificial language enthusiast, Otto Jespersen, characterised Volapük as 'a most curious mixture of good and bad'.[8] To its credit, he argued, it exhibited perfect regularity of all its forms, a fullness of vocabulary and a phonetic alphabet (not to everyone's liking). On the negative side, however, was the often asserted claim that nearly everything in the language rested upon the individual fancies or whims of its creator. Nevertheless, Volapük was the first artificial language to attract genuine popular support. No other constructed language had won more than a handful of enthusiasts or had seemed poised actually to become an international auxiliary language. In comparison with earlier *a priori* languages, Volapük must have looked eminently simple and practical. It might have used a complicated grammar and abjured internationally recognisable roots, but it remains not only an easier language to learn than the overwhelming majority of its predecessors, but also much more regular and straightforward than any natural language. Though not an attractive looking or sounding language to West Europeans, Volapük could satisfactorily convey written and spoken words; indeed, it was successfully used for both these purposes during its brief hey-day. Schleyer's rigidity concerning his linguistic 'child' was ill-advised, yet frequent changes in a language to answer the inevitable quibbles of individual critics is unlikely to prove attractive to the potential learner. Summing up Volapük, Guérard acknowledged that 'To Father Schleyer we owe the decisive step in the history of international languages' as 'his Volapük did not remain a paper proposal, a Utopian dream; it was actually used by all sorts and conditions of men.' In Guérard's words, 'Schleyer is the blazer of the trail.'[9] From our perspective, these words perhaps appear somewhat exaggerated; an artificial international language is no closer now than then. Undoubtedly, however, Volapük marked an important stage in the history of artificial languages.

Volapük itself spawned a number of descendants which quickly disappeared with little trace: Bopal, Spelin, Dil, Balta and Orba, for example, emerged in the last two decades of the nineteenth century, but only their rather exotic names now arouse curiosity. Of much greater lasting significance, however, was the creation of a Jewish oculist from Bialystok in Eastern Poland, called Ludwig Lazarus Zamenhof.

THE BIRTH OF ESPERANTO

Zamenhof, eldest son of a school language teacher and later Government censor, was born in December 1859 in Russian Poland. His early attraction to the idea of a universal language was motivated primarily by humanitarian considerations stemming from childhood experiences. As he later wrote:

This place where I was born and spent my childhood gave the direction to all my future endeavours. In Bialystok the population consisted of four diverse elements: Russians, Poles, Germans and Jews; each spoke a different language and was hostile to the other elements. In this town, more than anywhere else, an impressionable nature feels the heavy burden of linguistic differences and is convinced, at every step, that the diversity of languages is the only, or at least the main cause, that separates the human family and divides it into conflicting groups. I was brought up as an idealist; I was taught that all men were brothers, and, meanwhile, in the street, in the square, everything at every step made me feel that men did not exist, only Russians, Poles, Germans, Jews and so on.[10]

The young Zamenhof used Russian in the home but studied French, German, Latin, Greek and later English in school, Hebrew in the synagogue, heard Yiddish in the street and spoke Polish fluently. In particular, he was struck by the grammatical simplicity of English which he believed illustrated that greatness and beauty in a language does not necessarily require a complicated grammar. His earliest projects for an artificial language were drafted at the precocious age of 15, and before he left the Gymnasium in Warsaw, where his family had moved, he had elaborated a language which could be both written and spoken (his interest in the language problem was evident at an even younger age; when only ten he had apparently written a five-act tragedy on the Tower of Babel theme, the tower in this case being located in Bialystock and its builders the town's inhabitants).[11] Zamenhof's work was then interrupted, at his father's insistence, during his medical studies at Moscow University (one of the few professions open to Jews), only to be resumed on returning to medical practice in Poland. He considered renouncing his own language proposals on encountering Volapük, but decided after initial enthusiasm that Schleyer's language was difficult to learn and did not fully answer the needs of an international language.

After some initial difficulties in obtaining sufficient funds, Zamenhof published his language scheme in 1887 in a Russian edition entitled *Mezhdunarodny yazyk: predislovie i polny uchebnik* ('An international language: introduction and complete manual'). He used the pseudonym, Doktoro Esperanto (one who hopes) rather than his own name in case any suspicion of eccentricity should harm his livelihood. As he wrote:

I felt that I stood before the Rubicon, and that from the day my brochure had appeared I could no longer withdraw. I was fully aware of the fate which awaited a doctor, depending on public good-will, if his clientele saw in him a dreamer occupying himself with 'outside interests'. I felt that I had staked my future and that of my family on one throw of a card. But I could not relinquish the idea which had permeated my whole body and soul, so . . . I crossed the Rubicon.[12]

The language described in this first short publication of just 28 pages was called 'Lingvo Internacia', but the pseudonym of its author soon replaced it as the name. The booklet contained an introduction to the language, several passages illustrating its use, a complete grammar of 16 rules, a vocabulary of around 900 roots and several promissory forms. Translations quickly appeared in Polish, French and German, and in 1889 Holt published an English edition in New York entitled *An attempt towards an international language*.[13] Zamenhof began by stating that 'I need not dilate upon the immense importance for Humanity of the existence of an International Language, one that could be adopted by all nations and be the common property of the whole world, without belonging in any way to any existing nationality.' He listed three major problems which must be solved.

1   The language must be extremely easy, so that it could be learnt without difficulty.

2 It must be able to serve from the outset as a viable intermediary for international communication.

3 'Means must be found to overcome the indifference of the bulk of mankind, and to cause the masses to make use of the language offered as a living tongue and not solely to be used with the aid of a dictionary.'

Eight promissory forms were included at the end of the work which Zamenhof hoped would be completed and returned to him. They read: 'I, the undersigned, promise to learn the international language proposed by Dr Esperanto, if it appears that ten million people have publicly given the same promise.' On the verso was space for name and address. When the number of promissory notes returned reached ten million, a book listing all the names and addresses of signatories was to be published 'and the day after its appearance the problem will have been solved'. Zamenhof also appealed to those so willing to sign the form unconditionally.

From the outset, in other words, Zamenhof was fully aware of the principal problem faced by all artificial languages: how can people be induced to learn a language (and no matter how easy this may be, some effort is required) when they have no guarantee that those with whom they wish to communicate across a linguistic frontier will have done likewise? Alas, Zamenhof was never able to publish his book of names and addresses, but he did publish in 1889 a register of Esperantists who had successfully translated a short text into Esperanto. This *Adresaro,* listing 1,000 Esperantists, enabled supporters to contact one another. Responses were now forthcoming and in fact a supplementary book, *Dua libro de la Lingvo Internacia,* containing 50 pages, had already been published entirely in the new language in 1888, followed by a second supplement in the following year. As enthusiasm for Volapük waned, interest grew in this new challenger, Esperanto. Many of its early adherents were from the Russian Empire, but then Leopold Einstein, one of the most energetic members of the large World Language Club in Nuremberg (Nürnberger Weltsprach-Verein), transferred his allegiance from Volapük to Esperanto. The first Esperanto Society was established in this German city, hitherto the centre of Volapük, at the end of 1888, and in autumn 1889 it produced the first Esperanto journal, a monthly entitled *La Esperantisto.* At first it included some articles in French and German, but it quickly became an all-Esperanto journal, and was largely concerned with the development of the language and the movement. By 1890, Zamenhof himself was supervising its publication and it became crucial as a source of his authority in language matters. This journal continued to appear on a regular basis, despite financial difficulties, until 1895 when it included an article by Leo Tolstoy on 'Reason and belief', to which the Russian censors took exception. The ban imposed upon *La Esperantisto* throughout the Tsarist Empire cost the journal nearly three-quarters of its readership. (Esperanto publications were not again allowed in Russia until after the 1905 Revolution.)

Despite this setback, Esperanto was undoubtedly making headway. A second Esperanto journal, *La Mondlingvisto,* had appeared in Sofia in 1889, followed in 1895 by *Lingvo Internacia* from Uppsala (and later Budapest and Paris) which remained the central organ of the Esperanto movement until the outbreak of the First World War. By 1891 33 textbooks, propaganda booklets or dictionaries on Esperanto had been published in 12 languages and clubs were being formed in a growing circle of countries. According to one estimate, 15,000 people had by now learnt the language.[14]

During these early years the major topic of discussion and dissension was the reform of the language which, as Marjorie Boulton says in her valuable biography of Zamenhof, 'in the light of subsequent experience seem drearily trivial [and] wasted the energies of many admirable people, including Zamenhof himself'.[15] Yet the recent experience of the Volapük movement demonstrated that such disputes over linguistic modifications could prove fatal. Zamenhof had tackled this problem in his first publication by conceding modestly: 'I am far from believing that [my invention] is so perfect that it cannot be surpassed, amended or improved . . . I am but a mortal and may easily fall into error.' Before compiling a complete dictionary, issuing a newspaper, etc., he therefore decided to wait for one year from publication 'in the hope that men of letters would give me their views upon my proposal'. Any suggestions could then be considered and changes made before 'the Language will then take on its permanent and definite form'.[16] By 1893, Zamenhof was able to establish the League of Esperantists, consisting of all subscribers to *La Esperantisto,* to whom he promised to submit all proposals for changes in the language. A democratic referendum would then be held by August 1894. In the event, a considerable majority favoured retaining the language unchanged, a view apparently supported by Zamenhof himself. Many of the early disputes over reform centred upon relatively minor points, such as those of circumflexed letters in the alphabet, whether 'kaj' or 'et' should be used for the word 'and', whether the adjective should end in 'a' or 'e', and the inclusion of an accusative case; such linguistic thorns still irritate the Esperanto movement (see chapter 5 for an introduction to the main features of the language and a discussion of its contemporary situation).

THE EARLY ESPERANTO MOVEMENT

The discussion over language reform being settled, at least temporarily, Esperanto continued to gain ground. It was no longer a language mainly supported by Slavs in Poland and Russia; Germany, France, Spain, Italy, Switzerland, Bulgaria, Rumania, Austria-Hungary, Holland, the United States, Mexico and Chile all had national Esperanto societies. Smaller-scale activities were also taking place in Brazil, Argentina, Peru, Bolivia, Uruguay, Venezuela, Cuba, Australia, New Zealand, Japan and North Africa.[17] The growth of Esperanto was particularly striking in France. The French Society for the Propagation of Esperanto had been founded in 1898, and the richest and most active private organisation in France, the Touring Club, with over 100,000 members, gave Esperanto its powerful support.[18] The first Esperanto club in Britain was established in Keighley in 1902. Two years later the British Esperanto Association, with its journal *The British Esperantist,* was formed in time for the First Universal Congress of Esperanto, which convened almost 700 delegates from 20 countries. The Congress met in the French Channel port of Boulogne in August 1905. According to Edmond Privat, Zamenhof awaited the inaugural Congress 'with strange apprehension' and at first was doubtful even whether he would attend, given the long and expensive journey and his unfamiliarity with public appearances.[19] In the event, however, he was present to address the assembled Esperantists in their new language. Although by no means a demagogic orator, his speech was rousing and confident by all accounts. Esperantists should not see their cause as in any way peculiar or utopian:

We shall show the world that mutual understanding among people of different nations is perfectly possible, that for this purpose it is not necessary for one nation to humiliate and swallow up another, that the barrier between the peoples is not something inevitable and eternal, that understanding between creatures of the same species is no fantastic dream, but a perfectly natural phenomenon, which has only been long delayed by very sad and shameful circumstances, but which had to come sooner or later and which has now come, which is now taking its first very timid steps, but which, once it has begun to move, will not stop, and will soon become so mighty in the world that our grandchildren will even find it hard to believe that it was ever otherwise, that once for centuries human beings, the kings of the earth, did not understand one another.[20]

It is all too easy now, of course, to scoff at this optimism, but the Congress did prove that Esperanto, like Volapük before it, was a practical language in which people of different nationalities could converse, debate, sing, recite and worship. A group of amateur actors from six different countries even performed a Molière farce in Esperanto. With its new green flag, the Esperanto movement appeared to be marching towards an attainable goal: the establishment of a universal language. But in reality its troubles were far from over.

HOMARANISMO

Zamenhof believed that the time was now ripe to establish an authoritative foundation for the language, and in 1905 the *Fundamento de Esperanto* was published. It contained the Sixteen Rules of grammar first published in 1887, a vocabulary of 1,800 roots with translations into English, French, German, Russian and Polish (first published 1894) and examples of the construction of everyday sentences (which had also originally appeared in 1894). As Zamenhof stated categorically in its Introduction:

When our language has been officially accepted by the *governments* of the most important nations and such nations by a special *law* guarantee to Esperanto certain life and use, and full safety against all personal whims or disputes, then an authoritative committee, elected by agreement by such governments, will have the right to make, once and for all, all changes desired in the foundation of the language, *if* such changes show themselves to be necessary; but *until this time* the foundation of Esperanto must most strictly remain absolutely unchanged, because severe untouchability of our foundation is the most important cause of our progress up to now, and the most important condition for our regular and peaceful future progress.[21]

That is to say, Esperanto was now stabilised in its essential forms; it could and would change slowly through usage, as any other living language does, but such modifications would be evolutionary rather than revolutionary. The *Fundamento* established the structure of Esperanto, once and for all, and indeed it still remains the corner stone of Esperanto. For one Esperantist, the *Fundamento* has 'lent to the language the same powerful force of inertia that tradition has in the life of ethnic and national languages, and which is the essential condition for preserving the permanence and stability of their growth'.[22] For another, the *Fundamento* had an important psychological as well as linguistic value, providing Esperantists with a taboo around which they could unite against those who tried to violate it; their aggression could be directed safely outwards instead of being self-inflicted.[23] This unity was about to be tested.

At the Congress in Boulogne, Zamenhof had submitted a Declaration on Esperanto which has since been a fundamental document for the movement.[24] In it he renounced his own personal rights and privileges over the language and stipulated that 'the only obligatory basis for Esperantists of all time as the foundation of the language Esperanto is the booklet, *Fundamento de Esperanto*'. The first paragraph in this Declaration had been included in response to fears expressed by leading French Esperantists: they were concerned to safeguard the political and religious neutrality of the language. It read:

Esperantism is the endeavour to spread throughout the world the use of a neutral language, which, without intruding itself into the internal life of peoples and in no way aiming at displacing the existing national languages, would provide people of different nations with the means of mutual understanding . . . Every other idea or hope which any Esperantist may associate with Esperantism will be purely his own personal affair, for which Esperantism is not answerable.

This desire for a neutral language was a reaction of the rationalistic West European psyche to the idealism of the Russian Esperantists, who played a very important role in the early years of the movement. Zamenhof himself, however, did not entirely share this concept of neutrality. He also came from an East European background in which ethnic groups had fought against one another in the oppressive environment of the Tsarist Empire. The personal efforts and sacrifices which he had made were neither motivated merely by an intellectual curiosity regarding linguistics nor simply by the desire to provide an international auxiliary language for business or pleasure. His was a greater goal: peace, tolerance and human unity. In place of the Jewish faith which Zamenhof had abandoned in youth, he became attracted by the life and teachings of a Jewish rabbi called Hillel who had lived during the reign of Herod. Zamenhof conceived the idea of a world religion which should help to reconcile rather than replace other religions, promoting tolerance and respect, characteristics so palpably lacking in the Poland of his own childhood. Using a pseudonym, in 1901 he had published a work in Russian entitled *Hillelism,* followed in 1906 by an anonymous article 'Dogmoj de Hilelismo' (The dogmas of hillelism) in *Ruslanda Esperantisto,* once again legalised after the 1905 Revolution. He hoped that Hillelist temples would be set up to provide meeting places for Hillelists of different languages. A Hillelist would regard all peoples as of equal worth and every country as belonging to all its inhabitants, regardless of ethnic, religious or linguistic affiliations. In a fuller version of the dogma published in the same year in Russian and Esperanto, Zamenhof changed the name of this 'world religion' to Homaranismo (Homarano means a member of the human race), probably because of the Jewish connotations of Hillelism.

Such developments instigated by the creator of Esperanto were not to the liking of all his associates, many of whom saw Esperanto as a language and nothing more. In particular, the leading French Esperantist, Louis de Beaufront, opposed this idealistic trend which he saw as a threat to the movement. The influence of de Beaufront on the early Esperantist movement was considerable. After his break with it, de Beaufront was reviled by the Esperantists, but in 1905 the journal of the British Esperanto Association described him as Zamenhof's 'oldest and hardest-working lieutenant', the 'French apostle of Esperanto who more than any living person has rendered possible the existing development of the movement in Western Europe and throughout the world'.[25] Later, his new Idist colleagues (see below) also employed a biblical metaphor, claiming 'It is not too much to say that the early extension and magnitude of the Esperanto movement originated with de Beaufront' who was 'the St. Paul'.[26] Privat offered a more balanced, if still colourful, assessment:

In more than one large movement a second person has been evident by the side of the initiator; on account of his energy the former occupies a separate place among the rest, and becomes, as it were, the organisational and legislative chief for a certain period. By the side of Father Schleyer, Volapük had Kerckhoffs. The Reformation in the Sixteenth Century had beside Luther the powerful Calvin. Esperanto once had de Beaufront.[27]

De Beaufront emphasised the practical use of Esperanto and was suspicious of any religious or mystical overtones, fearing that they would undermine the growing respectability of the language. As President of the Société pour la propagation d'Espéranto and editor of a new journal, *L'Espérantiste,* he was able to play an increasingly powerful role. He worked to attract as sympathisers distinguished figures in French society regardless of whether they were actually able to speak Esperanto, and in this objective had considerable success. Such people might be attracted by the practical uses of an international language or even its intellectual interest, but were unlikely to associate themselves with a utopian crusade in which they might be exposed to ridicule.

Despite some disagreements with the French leadership, Zamenhof decided to go ahead with his religious plans. He had been encouraged by the enthusiastic reception to his speech at the Boulogne Congress, which had included references to the 'brotherhood of man' and had concluded with a prayer in which he beseeched God to unite humanity and establish the rule of love and truth on earth. He decided to confront the issue in his speech at the Second Esperanto Congress which took place in Geneva in 1906 and was attended by 818 delegates from 30 countries. Although Zamenhof deleted any reference to Homaranismo in his opening speech, he intoned to loud applause:

For fear of possibly displeasing those persons who want to use Esperanto only for matters useful to themselves, we are all to tear out of our hearts that part of Esperantism which is the most important, the most sacred, that idea which is the principal aim of the Esperanto movement . . . If we, the first fighters for Esperanto, are to be compelled to give up all that is ideal in our work, we will indignantly tear up and burn all that we have written for Esperanto, sorrowfully bring to naught the labours and sacrifices of our whole lives, cast far away the green star on our breast, and cry out with loathing: 'With such an Esperanto, which is merely to serve exclusively the objects of trade and practical utility, we will have nothing in common.'[28]

Despite continued reservations by some Esperantists, Zamenhof himself never abandoned his doctrine of Homaranismo, although in his utterances he now stressed the secular rather than the religious idealism of Esperanto. In 1913 he published a pamphlet in Madrid, this time under his own name, in which he further developed its principles and looked towards the Universal Congress scheduled to take place in Paris the following year, where he intended once again to take up the theme of Homaranismo and propose formally its foundation.[29] The outbreak of War prevented his attendance at the depleted Congress, however, and within a few years Zamenhof was dead (see below). The idealistic strain in the Esperanto movement has nevertheless proved persistent, and Zamenhof was probably correct in believing that without it support would quickly have dwindled. The enthusiasm and commitment necessary to sustain long-term involvement in a movement whose objectives are unlikely to be realised, at least in the immediate future, cannot be cultivated on a tasteless diet of practical convenience: a more highly spiced flavour of idealism must be added if the dish is to remain palatable.

THE IDO SCHISM

Although Esperanto had proved both its linguistic versatility and its ability to attract and retain an enthusiastic and growing body of supporters, it was still far from its goal of adoption as the universal language. The selection of an artificial language for such a role by an authoritative international assembly would greatly strengthen its chances of widespread acceptance: and the Esperantists, naturally, hoped and assumed that any such assembly would select Esperanto from amongst any rival contenders. As the British Esperantist wrote:

To us who know what Esperanto is, and still more so to those of us who have studied other systems, it is hardly conceivable that any serious rival to our beloved language will be found on the score of *suitability to requirements.* Add to this the actually acquired success of Esperanto, and we may confidently assume that, even if such rival did exist, and even if it could be proved to be *better* than Esperanto, the verdict would be in favour of Esperanto, because it already holds the field.[30]

Many Esperantists therefore greeted with approval the idea of a Délégation pour l'adoption d'une langue auxiliaire internationale, suggested by two Frenchmen, the philosopher, Louis Couturat and the mathematician,

Léopold Leau (who were amongst the French intellectuals recruited to the Esperantist ranks by de Beaufront around the turn of the century).

In a 'Declaration', produced at its inaugural meeting in Paris in January 1901, the Delegation stated that a successful international language must satisfy the following conditions:

1 it must fulfil the needs of the ordinary intercourse of social life, of commercial communications, and of scientific and philosophic relations;
2 it must be easily acquired by every person of average elementary education, and especially by persons of European civilisation;
3 it must not be one of the national languages.[31]

The Delegation, to comprise people who appreciated the need for an international language, would eventually present the problem of selection to the International Association of Academies, which included 18 academies of Europe and America and held a general assembly every three years. If the latter refused to cooperate then a Committee of the Delegation would choose an international language. With Couturat as treasurer and Leau as secretary, the Delegation by 1907 had the support of 310 societies and 1,250 individual scientists and university professors. Nevertheless, the International Association of Academies declined to act and therefore a Committee was elected to carry out this task. It held a long series of meetings in Paris and discussed the chief language projects which had been submitted, helped by the detailed comparative study of artificial languages published by Couturat and Leau in 1903, their *Histoire de la langue universelle,* and its supplement, *Les nouvelles langues internationales,* which appeared in 1907. Serious consideration was reserved for two schemes: Esperanto and a language called Idiom Neutral. Esperanto was defended by de Beaufront in Zamenhof's absence, whilst Otto Jespersen presented the rival case (the Delegation had decided that authors of language projects themselves should not be elected to the Committee).

Idiom Neutral, the work of some former Volapükists, had been published in 1902. The International Academy of Volapük had changed its name at the end of the century to the Akademi internasional de lingu universal (International Academy of the Universal Language), directed, like its predecessor, since 1893 by a railway engineer and pioneer of Volapük in Russia, V.K. Rosenberger (after a schism in the movement, Kerckhoffs had resigned in December 1892). Largely as a result of his own work, but

with the approval of the Academy, Rosenberger had formulated a new
language scheme to be called Idiom Neutral. Although formally based
upon Volapük, the new project in fact differed quite fundamentally from
its ill-fated parent. Idiom Neutral was an *a posteriori* language with a
vocabulary based upon radicals found in the principal European languages,
and omitting the arbitrary morphological rules of its predecessor (see
above). According to Couturat and Leau (admittedly active participants
themselves in the international language debate by this time and therefore
perhaps less than objective in their judgements of contemporary schemes),
Idiom Neutral was too *a posteriori,* especially in its resemblance to
French.[32] In their efforts to avoid the pro-German inclination of Volapük,
the former Volapükists may have erred too much on the side of the
Romance languages.

Whatever the relative merits of Idiom Neutral and Esperanto, however,
the Committee of the Delegation had not reached agreement on the
selection of a universal language when Couturat presented it with a
pamphlet written under the pseudonym Ido, setting out a language scheme
which bore a considerable resemblance to Esperanto.[33] The word Ido in
fact is an Esperanto suffix meaning 'derived from', and might therefore be
translated as 'Offspring'. The appearance of Ido was apparently decisive
and the Committee at last felt able to reach a verdict: 'In principle it has
decided upon Esperanto, on account of its comparative perfection and the
many and various practical applications it has already had, on condition
that some modifications be made by the Standing Commission along the
lines defined by the report of the Secretaries and by the project Ido, in
agreement, if possible, with the Esperantists' Language Committee.'[34]

The activities of the Delegation and its Committee had already created
controversy within the Esperanto movement. There was considerable
disunity on the question of the Delegation's authority to select a universal
language. In addition, the split widened between conservatives and
reformists in the Esperanto ranks. Ironically, it is argued by Forster that
one reason why Zamenhof probably chose de Beaufront as his
representative on the Committee, despite their strained relations over the
Homaranismo issue, was just because of his linguistic conservatism.[35] It
was in an already strained and uncertain atmosphere, therefore, that the
proposal for modification of Esperanto in the light of the Ido project was
received by the Esperantists. Perhaps the proposal was never really intended
to be successful. In any event, Zamenhof refused to accept the Committee's

decision or the Delegation's authority, and in January 1908 broke completely with the latter. There could be no question of modifying Esperanto at this stage for the sake of the Committee or anyone else. The ensuing acrimonious dispute was not lessened by de Beaufront's confession that he was the inventor of Ido (although very considerable doubt exists over the truth of this claim and it seems probable that in fact Couturat was its author).[36] Dictionaries and grammars for a somewhat reformed version of the original Ido project soon were published and a monthly journal, *Progreso,* was launched by Couturat in March 1908, which continued until his death in a car accident in August 1914. After some discussion, including an approach to Zamenhof by Couturat for permission to call the language 'Simplified Esperanto', it was decided to leave its name as Ido. Although the majority of Esperantists remained loyal, the Ido schism demonstrated the ever-present threat of internal disintegration which faces artificial language movements. According to Forster, an estimated 25 per cent or so of the leadership of the Esperanto movement became Idists, but the rank and file largely remained steadfast.[37] In the belief that the threat of further schisms could be countered by stronger organisation, the Universala Esperanto-Asocio (UEA) was founded in 1908 (known in English as the Universal Esperanto Association). The Fourth Universal Esperanto Congress, held in August of that year in Dresden, demonstrated that the Esperanto movement might have been shaken but was not destroyed; 1,368 participants gathered from 40 countries.

The Committee of the Delegation, on the other hand, ultimately failed in its task of selecting a language on which all interested parties would agree. It unanimously approved the Ido project and in October 1907 appointed a permanent Commission to settle the details of the language. The Delegation itself was then finally dissolved in 1910, having founded the Union for the International Language, whose mission was to develop and propagate the 'International Language of the Delegation'. The Union set up headquarters in Zurich and appointed a Committee and an Academy to direct its day-to-day activities. De Beaufront had continued his editorship of *L'Espérantiste,* but gradually it began to be written in Ido rather than Esperanto; as an Idist journal it continued to appear until the First World War.

According to Louis Couturat, 'The superiority of Ido over Esperanto is so striking and is so incontestably borne out by practical experience that one can now really speak, after the Volapük and Esperanto periods, of a third world-language movement which has started off with a reaction-velocity hitherto unknown in this department of knowledge.'[38] Yet Couturat was hardly an objective observer; Bertrand Russell, who knew him through a shared interest in mathematical logic, commented: 'According to his conversation, no human beings in the whole previous history of the human race had ever been quite so depraved as the Esperantists. He lamented that the word Ido did not lend itself to the formation of a word similar to Esperantist. I suggested "idiot", but he was not quite pleased.'[39]

Ido has never succeeded in overtaking the popularity of Esperanto, although it quickly acquired more supporters than any other scheme with the exception of its major rival. By 1911 it had 200 groups around the world of which 40 were in France, but it suffered even worse in the First World War than did Esperanto.[40] It continues to survive today, though a much smaller movement than Esperanto, and the antipathy between the supporters of the two languages remains as bitter as ever (see chapter 6). As an example of the insults exchanged between the faithful of each camp, a leading Esperantist asked:

What, then, now remains of Ido? An embalmed doll, wound in the swaddling-clothes of dogmatic logic . . . and it will never die, because it never began to live. The glorious Paris philosopher [Couturat] was not capable of inspiring into it that animating spirit which the unknown Bialystok student [Zamenhof] gave to his creation. That proves that one can be an excellent anatomist and a bad midwife, and that neither erudition nor pride are ever a substitute for love.[41]

From the other side, an Idist could write in 1919 that 'The deterioration of [Esperanto] which had already commenced before [the schism] continued now unchecked and is still continuing so that the language has become so overcharged with absurdities as to be entirely unfit for the role of an international language.'[42]

THE OUTBREAK OF WAR

Following the Fourth Universal Esperanto Congress in Dresden, annual congresses were held in Barcelona, Washington, Antwerp, Cracow and Berne. The Esperanto movement seemed fully recovered from the Ido schism, and indeed it was widely believed by its supporters that the next Congress, planned to open on 2 August 1914, would herald the final triumph of Esperanto. Zamenhof and his wife wished to attend, but *en route* for Paris they were stopped on 1 August in Cologne; Germany had declared war on Russia and the Zamenhofs now found themselves enemy aliens (the German-Russian border was closed and they finally reached Warsaw via Sweden, Finland and St Petersberg). The Tenth Universal Esperanto Congress did in fact convene but its proceedings, as those of the Esperanto movement in general, were severely curtailed by the War. Some idea of the setback can be seen from table 4.1.[43] Although the number of books published in Esperanto in 1918 showed a small increase on 1914, in other respects the steady rate of growth from the 1890s until 1914 was reversed and the position much worse by 1918.

Table 4.1   Growth rate in the Esperanto movement, 1890—1918

Numbers	1890	1895	1900	1905	1909	1914	1918
Local societies and organisations	3	8	26	308	1,447	c.1,800	c.1,200
Journals	1	1	3	36	91	118	c.35
Local reps in UEA*	—	—	—	—	578	1,288	630
Books	28	88	123	211	133	+2,700	+2,900

*UEA founded 1908

The Geneva office of the UEA continued its work throughout the war, acting as a forwarding office for personal communications between belligerents and handling altogether 200,000 letters. Nevertheless, the First World War presented a disappointing setback to the movement. The German and French governments did issue propaganda material in Esperanto, a practical, official recognition of the role which an international language could play, the International Red Cross recommended Red Cross workers to learn it, and the YMCA distributed thousands of lesson books to prisoner of war camps in various countries.[44] Nonetheless, mass conflict can hardly present the ideal setting for a language of international discourse, and the movement only continued to advance outside the theatres of war in South America, Australasia and the

United States, where a small Eleventh Universal Congress was convened in San Francisco in 1915 (the last until 1920).

By the termination of hostilities, many Esperantists on both sides had been killed and Zamenhof himself was no longer present to guide the movement; he had died of heart trouble at the comparatively young age of 57 in Warsaw in April 1917. The Esperanto movement would have to be rebuilt if it was to face the years of peace and reconstruction ahead with any expectation of success.

ZAMENHOF

What sort of a man was the Russian Jew from Poland who created an artificial language which has survived more than a century and which still remains by far the best-known constructed scheme of its kind? Many of the biographical accounts have been written, not surprisingly, by Esperantists for whom he seems to be little short of a saint. Here, for example, is a description of Zamenhof as a child, written by an eminent Swiss Esperantist who knew him personally: 'Wise, modest, thoughtful, studious, never noisy, although a little obstinate, he always avoided giving pain to others. At school he revealed exceptional ability . . . His teachers admired him . . . As a small child he had been pale and weak, but he became a gay and vigorous boy, and a splendid organiser of parties and excursions. As the life and soul of their amusements, he was the centre of a circle of brothers, sisters, and schoolfellows.'[45]

Boulton tells us that although Zamenhof was sickly, small and frail in his early years he was also 'precociously intelligent'.[46] Another observer attributes much of the success that Esperanto achieved 'to the wide-visioned outlook of its creator, who was throughout his life a practical-minded idealist'. He possessed 'a sound perception of the magnitude of the problem' he had chosen to tackle, 'the necessary patience and judgement to carry through his task' and also 'those rare qualities of understanding which served to attract . . . the right type of adherent to carry it through its early days'.[47]

The critics of Esperanto have often been less fulsome in their assessment of Zamenhof. One American commentator, for example, has complained, 'Zamenhof was not a philologist or linguistic authority, but an oculist who became somewhat more interested in his Esperanto than in eyesight.' In constructing the language he 'displayed a limited imagination tightly mired (sic) in the concepts of a Victorian Latin-oriented grammar'. Finally, the luckless language constructor is accused of sexist tendencies, as his language 'reflects with a vengeance the patriarchal spirit of Zamenhof's day': a reference to the suffix 'ino' which is frequently added to a male noun to form its feminine equivalent.[48]

Both the sycophantic and vitriolic assessments should be treated with care. There can be little doubt, however, that Zamenhof was a talented linguist with more than a passing flair for language construction. Whatever minor criticisms might be levelled at Esperanto, it has proved its practicality as a language in all spheres of written and spoken discourse (see chapter 5). A picture emerges of the man as a rather shy, unassuming figure, and perhaps this asset enabled him to work alongside others rather than adopting a dictatorial role which could have proved fatal. At the same time, it would be wrong to underestimate Zamenhof's personal authority; not only was he extremely influential when alive, but he has been venerated by his followers since his death. Given the rather loose organisation of the Esperanto movement in its early years, Zamenhof inevitably played a crucial role in all aspects of decision making. Despite some inevitable clashes of personality, however, it remains remarkable that Zamenhof was able to get along with most of his co-workers so successfully, not a terribly common trait in the annals of artificial languages. Rank-and-file Esperantists held this modest man in the highest esteem, and even allowing for a measure of hagiography in retrospective studies, it is difficult to avoid the conclusion that Ludwig Zamenhof was a thoroughly pleasant man who happened to be driven by an ideal: to establish a common language for all mankind.

THE WORLD AT THE TURN OF THE CENTURY

Artificial languages were not the only manifestation of a growing sense of international interdependence in the latter half of the nineteenth century. From around 1860 there was an enormous increase in the number of international organisations, both governmental and non-governmental. In the realm of communication the most noteworthy development was the establishment in 1865 of the Telegraphic Union and in 1874 the International Postal Union. Such a growth of transnational communication only emphasised, however, the obstacle which language created to effective communication. The dominant role of English in large parts of the world was still in the future and an artificial language must have seemed the most obvious and fruitful answer to this barrier.

New industrial techniques required both increasing supplies of raw materials from all parts of the world and also an international market to absorb their products which could not be confined to a limited domestic demand. Related to the drive for markets was the final great imperial expansion in the last decades of the nineteenth century when European countries scrambled to snatch the remaining corners of Africa and Asia. Developments in transport on both land and sea further encouraged international trade. Economic activity was now conducted on a global scale and an efficient communication network was essential to its success.

In Western Europe, at least, economic and social conditions were gradually improving and education was no longer the privilege of a small minority. Widening circles of the population were becoming involved in political and social causes, in some cases on an international scale. Pacifist, free-trade and socialist ideas, for example, attracted international support. One of the fundamental beliefs of Marx and his followers was that socialism must be an international movement. The First International had been formed in 1864, followed by the Second International in 1889; the International Socialist Bureau was established in Brussels a little later, in 1900. An annual Universal Peace Congress was held from 1889 and an International Peace Bureau was set up in Berne in 1892. Five years later the Nobel Peace Prize was first awarded. As Anderson has commented, 'the result of this was that the decade before 1914 probably saw a more widespread belief in the possibility of international cooperation and a more general optimism as to the possibility of achieving permanent peace between the great powers than had ever been known before.'[49]

It is in this context that Volapük and then Esperanto were launched into a world in which there was a growing realisation that continued well-being required international cooperation, and that a failure to achieve this cooperation threatened war on a scale hitherto unknown. In a sense, conditions were now ripe for an artificial language which actually offered a means of simple and practical communication between peoples speaking mutually unintelligible natural languages.

Yet this internationalist strand in nineteenth-century history was not alone; it was interwoven with a different and ultimately much more powerful warp. A sense of national identity had been growing in Europe since the Napoleonic Wars. By the later decades of the century, despite the continued extension of international trade, a period of strident economic nationalism was setting in, accompanied by rising tariff barriers and frequent, if relatively minor, wars. Against the powerful ties of national identity, the various international unions and associations had little or no emotional appeal for the ordinary man and woman, even supposing that the latter were aware of their existence. The popular imagination was captured much more effectively by nationalist than internationalist ideals, and against a national call to arms the artificial language movement was ultimately to be proven impotent.

PART II

Artificial Languages in the Contemporary World

5

Esperanto

Countless language schemes have been constructed since the days when the likes of George Dalgarno and John Wilkins pondered over their complicated philosophical languages in the seventeenth century; a few schemes have even achieved limited, if short-lived, success. Today, however, few of us would be capable of naming more than one or two such languages from the several hundred available, and in all probability only one would come readily to mind: Esperanto. Indeed, 'Esperanto' has now become almost synonymous with the term 'artificial language'.

The emergence of Esperanto in an obscure corner of Eastern Europe towards the end of the last century and its early history, when the language gained an enthusiastic support in Europe and then further afield, has already been described in the previous chapter. Since those youthful days before the First World War, it has gone on to prove its suitability as a medium of both spoken and written communication for everyday as well as more specialised affairs. Esperanto has been used at international conferences, in radio and television broadcasts, for books, journals, newspapers and trade literature, and in social gatherings of all kinds. Its utility has been discussed at the highest international forums. In the educational sphere, despite considerable resistance from some quarters, it has achieved a measure of academic respectability, and can now be studied in schools and universities as well as privately by using a variety of self-instructional aids. An organised Esperanto movement exists in many countries, which nurtures and propagates the language at local, national and international levels. The undoubted resilience of Esperanto and the successes achieved by the Esperanto movement explain why it has been afforded a more detailed investigation in this chapter than any one of its rivals receives in the following chapter. It is instructive to examine the scheme which has come closest to attaining its goal of selection as an international auxiliary language; it is equally instructive, of course, to consider why this goal has remained so elusive, even in the case of Esperanto.

THE MOVEMENT

It is extremely difficult to estimate with any accuracy the number of people in the world today who are proficient in Esperanto. Indeed, it is by no means straightforward even to define what is actually meant by 'proficiency' in Esperanto. There are a few individuals who speak Esperanto as their first language, children of Esperanto-speaking parents who have acquired the language at the hearth (the Universal Esperanto Association (UEA) maintains a register of such native speakers). For the vast majority of Esperantists, however, it is a second language learnt by choice in classes of one kind or another or by private study. The level of proficiency can therefore range from spoken and/or literary fluency of a very high standard to the merest outline of Esperanto grammar with a smattering of vocabulary. It is possible to attain various qualifications in the language, but the possession of an academic certificate or diploma alone can never represent a satisfactory measure of proficiency. In practice, a knowledge of Esperanto must be credited to those who so claim it, whatever their real level of ability (and people are as apt to underestimate as to overestimate their achievements).

Apart from the large measure of subjectivity involved in assessing proficiency in Esperanto (or any other language for that matter) it is impossible to count reliably how many people would claim to know Esperanto. Available estimates, even when made by Esperantists or sympathisers with their cause, differ very considerably from as few as several hundred thousand who are using Esperanto 'seriously'[1] (no more than the population of a medium-sized British city) to as many as 15 million[2] (about the population of Czechoslovakia). The UEA, which functions as the international headquarters of the Esperanto movement and is located in Rotterdam, had some 31,000 members in 1979, but some national Esperanto associations are not affiliated to the world movement. (UEA members fall into two categories; Associate Members — persons who belong to an affiliated national Esperanto organisation; and Individual Members — persons who are directly and personally members of the UEA.) Furthermore, it cannot be assumed that local Esperantist clubs in towns and cities will have affiliated to the national association in their country. In 1964 the UEA carried out a survey of local groups in an attempt to assess their size. It reported a total membership of 36,346 (excluding the USSR for which figures were not available), 86 per cent of which resided in Europe. Bulgaria had both the greatest number of individual groups (139) and the highest number of individual members (6,025), followed by Poland (69 and 3,493 respectively), Czechoslovakia (101 and 3,280), Hungary (101 and 2,418) and the leading non-European country, Japan, with 75 groups and 2,148 members. Britain at that time had 59 groups with 1,443 members.[3] These figures from the UEA survey represent a minimum number of active Esperantists as in certain countries it was clear that many did not reply. Esperantists themselves often claim much higher numbers because they argue that many people who have some knowledge of Esperanto and interest in the language do not even belong to a local Esperanto group. Pierre Janton, for example, cites editions of certain Esperanto textbooks and dictionaries intended for Polish users which have been rapidly sold out despite the publication of around 20,000 copies (five times the number of Poles who actually belong to local groups). The Chinese Esperanto League had only 500 adherents but the works of Mao Tse-tung were published in Esperanto in tens of thousands of copies.[4]

As one critic of Esperanto comented, however: 'The leading Esperantists constitute an enthusiastic group with a fondness for large numbers and an astonishing forgetfulness of the fact that a majority of those who purchase their textbooks and leaflets fail to make any particular study or use of the language after the first interest has worn away.'[5] It seems clear, at any rate, that the number of organised and effective Esperantists is less than 50,000, although a much greater number of people have some knowledge of the language or at least some familiarity with the Esperanto movement and sympathy for its cause.

A disappointing aspect of membership statistics for Esperantists must be the levelling off which now seems to have occurred. In its early years the movement made rapid progress, but this was halted by the outbreak of war in 1914. After the inevitable setback caused by such a protracted, bitter and extensive international conflict, the Esperanto movement slowly began to recover, despite active state persecution in some countries, most notably the Soviet Union and Nazi Germany (see p. 100). By 1939 it was once again thriving, only to be crippled for a second time by a world conflagration. More recently, Esperantism appears to have reached a plateau far below the level of support necessary if it is to become a universal language, and from which any further ascent is proving difficult. Membership of the UEA in Western Europe has in fact declined in recent years, but this has been compensated by a large influx of new adherents from Eastern Europe.

If success is measured by standards other than membership statistics, then Esperanto presents a much stronger profile. The movement has certainly achieved an international status, and in 1975 national associations could be found in 64 states. Indeed, there can be few countries which do not have at least one group of dedicated Esperantists. The annual Universal Congress of the UEA may gather as many as 5,000 people from 50 or so countries, depending upon the accessibility and attractiveness of its venue (the Congress is held at a different site each year). Specialist international associations of Esperantists represent the interests of the most diverse groups, including students, journalists, railway workers, musicians, ornithologists, philatelists, spiritualists, the blind and many others. An international network of UEA 'delegates' has been established which can be used by Esperantists when travelling abroad; the local delegate can be contacted for help with accommodation, sight-seeing or organising a meeting with the local Esperantist club.

Esperanto has also achieved a measure of success as an academic subject. According to Mario Pei, it was taught to at least 16,300 students at 427 schools in 37 countries during the academic year 1965—6, while Cavanagh claims over 600 schools and 31 universities.[6] The introduction of Esperanto into educational curricula, especially in schools, is a longstanding objective of Esperanto associations. If the language is to acquire more speakers then schools have a vital role to play. The results, however, have not always satisfied the Esperantists. As the *Newsletter* of the British Esperanto Association (BEA) lamented in its first issue which appeared in November 1972:

It is continually exasperating to rediscover how few people, despite all our efforts, have been made aware of the bare and simple facts about Esperanto. Until they know, they will not demand Esperanto for their children — instead of a totally unattainable French — and until they demand it in large determined numbers they will not succeed. Until the children have had it in the schools for a generation Esperanto *cannot* be a universal language.

More success has been achieved at the tertiary education level, where Esperanto courses may be offered as options within a programme. London University, for example, has recently introduced Esperanto as a part of a degree in linguistics.

Whatever conclusions might be drawn from the contradictory estimates about the number of Esperantists, there can be no doubt that the language has proved its worth as a literary language. Zamenhof himself led the way with his translations of such works as *Hamlet* and Gogol's *The Government inspector* as well as the Old Testament. Since then, works by Homer, Dante, Byron, Dickens, Goethe, Schiller, Tolstoy, Pushkin, Cervantes, Ibsen and many others have appeared in Esperanto translation (as have the entire Bible and Koran). Interestingly, many works have been translated between 'difficult' natural languages via an Esperanto edition: a Japanese translation of a Czech book may have been prepared from an Esperanto version of the original Czech text. The catalogue of Esperanto translations by itself is no mean achievement, but Esperanto is unique amongst artificial languages in that it has also been employed extensively as a literary medium for original works of all kinds, including a good deal of poetry. An Esperantist, Margaret Hagler, explains in her important study of this topic:

Esperanto began its literary career with certain important advantages. Its vocabulary, grammar and syntax are a blend of Greco-Latin, the Romance tongues, and elements from, or similar to, those of German, Russian and other Indo-European languages, though without the iregularities of these tongues. This combination gives Esperanto a historical depth lacking in *a priori* constructed languages, for in its vocabulary, Esperanto distills the rich cultural heritage of the Indo-European language family.[7]

According to Lapenna, 416 works were published in Esperanto just between 1961 and 1969, and of these 109 were originals.[8] Since its earliest years, Esperanto has also been employed as a language of scientific communication. Journals containing either full articles or abstracts of articles in Esperanto have been published recently in the fields of agriculture, astronomy, botany, computing, geology, mathematics, medicine and physics. Works of philosophy, religion, psychology, law, linguistics, history, economics, geography and politics have also appeared. Esperanto publishing houses can be found in a number of countries in

Europe, North and South America, and the Far East. Turning to a different medium of communication, 15 or so radio stations in 12 countries broadcast in the language, a step first taken in 1922 by stations in Newark in the United States and in London.[9]

ESPERANTO AND INTERNATIONAL ORGANISATIONS

It comes as no great surprise to find that the supporters of a language which is intended ultimately to assume a universal role should always have attached importance to its acceptance by international organisations. Before the First World War, however, there was no suitable international body which could be approached. With the formation of the League of Nations in 1920, the Esperantist movement could now focus its hopes on an inter-governmental organisation whose objective, as set out in its Covenant, was 'to promote international cooperation and to achieve international peace and security'. During its first two Assemblies, delegates from a number of League members, including Brazil, China, Haiti, Italy, Japan, India and South Africa, presented resolutions suggesting that the League should recommend the universal teaching of Esperanto in schools as an international auxiliary language. The Second Assembly then requested the League Secretariat to prepare a complete report on this matter.

The Report of the General Secretariat, adopted by the Third Assembly of the League of Nations in 1922, stated that Esperanto was the most widely spoken artificial language in universal congresses, in travel, in international offices 'and even in the theatre'. It was beginning to attain a literary style and already possessed a library of some 4,000 printed works, both in translation and originals. Teachers of the language were to be found in quite a large number of countries; according to the Report, Esperanto was taught in certain of the primary or secondary schools in about 320 towns in 17 different countries, and in evening classes in about 1,200 towns in 39 countries. The Albanian Cabinet, in a Decree of June 1922, had even decided to make Esperanto a compulsory subject in secondary and higher education, whilst in Madrid, Brunswick, Dresden, Edinburgh and Lisbon, Esperanto was apparently taught in the police schools 'where the police sergeants are trained to help foreigners in the street'. Hungarian police sergeants were also singled out for Esperanto courses, along with postmen and blind students, and in Portugal, at least, the armed forces were not to be outdone by their civilian counterparts: the Ministries of War and Navy authorised candidates who had obtained the Esperanto diploma to wear a special badge on their uniforms.[10]

Although the Third Assembly of the League of Nations unanimously accepted this detailed and favourable report, it felt unable to adopt a resolution urging its members to introduce Esperanto into the school curriculum. France, in particular, expressed opposition to Esperanto and argued that a recommendation on teaching that language in schools would be an unwarrantable interference in the internal affairs of member states. Sweden and Norway both favoured English as an international language while Denmark spoke for another artificial language, Ido. The Brazilian delegate attacked Esperanto as 'a language of ne'er-do-wells and communists'.[11] Following a resolution of the League in 1924 recommending that Esperanto be accepted as a 'clear' language in telegrams, however, the International Telegraphic Union did change its rules in 1925 in order to accept Esperanto for telegraphy.

In more recent years, the Esperanto movement has directed attention towards the successors of the League of Nations: the United Nations, Unesco and the European Communities. The General Conference of Unesco accepted a resolution in 1954 by which it recognised that the aims of Esperanto in furthering international intellectual exchanges and in bringing the peoples of the world together were in accordance with Unesco aims and ideals. This resolution was greeted enthusiastically by Esperantists and encouraged the UEA to turn its attention to the United Nations. In 1966 the UEA presented the Secretariat of the United Nations with a proposal signed by 920,954 people in 74 countries, and by 3,843 organisations with a combined membership of 71,165,500. The Proposal read in full:

Giving whole-hearted support to the efforts of the United Nations to further cooperation between the peoples of the world in order to dispel international tensions and consolidate world peace; but being profoundly convinced that the multiplicity of languages represents one of the most serious obstacles to the further intensification and development of international cooperation at all levels; taking into consideration the resolution of 10th December 1954, whereby the General Conference of UNESCO took note of 'the results attained by Esperanto in the field of international intellectual relations and in the rapprochement of the peoples of the world';

We now propose that the United Nations solve the language problem both by real and effective aid to the propagation of the neutral International Language Esperanto, and by recommending Member States to further the teaching of the language and to encourage its use in international relations between the peoples of the world.[12]

To the chagrin of the UEA, however, this proposal was never passed to the member states by the Secretariat. Furthermore, the United Nations has not chosen to set its member states an example by adopting the international language for its own deliberations. Nor, of course, have the European Communities, although the Commission is now planning to use Esperanto as a bridge language in its machine translation programme. In an endeavour to reduce its vast expenditure on translation, the Commission for several years has been using a computer to accomplish a part of this work. It intends to introduce a new machine translation system, Eurotra, by the end of the 1980s, which will be able to translate each Community language into Esperanto as an intermediate stage before converting it into the required target language.

Despite these setbacks, Esperanto has proved an effective medium of communication in international gatherings since its earliest days. The UEA congresses are held exclusively in Esperanto and the language is not only used in the formal sessions but also in the many social gatherings which are associated with this annual event.

PERSECUTION

Unhappily, instances of linguistic persecution are by no means rare. In most cases persecution is part of an attempt to impose the dominant language of a country upon another linguistic community within its borders, and may be just one of several sanctions intended to weaken the cohesion of an ethnic minority and facilitate its assimilation into the majority culture. Linguistic diversity has often been seen as a threat to the political and economic integrity of a state. It is more surprising, perhaps, that a language such as Esperanto, which is not linked with any particular ethnic group but is the common property of all peoples and countries, should have attracted political repression. Yet more than one government has tried to eradicate Esperanto from its territories, or at least to harass its supporters and suppress its literature. From its earliest days the Esperanto movement had to contend with problems from the Tsarist censorship in the Russian Empire, and even in inter-war France, to cite a further example, the movement experienced a brief interval of governmental disapproval. The teaching of Esperanto was prohibited in all state schools from June 1922 until September 1924; the Minister of Education emphasised that 'French will always be the language of civilisation', and pointed to the dangers of teaching Esperanto.[13] But it was in the 1930s that Esperantists encountered their greatest difficulties, and above all in Hitler's Germany and Stalin's Soviet Union.

As far as Hitler was concerned, Esperanto was part of a Jewish cosmopolitan conspiracy, and as such was the object of early vilification in *Mein Kampf*. Denouncing the language and its supporters, he wrote that the Jews would attempt to establish a universal language like Esperanto in order to rule the world:

As long as the Jew has not become the master of the other peoples, he must speak their languages whether he likes it or not, but as soon as they become his slaves, they would all have to learn a universal language (Esperanto, for instance) so that by this additional means the Jews could more easily dominate them.[14]

To make matters worse, if this were possible, Esperanto was not only associated with Jews in Nazi thinking, but also with socialist and communist organisations in Germany and elsewhere, a view not entirely without foundation. It is not really surprising that idealist and internationalist socialist movements should establish common ground with at least certain sections of the Esperanto movement (see below). Upon Hitler's seizure of power in 1933, the socialist and communist Esperanto organisations in Germany (the Socialista Esperanto-Asocio and the Germana Laborista Esperanto-Asocio) were quickly disbanded, but the remaining Esperanto groups continued an uneasy and fragile relationship with the Nazi Government. Despite efforts to placate the authorities, including arguments advanced to persuade the Nazis that Esperanto purified the German language by preventing the assimilation of foreign words, and even the founding of a new movement, the Neue Deutsche Esperanto-Bewegung, whose constitution excluded Jews and which claimed close relations with the Gestapo, Esperanto teaching was banned in 1935. A month later Heinrich Himmler, chief of the Gestapo, reported that 'a large proportion of the members of Esperanto organisations have proved to be under suspicion of anti-State activities', and in the following year all organised operations by Esperantists were suppressed.[15] Similar measures were subsequently introduced into Nazi-occupied Europe, although the movement was allowed to continue in Norway and Denmark and, to an extent, in France also. After the German invasion of Poland, the Gestapo chief in Warsaw received specific orders to imprison members of the Zamenhof family. Zamenhof's son was shot and both his daughters died in the Treblinka concentration camp (his daughter-in-law and grandson escaped *en route* to Treblinka and survived the war).[16] In Fascist Italy, affairs were a little better though the Italian Esperanto Federation felt it advisable to release pro-regime statements, and in 1939 expelled all Jewish members. Despite these measures, it still disappeared completely during the war years.

After the Second World War, the problem of accepting German Esperantists once again into the international movement had to be tackled. A new German Esperanto Association was formed in 1947 in the western zones of Germany and a few Germans attended the first post-war World Congress in Berne in that same year. One offered to greet the Congress in the name of the German Esperantists, but withdrew his suggestion when Yugoslav, Polish and Jewish Esperantists threatened to walk out in protest.[17] Understandably, bitter memories die hard even in an organisation dedicated to international cooperation and the brotherhood of man. By 1955, however, the German Esperanto Association had again been admitted to the UEA, and indeed the 1951 World Congress had already been held in a city closely linked with the career of Adolf Hitler: Munich.

In contrast, the attitude of the Soviet regime at first had been favourable towards Esperanto.[18] The language had been viewed with some suspicion by the Tsarist authorities, but after the Revolution the position was reversed. There was much in the Esperantist ideals which could appeal to the new rulers in Soviet Russia, intent upon establishing a unified world without class or state divisions, an international fraternity of the toiling masses. Local and national associations of Esperantist workers had already been formed before the First World War in a number of countries, journals had been published, and the UEA had established a workers' section in 1911. Initially, at any rate, the Bolsheviks had no cause to distrust Esperanto. As early as 1919 the People's Commissariat of Education decided to introduce Esperanto into schools, although with little effect, and the Soviet Republic Esperanto Union (SEU) was founded in 1921 with the intention of using Esperanto to promote revolutionary ideas in the rest of the world. Soviet Esperantists were encouraged to study and communicate internationally in the language, and the Soviet Government was even the first to issue postage stamps in Esperanto. By 1931 the SEU had 3,657 members, 17 per cent of whom were also Communist Party members and a further 23 per cent Komsomolists (members of the Communist youth movement); by the end of 1934 SEU membership had grown to almost 9,000.[19]

The friendly attitude of the Communist Party leadership was not to last long, however. The Esperanto movement in the USSR was no more able to stand aside from the political unheavals which were taking place in the highest echelons of the Party and country at large than any other group. The consolidation of power in the hands of Stalin, the introduction of the doctrine of 'socialism in one country', the draconian economic and social measures quickly introduced and the atmosphere of suspicion, even paranoia, permeating all aspects of life in the country: none of these changes boded well for Esperanto (nor, if it is true as one Soviet defector has claimed, did the fact that Stalin had once considered Esperanto as a future world language but had abandoned the idea after unsuccessfully trying to learn it; personal setbacks to the Soviet leader were not to his liking).[20] Reports of economic sabotage directed against Soviet industry by agents of the imperialist powers and a rabid fear of spies and traitors which was frantically whipped up by the Communist Party, were scarcely likely to favour a language whose objective was to facilitate formal and informal contacts between Soviet citizens and the capitalist world.

Difficulties developed in particular between the Esperantist movement in the Soviet Union and the Sennacieca Asocio Tutmonda (SAT), the 'World Association of Those Without a Nationality'. The inaugural meeting of SAT had taken place in 1921 at which the use of Esperanto in the class struggle was emphasised and the UEA condemned for its political neutrality. All class-conscious members of the proletariat were urged to join SAT, which thereafter held its own world congresses. For a time it even forbad the simultaneous membership of SAT and any bourgeois Esperanto organisation unless there was no local Esperanto workers' group available. The Third Communist International (or Comintern, as it was usually known) with its headquarters in Moscow and politically subservient to the Soviet leadership, expected SAT to follow its directives. Such a course of action, however, could not be guaranteed. Although many communists, including those from the Soviet Union, were active in SAT, it also included social democrats and anarchists who were increasingly vilified by the Comintern and its Soviet masters as the most dangerous of class enemies (the Soviet attitude to social democrats did briefly change in the mid-thirties at the time of the popular front policy). Relations between the SEU and SAT steadily worsened, and the SAT World Congress held in London in 1930 was not attended by any Soviet delegates. By 1931 the breakdown between the two organisations was complete. The SEU now joined a newly-formed Internacio de Proletaraj Esperantistoj (International of Proletarian Esperantists) which was orthodoxly pro-Soviet and completely dominated by the Comintern.

By the mid-thirties any contacts between Soviet citizens and the outside world had become highly suspicious. E.K. Drezen, President of the SEU, was arrested in 1935 (and shot in 1937), followed by many other Esperantists, who were executed or incarcerated in camps as members of an international espionage organisation or simply as anti-Soviet elements. After the Soviet invasion of the Baltic States in 1939, for example, the People's Commissariat for Internal Affairs (NKVD) in the newly-established Lithuanian Soviet Socialist Republic issued a 'strictly secret' order; all anti-Soviet and socially-alien elements were to be identified and registered, and category j of the 14 categories included 'Persons who have personal contacts and correspondence abroad, or with foreign embassies and consulates, Esperantists and philatelists'.[21] Esperantists like Drezen who had employed their language in the service of proletarian internationalism found themselves accused as enemies of the state and dealt with accordingly in Stalin's repression. As Solzhenitsyn has pointed out, amongst the 'lashing waves' of the purges 'certain modest, changeless wavelets always got lost; they were little heard of, but they, too, kept flowing on and on'. Included in these wavelets 'There were Esperantists — a harmful group which Stalin undertook to smoke out during the years when Hitler was doing the same thing'.[22] A recent estimate maintains that 30,000 Esperantists were arrested and 2,000 of them killed during the Stalinist terror.[23] This may seem high when compared with the figure of 9,000 members in the SEU in 1934 which was quoted above. When account is taken of the fate which befell the families of arrested citizens in Stalinist Russia, however, this estimate is more credible.

Esperanto was effectively suppressed not only in the Soviet Union, but after the Second World War also in Soviet-occupied Eastern Europe, to varying degrees of severity. Only with the death of Stalin in 1953 and Khrushchev's subsequent period of de-Stalinisation, inaugurated in 1956, did Esperanto once again have an opportunity slowly and painfully to revive. In 1963, following an insistent request from Bulgaria to the Central Committee of the Communist Party of the Soviet Union, a delegation of Soviet Esperantists did finally participate in an international Esperanto meeting: the 48th Universal Esperanto Congress held in Sofia (a Soviet delegation had last attended an Esperanto Universal Congress in 1931). Drezen was posthumously rehabilitated under Khrushchev, and it was officially admitted that the destruction of the SEU and the persecution of thousands of Esperantists had been based upon false accusations. It was only in 1979, however, that a national organisation was again established in the Soviet Union, although Esperanto has fared much better in some other East European countries (but not in Rumania or Albania). SAT continues to exist but still encounters difficulties in uniting membership from the communist as well as the non-communist worlds. Ironically, the revival of Esperantist fortunes in Eastern Europe has been associated with the UEA rather than SAT. The Mondpaca Esperanto-Movado (World Peace Movement) was founded in 1953 in Vienna, and this organisation now takes a political line acceptable to the Warsaw Pact countries and attracts support from communist countries as well as from communists in capitalist countries.[24] It uses the slogan, 'Esperanto is an instrument in the struggle for peace'. According to M.I. Isayev, Esperantists in the Soviet Union have formed circles that meet at houses of culture, clubs and institutions of higher learning in almost all the national republics. Contacts with Esperantists abroad are organised by the Esperanto Commission of the Union of Soviet Friendship Societies. Apparently, a large number of books and brochures are published in Esperanto, including the Russian classics, as well as proceedings of the Party Congresses and speeches by prominent figures in the Communist Party and the Soviet Goverment.[25] More enticing, perhaps, for the Soviet Esperantist is the opportunity to receive journals in Esperanto from the West devoted to such subjects as Catholicism, Bible studies, Socialism, and so on, presenting views unlikely to be encountered in local publications (although such journals may encounter difficulties in reaching their subscribers).[26]

THE ESPERANTISTS: A BRITISH CASE STUDY

Despite the international scope and objectives of Esperanto, for many rank-and-file Esperantists their movement is one to be enjoyed at the local or national rather than the international level. They might attend some of the more accessible Universal Congresses or use their language whilst holidaying abroad, but most of the social gatherings which are so much a part of the Esperanto movement will be enjoyed much closer to home. It is therefore important to consider the movement at 'grass roots' as well as on the grander international stage, and for this purpose the British Esperantists have been chosen (although this is not to imply that they are in any way especially typical of the movement at large; indeed, it is arguable that national Esperantist movements are as much a product of their local environment as of the internationalist ideals and common language shared by all Esperantists).

Esperanto initially did not make much headway in Britain, perhaps because there was no strong Volapük movement from which to attract supporters and because no powerful individual emerged to champion the language. Fifteen years elapsed between the publication of Zamenhof's first pamphlet on the language and the founding of an Esperanto society in 1902 by a local journalist in the Yorkshire town of Keighley. Once this first step had been taken, however, events developed apace and in the following year a second Esperanto society was started in London and a journal, *The Esperantist*, began publication. Shortly afterwards, the BEA was formed with its organ, *The British Esperantist* (in which was incorporated *The Esperantist*). Local clubs quickly multiplied around the country and annual congresses were held from 1908 onwards, following the Third Universal Esperanto Congress which had been organised in Cambridge in 1907 (and which Zamenhof himself attended).

The growth of the new movement was inevitably set back (as elsewhere) by the First World War, but the BEA recovered well and by 1931 could boast a membership in excess of 2,000. Although this proved to be an inter-war high-point, after the Second World War membership surged above 3,000. Such success was short-lived, however, and in recent years the number of members has scarcely exceeded 1,000. Taking two fairly typical recent years, the Annual Report of the BEA for 1981 revealed a membership of 1,253 (including 43 juniors). This represented a net loss of 29 compared with the previous year (although 123 new members had joined, 152 had left).[27]

Whatever the reasons for this disappointing picture, it cannot be blamed on any indifference towards recruitment by the leaders of the British movement. Esperantists are constantly urged at every opportunity to publicise the cause and to proselytise amongst friends and acquaintances. The *Newsletter* of the BEA, for example, reminded its readers that they should consider the following questions: 'Have I asked anyone *this week* to become an Associate of the BEA?; How many people have I spoken to *this week* about Esperanto?'[28] At a more general level, publicity in the press, on radio and on television is given great significance, and Esperantists endeavour to keep their language in the public eye. In 1974, for instance, the Press and Public Relations Committee of the BEA reported that it had met its target of two press cuttings per day throughout the year, a rise of five per cent compared with 1973. Nearly half of these items were 'letters to the editor', mostly sent by members of the Press Panel. This high level of press visibility had declined by 1982, however, to just one cutting per week, prompting a rebuke from the President of the BEA. As he informed the readership of *Esperanto News:* 'In view of the progress we have made in the past few years it is imperative that we not only keep up our efforts, but that we increase them in order to improve this progress. The continuous appearance of articles and news items, even more than letters, will keep Esperanto before the public.' In his opinion, 'Articles appear to be unbiased and factual, but letters present a point of view.' Esperantists were urged to 'exploit every possibility, report as often as possible on group and federation meetings, seminars etc, and don't forget that the same report can be sent to several papers as long as it can be related to someone or something in the area'. He advised the local Esperanto clubs that 'If there is not already a Press or Publicity Officer in your group then elect one NOW.'[29] As regards broadcasting, the BBC actually started some overseas broadcasts in Esperanto in 1967, but they were suppressed 'by higher authority' after the third programme.[30] Repeated requests from Esperantists that the BBC should resume this service have met with a deaf ear.

Special attention is devoted by the British Esperantists to education and the teaching of Esperanto in schools. Parents are urged to write to their Member of Parliament about the need to offer Esperanto in the curriculum, and also are encouraged to discuss this matter with their child's headteacher. Political lobbying is also dealt with in a more organised fashion through the Esperanto Parliamentary Group which currently has around 150 members, mostly drawn from the Labour Party (although only a handful of the Group can actually speak Esperanto). Parliamentary interest in the language has increased in recent years, probably helped by Britain's membership of a multilingual European Communities.

The organisational structure of the Esperantist movement in Britain is relatively decentralised. The BEA meets just once a year at its national Congress; apart from this, activities are carried out in the many local organisations scattered throughout the country. The BEA itself is governed by a Council of around 100 members, consisting of national officers and representatives of regional and specialist groups affiliated to the BEA. The Council itself only meets four times per year (one of these meetings being at the BEA Congress), and effective policy making is done by the Executive of the Council which has 13 members and meets more regularly. Strangely, the Annual General Meeting of the BEA is held in English and not in Esperanto (as are also the meetings of the Executive and Council), but this is because its legal status requires that its business is conducted in a language comprehensible to all. There is in fact no requirement to speak the language in order to join the BEA as it is an organisation of *supporters* of Esperanto, not speakers. At the same time, there is no obligation upon individual speakers of Esperanto or even local Esperanto groups to affiliate to the BEA. About half of those interested enough to join a local group are not members of the national organisation.

The local Esperanto groups tend to be created on local initiative. Anyone can form such a group, which usually will affiliate to the BEA once it begins to become established. The groups organise language classes for beginners, campaign for Esperanto in the local press, schools and the public library (where they urge the purchase of Esperanto literature) and carry out the sort of social activities frequently found in local organisations: talks, dances, holidays, etc. Local groups can join together in regional federations which usually conduct their proceedings in Esperanto. Some well-established local groups will also use Esperanto as the medium of communication, others will conduct their meetings normally in Esperanto but business meetings may be in English or even held bilingually, whilst groups comprising mainly beginners will speak English most of the time. The BEA runs an information service about Esperanto for both its own members and the general public, publishes two journals (*Esperanto news,* mainly in English, and *La Brita Esperantista,* mainly in Esperanto) and gives members access to the Butler Esperanto Library in London.

As well as local groups and regional federations, many specialist Esperanto groups have been formed as a focus for Esperantists with particular interests. The Socialist Esperantists have an especially long history of organised activity. The British League of Esperantist Socialists was founded as long ago as 1907, when a few local groups were set up, but it soon became dormant. It was revived in 1920 and in 1927 changed its name to the Brita Laborista Esperanto-Asocio (British Workers' Esperanto Association). The split between SAT, representing the socialists, and the IPE (Internacio de Proletaraj Esperantistoj), the pro-Moscow organisation, in the early thirties (see above) divided the British Socialist Esperantists. The Brita Laborista Esperanto-Asocio voted in 1932 to affiliate to the IPE rather than SAT — the meeting was apparently packed with communists, not all of whom were Esperantists — and the remaining SAT supporters then formed SAT en Britio. This group still exists, but its membership is both small and elderly. In 1977 the Trade Union and Cooperative Esperanto Group was formed within the BEA, which has won support from a number of trade union leaders. In 1980 Sir Harold Wilson accepted nomination as Vice-President of the Group; he had learned a little Esperanto as a 14-year-old scout when he attended an Esperanto International Scout Camp in the Netherlands. Reflecting a traditional moderation in British political life, the divide between 'socialist' and 'neutral' Esperantists has been much weaker than in many other countries.[31]

The Esperanto movement in Britain suggests a curious mixture of idealism, fanaticism and eccentricity, at least to many outsiders. As Peter Forster comments, in this country Esperanto occupies 'a decidedly marginal position', no doubt related in part to the widely held view in the English-speaking world that English is already *the* international language. As a consequence, those who support Esperanto in Britain 'tend to be deviant in certain other respects: a deviance syndrome is evident'.[32] It is therefore interesting to examine some data on the social composition of the British Esperanto movement. In 1968 Forster, a British sociologist, sent a questionnaire to a representative sample of members in the British Esperanto Association and received a response of over 80 per cent. His most interesting results are summarised below.[33]

Men outnumber women in the BEA by two to one, and almost half the members are over 60 years of age. Of the women, a large proportion are unmarried. Manual workers are very much under-represented in a predominantly middle-class movement, with teachers being particularly well-represented (as in other social movements such as the Campaign for Nuclear Disarmament). In Forster's words, 'Esperanto opens up the world to those who, while having aspirations to higher status than they possess, find no outlet for these in the wider society.'[34] The membership is relatively highly-educated, but interestingly, 20 per cent have no knowledge whatsoever of any language other than English and Esperanto. As regards political persuasion, the Labour Party appears to be stronger in the BEA than in the population at large and the Conservative Party weaker, with more than proportionate support for minority parties. Turning to religion, non-conformists are over-represented but even more so are atheists and agnostics. Nine per cent of members in 1968 were vegetarian, a very high percentage for that time when vegetarianism was much less common than today. A fairly typical Esperantist, therefore might be a rather well-educated, unmarried, middle-aged, female teacher who votes Labour, does not believe in God and never eats meat.

Forster himself concludes that 'the overwhelming majority of Esperantists in Britain do not seem particularly deviant in their orientations', although 'members also tend to be rather elderly, and some orientations (e.g. agnosticism) which are not now considered as particularly deviant may be more so for the generation concerned.' He does concede that although the 'cranks' are not numerically strong they are 'often noticeable'. There is a consistent strain which rejects the urban industrial society and relates to what is 'natural'. So, Forster found a greater than average representation of vegetarians and pacifists — even vegetarian pacifists — who are fully accepted in the Esperanto movement.

The BEA is not unaware of some of these characteristics shared by many of its members, nor oblivious to the need to create the right kind of image for the movement amongst the non-believers. In recent years it has attempted to modernise the Esperanto image and break away from its elderly, middle-class social composition. The photographs in *Introducing . . . esperanto association of britain* (and note the gimmick of using lower case letters throughout), for example, all show young Esperantists dressed informally (and therefore conventionally) and enjoying themselves at various social events. Despite such propaganda, the actual activities of the youth movement seem quaintly outmoded, more in keeping, perhaps, with the grandparents of today's youngsters than the offspring of the 'swinging sixties'. Take, for example, the Young British Esperantists' house meeting organised in Grimsby over the New Year 1981—2: 'Seven teenagers took part, most of whom had only been learning Esperanto a few months. There was a New Year's Party with games and songs, and on New Year's Day the Grimsby Esperanto Society was invited to watch the sketches that had been prepared and to join in some Christmas singing in Esperanto.'[35] Again, in an attempt to break away from the 'crank' image, the BEA has tried to improve the quality of local group activities. Speakers at a public meeting, for instance, are requested to look like an intellectual (whatever this means) whilst not behaving in any way like an eccentric: contradictory advice, some might argue.

This crankiness aspect of the Esperanto movement is by no means unique to Britain, and has often provoked the wrath of certain Esperantist leaders. Ivo Lapenna, later to become President of the Universal Esperanto Association, had this to say about the Berne World Congress held in 1947:

Among those present were only a few workers, and a similarly small number of intellectuals. As far as I know there was not a single peasant present. Thus in social composition the congress was largely petty-bourgeois with a strong and accented religious-mystical-spiritualistic colour, with a mass of naivities and frivolities, which can only compromise the cause of the International Language . . . Do people still not understand that one of the most serious hindrances to the dissemination of Esperanto among serious people is exactly that strange mysticism which incessantly encircles the movement? In the eyes of the masses we make a laughing-stock of ourselves and the cause of International Language by such frivolities . . .

Finally, there was certainly no shortage of cranks. On the contrary, they were abundant. One woman with green stockings explained to me that every lady Esperantist should wear only green stockings for propaganda purposes [green is the Esperanto colour]. One came to the ball in a dress, like a nightdress, with masses of green stars, large, medium and small [a star is the symbol of Esperanto]. I saw a loud yellow tie with an even louder green star woven into it. In general, one could see stars everywhere; on the chest, in the hair, on belts, rings, etc.[36]

Such apparel must indeed have caught the eye in those austere, early post-war years. At the Budapest World Congress in 1966, President

Lapenna reverted to this theme: 'What we need today is . . . not a sect of cranks in unusual clothes, but a cultural movement enjoying prestige and esteem. Fortunately we have attained this almost one hundred per cent. But unfortunately there still exists this "almost" which jeopardises the seriousness of our work, belittles the attainments, hinders new steps and puts a brake on progress.'[37] These attacks by Lapenna and like-minded Esperantists in turn produced ripostes about the need for tolerance and cooperation in the movement. It is perhaps inevitable that social movements such as Esperanto will attract cranks and eccentrics, but it is also difficult to deny that deviant behaviour by some members will gain more than its fair share of publicity and helps to create an image of Esperantists and Esperanto which is not conducive to winning wider support.

A LINGUISTIC OUTLINE

Many textbooks have been published during the last 100 years in a wide variety of languages setting out the fundamentals of Esperanto grammar, beginning with *Lingvo internacia,* Zamenhof's own pseudonymous work which appeared in 1887 (see chapter 4). Anyone desiring to study the language would be well advised to seek out a suitable textbook (or better still join an Esperanto course) such as Cresswell and Hartley's primer in the 'Teach Yourself' series.[38] All that can be attempted here is the merest outline of the language which may help to explain why Esperanto has proved so successful as an artificial language.

Esperanto closely resembles the languages in the Indo-European linguistic family, both in grammatical structure and in vocabulary; so much so, indeed, that it has been described as the most recent member of that family.[39] The alphabet contains 28 letters: 23 consonants and five vowels. The spelling and pronunciation of Esperanto are broadly phonetic as each letter, including the vowels, should have one sound only, which is always rendered by that one and only letter. There are no silent letters, and stress always falls on the penultimate syllable. The grammar is regular, avoiding the frequent exceptions to rules, the 'irregulars', which so plague natural languages and cause even children learning them as a first language initial difficulties, let alone the student tackling a second language. In the words of Cresswell and Hartley, the grammar is 'so ingeniously devised that in place of the usual maze of rules, occupying a sizeable volume, which most other languages present, we have only 16 short rules, which may be written comfortably on a sheet of notepaper'.[40] They are referring to the 'Sixteen Rules' in which Zamenhof first summarised his creation in 1887 and which were re-published in 1905 in the authoritative sourcebook of the language, the *Fundamento de Esperanto* (see above, p. 76—7; these rules are also reproduced below in Appendix I).

The vocabulary of Esperanto is largely based upon the Romance languages or drawn directly from Latin, with smaller roles for German, Russian, English and Polish. Nouns always end in the letter 'o'. The following examples reveal the close relationship between Latin and Esperanto:

Esperanto	*Latin*	*English*
akvo	aqua	water
domo	domus	house
tero	terra	earth
mano	manus	hand
patro	pater	father

Other Esperanto words are fairly easily recognisable from their English equivalents, especially when the rules for pronunciation of Esperanto have been studied:

Esperanto	*English*
birdo	bird
rivero	river
vilaĝo	village
kato	cat
elefanto	elephant

An important characteristic of Esperanto, much stressed by its advocates, is its receptivity to new words. Zamenhof himself created only a small proportion of its contemporary vocabulary. Rule 15 of the 'Sixteen Rules' provides one means of word building: 'The so-called "foreign words", i.e. words which the greater number of languages have derived from the same source, undergo no change in the international language, beyond conforming to its system of orthography.' Thus words like *nazio* (nazi), *tanko, parasuto* and *transistoro,* none of which existed in Zamenhof's day but which currently have a wide international usage, are now to be found in Esperanto. If no internationally-recognised word is available to express a concept and if it is impossible or too inconvenient to compound existing Esperanto roots, then a new word may be created. Esperanto is a living language which like any other language adapts to the changing environments in which its speakers are to be found. The Akademio de Esperanto is an international body of experts in the language whose task is to regulate any changes which are made, thus permitting flexibility whilst ensuring consistency, or so it is hoped.

The second major characteristic of Esperanto is its regularity of word formation. Just as all nouns end in the letter 'o', all adjectives end in 'a' and adverbs in 'e':

Esperanto	*English*
bona hundo	a good dog
bela domo	a beautiful house
juna viro	a young man
forta leono	a strong lion
bele	beautifully
forte	strongly

The plural form of nouns and adjectives always ends in 'j':

Esperanto	*English*
bonaj hundoj	good dogs
belaj domoj	beautiful houses
junaj viroj	young men
fortaj leonoj	strong lions

This regularity of formation is especially noticeable in the verbal forms, which are so often plagued by irregularities in natural languages. Even the verb 'to be' is regular in Esperanto:

Esperanto	*English*
mi estas	I am
vi estas	you are

li estas	he is
ŝi estas	she is
ĝi estas	it is
ni estas	we are
vi estas	you are
ili estas	they are

The second person plural is the same as the second person singular, and as is readily apparent from the above conjugation, person is indicated by personal pronouns: the verb ending remains constant throughout the conjugation. Different endings are used, however, to indicate other tenses. The past tense has the ending *is* (*ni estis,* we were); the future tense *os* (*li estos*, he will be); the conditional *us* (*ŝi estus*, she should be). The infinitive always ends in *i* (*esti,* to be) and the imperative in *u* (*venu,* come; *iru,* go).

In Esperanto, regularity of word formation is greatly facilitated by the use of prefixes and suffixes to provide a series of related words from one common root. They can be used with adjectives, adverbs and verbs as well as nouns. To take a few examples first, of prefixes:

GE- denotes people of both sexes taken together:

| gepatroj | parents |
| gefiloj | son(s) and daughter(s) |

MAL- gives the opposite of the word to which it is attached:

bela	beautiful
malbela	ugly
bona	good
malbona	bad

SEN- without:

| nuba | cloudy |
| sennuba | cloudless |

RE- repetition:

| legas | reads |
| relegas | re-reads |

or the return of a person or thing to its former place or condition:

iras	goes
reiras	returns

The following examples illustrate the use of suffixes in Esperanto:

-IN   denotes the feminine form of a word:

patro	father
patrino	mother
filo	son
filino	daughter

-EJ   place

lernas	learn
lernejo	school
preĝas	pray
preĝejo	church

-ET   diminutive form:

domo	house
dometo	cottage
dormas	sleeps
dormetas	dozes

-EG   indicates great size:

domego	mansion
dormegas	sleeps heavily

-AN   member of:

vilaĝo	village
vilaĝano	villager
Kristo	Christ
Kristano	Christian

Pierre Burney has likened this facility in Esperanto to a 'linguistic meccano'.[41] By attaching prefixes or suffixes to a common root, a whole family of words can easily be created. Thus *hundo* is dog, *hundino* a bitch, *hundido* a puppy, *hundidino* a bitch puppy, *hundego* a big dog, *hundinego* a big bitch, *hundidinego* a big bitch puppy, and so on.

Esperanto has two cases for nouns and adjectives; it uses a special form — an accusative form — to express the direct object of a verb or to show motion or direction to somewhere. The accusative ending in both singular and plural is 'n':

La amiko sendas leteron	The friend sends a letter
La amikoj sendas leterojn	The friends send letters
La viro iras en la domon	The man goes into the house

Numbers are based upon Latin forms and are combined in a straight-forward manner:

1	unu	11	dek unu
2	du	12	dek du
3	tri	20	dudek
4	kvar	30	tridek
5	kvin	100	cent
6	ses	101	cent unu
7	sep	112	cent dek du
8	ok	200	ducent
9	naŭ	1,000	mil
10	dek		

The consequence of Esperanto word formation rules is that an Esperanto dictionary is much more compact than its equivalent in a natural language. The most comprehensive dictionary, *La Plena ilustrita vortaro,* contains only about 16,000 roots, but these can be used to form ten times as many words.

LINGUISTIC CRITICISMS

For many Esperantists, their language is a model of regularity, simplicity and beauty. An early expression of confidence was issued by the *British Esperantist* in June 1906 in its 'Answers to correspondents'. The editor wrote that he did not wish to discuss matters relating to any proposed changes in the language because 'it is so wonderfully well made that there are very few, if any, points about it which its best experts would wish to unmake or to make otherwise, if they could put back the clock of time to the days of its making.'[42] More recently, in its 'Basic facts about the International Language' the Centre for Research and Documentation on the Language Problem of the UEA has emphasised that 'The grammar of Esperanto, synthesised from a number of languages, represents that essence of grammatical structure which is at one and the same time the basic minimum for the free expression of ideas, and yet is entirely sufficient.' Esperanto has become a living language 'satisfying all the demands not only of logical thought, but also of artistic expression'.[43] Then again, for Mario Pei, Esperanto 'combines to a superlative degree the four qualities that make constructed languages superior to natural ones: neutrality, standardisation, phonetisation, and simplicity of grammatical structure and word-formation'.[44]

Notwithstanding such confident assertions by its supporters, Esperanto has by no means evaded criticism. Indeed, all aspects of the language — grammar, vocabulary, orthography and pronunciation — have at one time or another been the object of critical examination. Discussion of language reform within the Esperanto movement was probably most active in its first few decades. The recent memory of linguistic disputes in the Volapük movement, which proved so damaging to its survival, was ever present, however, and helped to curb the inevitable calls for changes. Zamenhof himself did not favour major modifications of his language, a view ultimately supported by a ballot of Esperantists on certain proposals for reform which were made in the mid-1890s (see chapter 4). It is interesting to note, though, that argument still continues over these same points today.

An early and eminent critic of Esperanto was the Danish linguist, Otto Jespersen, although it should be noted that as a supporter of Ido, that great rival of Esperanto, he was no neutral bystander. First, Jespersen criticised the selection of Esperanto vocabulary. Before Zamenhof had decided to select vocabulary from the Romance and Germanic languages, supplemented by a stock of international words, he had chosen words quite arbitrarily. According to Jespersen, this had resulted in a series of *a priori* formations which would be more difficult to learn and use. Second, Esperanto pronunciation revealed a preference for sibilants and dipthongs, a consequence of Zamenhof's Slavonic mother tongue. Third, the orthographic use of circumflexed letters (ĉ, ĝ, ħ, ĵ, ŝ, ŭ), although quite common in various Roman alphabets, made the language more cumbersome to write and required special type fonts. Finally, many Esperanto words could not be recognised from their prototypes in existing languages, a criticism which had previously been emphatically made against another artificial language, Volapük (see chapter 4).[45]

These criticisms seem a little harsh. As regards pronunciation, for example, it is generally regarded that Esperanto has a rather pleasant sound not unlike Italian, with which it might easily be confused by someone unversed in either tongue. The use of circumflexed letters has been widely and strongly condemned, particularly by critics whose own alphabets do not make use of diacritic signs of any kind, and undoubtedly it does create problems for printers who may require special type. Furthermore, typewriters may require modification, and nowadays computer keyboards made for an American and British market will lack these circumflexed letters. Nevertheless, such orthographic points hardly loom into prominence when assessing the overall suitability of Esperanto as an effective language of written and spoken communication. In any case, the use of circumflexes has the advantage of helping to ensure that as far as is possible, Esperanto is a phonetic language: that each sound is represented by one letter only and that each letter only has one sound.

The criticisms levelled at Esperanto vocabulary are more telling, as they relate to the ease with which the language can be assimilated and employed. Indeed, many of the artificial forerunners to Esperanto had been justly and roundly attacked on this very matter (see chapters 2—4). The accusation of arbitrariness has often been made against Zamenhof's selection of roots, and certainly it is possible to identify those banes of the language learner, *faux amis*. The Esperanto word 'foresto', for example, does not mean forest (forêt in French) but absence. Other examples of words which might mislead the English Esperantist are 'sesono' which means 'one-sixth' and not season, and 'fosilo' which is a spade. Furthermore, despite Rule 15 of the famous Esperanto Sixteen Rules — that words which the greater number of languages have derived from the same source should be adopted by Esperanto — many words with a common root in European languages have not been used. To take one example, the word hospital (or hôpital in French, hospital in Spanish, Spital in German) is rendered in Esperanto by a totally unrelated word, 'malsanulejo'. This is produced by the word-building techniques employed in Esperanto which have already been discussed above. Thus 'sana' means health, 'malsana' means sick (the use of the prefix reverses the meaning of the root), 'malsanulo' means invalid (the suffix -ul is used to denote a person characterised by the idea contained in the root), and finally the additional suffix -ej indicates the place specially used for the object indicated by the root. It should also be noted that despite its widespread use of suffixes, Esperanto does NOT use suffixes such as -ion, -iv, -ment, etc., which make up a large part of international derivatives. Finally, of course, it may be that Esperanto is already using a word which is then adopted by other languages to express a completely different meaning; the word 'radar' could not be used by Esperanto for the system of ascertaining range and direction of objects by means of reflected electro-magnetic waves, because 'radaro' already means a clockwork mechanism.[46]

A recent critic of Esperanto, Nolting, has argued that much of Esperanto morphology was 'dictated by whims instead of a regard for function and simplicity'. Although he agrees that 'whims can produce more pleasing results than arid logic, for whimsicality is a component of art', he adds that 'many of Zamenhof's whims were an affront to both art and logic'. In defence of this assertion, Nolting cites the example of the Esperanto suffix -mal, which, as mentioned above, expresses the opposite meaning to that of the root to which it is attached. The choice of which one of a pair should carry the prefix is arbitrary (for example, to be 'left' in Esperanto is to be 'unright') or involves a value judgement (to be 'short' is to be 'untall' or to be 'thin' is to be 'unfat').[47]

Turning to criticisms of Esperanto grammar, the most popular target has probably been the use of an accusative case to express the direct object of a verb or motion towards something. Its supporters argue that it lends flexibility to the language, particularly useful in literature and poetry, because the word order need not be fixed in the one pattern, subject, verb, object. Its opponents state that this is scant compensation for the ensuing grammatical complication which has thereby been introduced into the language. Not surprisingly, one's response to this dispute is likely to be coloured by one's own native language: those of us from the English-speaking world are more likely to balk at the use of such an alien construction than those from, say, the slavonic language group where such a construction is familiar. The argument over the use of an accusative continues to rage in Britain even amongst 'card-carrying' Esperantists, as evidenced by a recent outburst in *Esperanto news*.[48]

This last point raises the interesting topic of precisely how international is Esperanto, from a linguistic point of view. Reflecting its late nineteenth-century origins, the structure and the vocabulary of Esperanto were modelled upon the European languages which belong to the Indo-European family. Notwithstanding claims sometimes made that in certain features, such as its simplicity of grammatical construction, it resembles Chinese, it was a pan-European (at best) rather than a pan-world language. This may well make it attractive to Europeans, but what of the rest of the world? It is no longer sufficient that an international language should suit the needs of European peoples; it must now be accessible to all, regardless of native language. In earlier times, of course, this was not so true, and some Esperantists, at any rate, had no inhibitions about extolling the virtues of their language's Europeanness. As one wrote as recently as 1930, any new auxiliary language 'should cater primarily for Europeans, since if they accept such a language it will be automatically taken up elsewhere, whilst a scheme based (for example) on Japanese, Malay, and Arabic, even if workable, would not attract the Western world, and would thus never become a general auxiliary tongue for the nations most in need of the boon'.[49] Such an argument is unlikely to be propounded today, of course; rather, the European orientation of Esperanto has become a weak chink at which its critics probe and which its supporters attempt to play down.

The former president of the UEA, Humphrey Tonkin, for example, urges that we must distinguish between vocabulary and structure. While the former is drawn from Indo-European languages the latter 'essentially transcends them'. According to Tonkin, 'Although Esperanto's agglutinative system of roots and endings conforms to Indo-European notions of parts of speech, the agglutination itself sets Esperanto off from most of the languages from which Zamenhof borrowed his lexicon'. Speakers of Japanese and Chinese are supposedly 'very much at home with the agglutinative morphology of Esperanto'.[50] A critic, Richard Lillie, believes, however, that artificial languages such as Esperanto are 'too ethno-centric and parochial to appeal to the millions of Asian people whose native tongues bear no resemblance to Latin-derived tongues'. On the other hand, he thinks that minor modifications to Esperanto — the addition of vocabulary from Asian languages, some grammatical changes, and the adoption of a non-Roman alphabet — would make it acceptable to Asians. Surprisingly, he argues that the last of those three modifications is the most important: 'In point of fact, the phonetic syllabaries of Korean, Japanese or Sanskrit are far more suited to describing the actual sounds of any language than is the Roman alphabet.'[51] Such modifications, of course, would radically alter Esperanto, with incalculable effects upon its existing speakers, without necessarily making it more linguistically acceptable to speakers of any specific natural language. The enormous differences between individual oriental languages, for example, would make the task of constructing a genuine inter-language extremely difficult — in all probability impossible — while at the same time ensuring that it was no longer easily intelligible to Europeans. Esperantists retort, in any case, that Esperanto is becoming less Indo-European as it develops, just because many of its users are non-Europeans and they are playing a part in extending its ever-evolving vocabulary.[52] This would seem a little disingenuous, and a most cursory perusal of an Esperanto text clearly shows that the language favours learners with certain mother tongues rather than others. A short passage, admittedly more than usually easy for the English speaker, should make this point clear:

La inteligenta persono lernas la interlingvon Esperanto rapide kaj facile. Esperanto estas la moderna, kultura lingvo por la internacia mondo. Simpla, fleksebla, praktika solvo de la problemo de universala interkompreno, Esperanto meritas vian seriozan konsideron. Lernu la interlingvon Esperanto.[53]

Other critics in turn have argued that if it is really true that Esperanto is losing its European bias through practical use by speakers from other parts of the world, then a new danger arises: that Esperanto will disintegrate into a number of increasingly unintelligible dialects, a charge Esperantists vigorously deny. This argument must remain largely theoretical as in fact the vast majority of Esperantists are still Europeans.

What of all these linguistic criticisms? Perhaps the most comforting thing for Esperantists is that really they are so slight. After all, it is inconceivable that any artificial language will ever be constructed which receives universal praise. If it is true that there are as many economic theories as there are economists, it surely must be so that there are as many ideas for a perfect language as there are linguists. It is hard to disagree too violently with Zamenhof's own comments made at the Sixth

Esperanto Universal Congress in Washington in 1910. Speculating on the changes which any committee set up to choose an international language might propose for Esperanto, he said:

If you will look through all the criticisms which have been made upon Esperanto in twenty-three years — and in fact Esperanto has already had many thousands of critics, and certainly not one, even the smallest, of its defects has remained undiscovered — you will find that the immense majority of these criticisms are simply personal caprices. The number of those proposals of change which really might have some practical value is so small that all of them together would not fill more than one small leaflet . . . but even among those very few hypothetical changes the most important are only a *seeming improvement,* and, in fact, after more mature consideration, might prove to be quite the reverse.[54]

Jespersen had made his criticisms, discussed briefly above, in the aftermath of the bitter feud between the supporters of Ido and Esperanto, but despite the poisonous atmosphere even he was generous enough to concede that the impefections of Esperanto did not prevent him from recognising 'the meritorious services of Zamenhof, who, at a time when the question of the best construction of an international language was not seriously discussed, succeeded in producing one which was in many respects superior to the attempts of that time, and which has proved in practice a serviceable, though very imperfect, means of international communication'.[55] And perhaps that should be the last word. Whatever its linguistic defects, Esperanto has by now proved that it is quite capable of functioning effectively in the many ways expected of an international language: in any case, the success or failure of any constructed language ultimately is unlikely to be determined primarily on linguistic issues.

LEARNING ESPERANTO

An important pre-requisite of any artificial language which has aspirations to mass support is that it should be relatively easy to learn. For anyone familiar with one or more European languages from the Indo-European group, Esperanto should not pose any great obstacles to acquisition, and certainly should be easier to learn than any natural language. Indeed, it would be surprising if this were not the case, given its basic *a posteriori* structure, its grammatical regularity, broadly phonetic spelling and pronunciation, and relatively consistent rules for word building from European roots. With a considerable measure of success it has managed to combine the texture or feel of a natural language with the logic of a constructed one.

The more dramatic claims for its ease of acquisition should perhaps be treated with some caution. According to Stanley Rundle, for example, 'a person of normal intelligence' could easily learn its 'regular and scientific' grammar in an hour, as it consists of 'only sixteen short rules'.[56] It may well be quite feasible to learn by rote these short rules very quickly but, of course, this is not the same as learning to use Esperanto. As William Solzbacher, then a member of the Academy of Esperanto and an eminent Esperantist in the United States, conceded at a Symposium on the Teaching of Esperanto in American universities and colleges:

I think that we should have no illusions that certain aspects of the Esperanto propaganda are serious obstacles to any kind of introduction in academic circles. Take the propagandists who say that this is the language that has only 16 rules, that it is absolutely phonetic and so on. Of course, for any linguist this is nonsense, something completely impossible.[57]

Like any other language, Esperanto can be used with infinitely varied degrees of fluency and precision. To speak or write it as a second language with subtlety and verve requires practice and aptitude. The Sixteen Rules provide a useful summary of the main grammatical characteristics of Esperanto: and nothing more. The President of the UEA, Professor Lapenna, offered a reasonable estimate of two or three hours per week of study for one year in order to acquire 'a solid groundwork of knowledge of Esperanto's grammatical structure and of five hundred or so selected roots, from which the language's agglutinative structure enables one to derive some five thousand words'.[58]

In part a consequence of the success achieved by Esperanto, in part an explanation of that success, a wide variety of excellent teaching aids are now available for the student of the language. The availability of a relatively large market (at least in comparison with other artificial language schemes) for teaching aids and the existence of a central organisation to encourage and in some cases support production and distribution has enabled books, cassettes, records and so on to be published which meet the needs of learners at different stages of study. It is only necessary to compare a course book in Esperanto with those available to explain many of the other constructed languages to appreciate the clarity and indeed the readability of the former. Perhaps most strikingly, Esperanto textbooks and other media aids are aimed at the ordinary person who may not know any foreign language or even possess any background information on the grammatical structure of any language, including his or her own native language. Undoubtedly, the availability of such aids has in turn made Esperanto accessible to an audience which could never be reached by abstruse technical grammars suitable for (if not actually intended for) only the most enthusiastic expert.

Not only are teaching aids available for Esperanto, but language courses are also regularly offered. In many cases local Esperanto groups will provide an opportunity to study the language with other beginners, where encouragement and an element of discipline, together with collective motivation and guidance, should simplify learning. In Britain, at any rate, residential language courses for various levels of achievement are offered from time to time, where the benefits of intensive study can be reaped. Again, such courses can only be provided when a language has reached a certain measure of popularity and when an organisational structure is available to make the necessary arrangements. Esperanto alone of any artificial language today is in a position to exploit these possibilities.

A number of controlled experiments have been conducted to measure the ease with which schoolchildren can acquire a facility in Esperanto compared with their achievements over a similar period in a modern language such as French. An English headmaster of a secondary modern school reports an experiment in which the 'A' stream pupils were taught French and the 'B' stream Esperanto. At the end of each year tests were given in French and Esperanto, the Esperanto tests being based on the French. The papers were marked by independent examiners and the results showed that only by the end of four years' study of French did the 'A' children slightly outshine the 'B' children's performance in Esperanto after just twelve months' study. Most of the children were taught by the same teacher, an honours graduate in French but a beginner in Esperanto. Later, Esperanto was taught for one year to both the 'A' and the 'B' streams, and the examination resulted in an average mark of 65 per cent for the As and 40 per cent for the Bs. In other words, the 'A' stream children were considerably better at language study than the 'B' streamers, yet when handicapped with French rather than Esperanto they failed quite significantly to outshine their weaker colleagues.[59] Apparently, American language teachers have reached similar conclusions; according to one report, Esperanto can be learnt five to ten times as fast as any other language.[60] A slightly more conservative assessment was reached by the teachers of a half-semester course at the University of Illinois; progress in Esperanto was about four times faster than in any national language.[61] It is unnecessary to accept the precise findings of these individual experiments in order to draw the conclusion that Esperanto can be learnt, by English-speaking pupils, with *relative* ease. It is also interesting to note the claims that the study of Esperanto actually facilitates the learning of other languages, simplifies the teaching of grammar and results in a better knowledge of the English language.[62]

THE ESPERANTO MOVEMENT

Esperantists always describe themselves as being part of a 'movement', although many local Esperanto associations are known as 'clubs'. The term 'movement' has been used throughout this study, and certainly it seems to convey better the evangelical and proselytising fervour of many members and does suggest similarities with certain minority religious and political movements: a belief in an ultimate and attainable goal, a certain sense of embattlement against the weight of apathy or hostility in society at large, a belief that at some future date the 'truth' of the cause will become clear to those who now scorn, a comradeship with those who have already accepted the faith, a tendency towards factionalism and heresy hunting, and so on. As C.K. Ogden, the creator of Basic English (see chapter 6) sarcastically commented of the Esperantists in the 1930s, 'They are, as it were, the Fundamentalists of a not very evolutionary Faith, and in the bitter internecine quarrels of the past forty-five years they have developed a method and style of controversy which is reminiscent of the religious logomachies of earlier ages.'[63]

Further common ground is provided by the tendency of such movements to attract more than their fair share of eccentrics or fanatics amongst the core of dedicated enthusiasts who devote endless time and money to the cause. Some aspects of the Esperanto movement in particular conjure the image of a religious sect. Forster quotes excerpts from several Esperanto songs which would perhaps better be described as hymns in terms both of their content and performance. To quote one example in English translation:

> To the Esperantists
> Here and overseas
> Our band of fellow idealists
> Turn themselves with love,
> Nowhere let it fail to prosper
> May it by God's gift
> Everywhere grow further through the years
> Up to tremendous fame.
> Let the nations live like families,
> Let brotherly friendship grow and envies cease;
> Soon human warfare
> And hate that has existed till now
> Owing to mutual understanding
> Disappear.
> High-idea'd peace-lover,
> Father of Esperanto,
> May Zamenhof always be
> Leader of us.
> The language will go everywhere,
> It will conquer the whole world
> Draw the nations together
> Through the blessing of God.[64]

In this one song are gathered the religious overtones of the movement, the veneration of Zamenhof and the concepts of international brotherhood and peace amongst nations which are such common themes in Esperantist tracts. As the proponent of a rival scheme, Alexander Gode, caustically remarked: 'There is something nostalgically beautiful about the naiveté of the true Esperantist's faith in the power of his language. One may be justified in suspecting that it is this faith in its often fanatical excesses that explains why Esperanto has progressed as far as it did, and not really the power of the language itself.'[65]

According to a Freudian psychologist, J. Flugel, for many Esperantists Zamenhof represents an ideal father, characterised by loving kindness and creative power. The movement has much in common with primitive Christianity: an almost exclusive predominance of the loving attitude towards the father; a tendency to regard all mankind as brothers; a very strong bond of kindness and sympathy between all those who take part in the movement; both appealed chiefly to the relatively poor, uninfluential and uncultured. At the same time, Zamenhof, by his renunciation of all special ownership, privilege or control with regard to Esperanto, was able in most cases to prevent the transference to himself of the more hostile aspects of the father-figure. For Flugel, linguistic activities are to some extent sublimations of sexual activities:

If the acquirement of each fresh language constitutes an additional gratifying manifestation of power (in the last resort sexual power) and diminishes the sense of inferiority (based ultimately on the fear of sexual impotence or castration), it is clear that the knowledge of a universal language which would enable its possessor to understand and be understood by the inhabitants of all the world would afford access to the completest possible satisfaction on this plane; being inferior only to the manifestly impossible alternative of a knowledge of *all* living tongues.[66]

Esperanto is not simply a movement but it is predominantly a European movement despite its internationalist ideology and objectives. Although its members are scattered over the globe, its heartland where most of its members are still found is Europe. Esperanto has not even made much headway in the New World; its national organisation in the United States, The Esperanto League for North America, can currently only claim about 700 members. But more than this, the language itself is Indo-European in structure and vocabulary (see above) and it grew out of a distinctly European environment. Zamenhof himself was a product of his East European Jewish background and the movement took root in a Europe in which large numbers of people linked by a common culture and outlook were perversely broken into many different nations, potentially in conflict one with another. This was a European civilisation from which several key elements — socialism, rationalism and idealism — were absorbed into the youthful Esperanto movement. The fact that these elements have now been dispersed around the world in one variety or another does little to detract from their essential Europeanness. The UEA has itself recognised its European bias and has attempted to correct it. Non-European membership has been encouraged by such measures as reducing subscriptions for members in poorer countries, establishing more Esperanto centres, cheaper distribution of literature, and so on. It remains to be seen whether such endeavours bring rewards.

The neutrality of the Esperanto movement in political matters has always been stressed by the UEA. Indeed, Esperantists have traditionally distrusted political action and have usually concentrated on converting individuals to their cause rather than influencing governments. As Zamenhof told the Esperanto World Congress in 1910:

The end for which we are working can be attained in two ways — either by work of private individuals, that is, by the masses of the people, or by decree of the Governments. Our purpose is most likely to be attained by the first method; for to a cause like ours the Governments generally come with their sanction and help only when everything is already quite prepared.[67]

Even the approaches made by the UEA towards the United Nations and Unesco were a departure from this tradition, and were not welcomed by all members.

Despite this neutrality, socialist ideology has been linked with Esperanto from its earliest days. SAT was formed in 1921 to counter the political neutrality of the UEA and in general to break away from its quasi-religious atmosphere which smothered the class consciousness of its proletarian members, to use the vocabulary of SAT. In times of 'Cold War' and ideological conflict, the neutrality favoured by the UEA is a delicate blossom which must be carefully tended if it is to survive the harsh political storms. Although SAT itself remains today a socialist organisation, it is virtually forbidden in most communist countries. On the other hand, the growing number of Esperantists in Eastern Europe (see above) could well pose problems in the future for the Esperantist movement. According to a report in *The Guardian,* for example, the Novosti Press Agency in Moscow has started using Esperanto for anti-nuclear war propaganda.[68] Fears about the exploitation of the movement as a communist front organisation have already been voiced, especially in the United States where a full-scale campaign against communist 'infiltration' was launched in the 1950s. The UEA policy is that publications of affiliated movements in communist countries can comment upon their own achievements but must not attack either the political neutrality of the UEA or the policies of other countries.[69] Such a neutral stance will not prove simple to sustain, yet a failure to do so could be disastrous for a movement with an international membership and a universal ideal.

6

The Challengers to Esperanto

Esperanto has undoubtedly proved itself to be more successful than any other artificial language in terms of winning and sustaining a world-wide movement of enthusiastic speakers. Of even more importance, perhaps, is its relatively high level of general visibility; its name at least is familiar to many who could adduce little else about artificial languages. Indeed, it would be no exaggeration to say that 'Esperanto' is commonly used synonymously for 'artificial language' (see chapter 5). Nonetheless, this success has not deterred language projectors from offering rival schemes whose alleged superiority will, it is fervently believed, ensure the attainment of the goal sought but not yet reached by Esperanto: adoption as an international auxiliary language. Some of these schemes bear a close resemblance in structure to Esperanto, whilst others have taken a different approach, on occasions reminiscent of the seventeenth-century language projects. This chapter will do no more than highlight a few of the more interesting or influential artificial languages which have been presented during this century as challengers to Esperanto.

In categorising these twentieth-century language schemes, it is again useful to make a distinction between *a priori* and *a posteriori* approaches, already discussed in relation to earlier schemes (see above p. 51). In the main, language projectors since the late nineteenth century have favoured an *a posteriori* structure, reflecting the more pragmatic nature of contemporary thinking. The primary motivation in most cases has been to design a workable international auxiliary language which can be easily learnt and used by everyone, rather than a more rigorous logical or philosophical language of the *a priori* kind, whose practical application as a medium of common discourse is less certain. Additionally, the very success of Esperanto, itself an *a posteriori* language, has encouraged the construction of languages which differ from it in detail rather than overall structure; a belief that the final triumph of Esperanto has only been prevented by the stubborn refusal of its supporters to introduce certain supposedly essential modifications has spurred on many language projectors.

In this chapter it will further prove useful to divide the *a posteriori* languages into two categories: those, like Esperanto, which can be considered autonomistic systems, and others, like Occidental and Latino sine flexione, which are naturalistic systems. In his paper, *On language making,*[1] H. Jacob defined an autonomistic system as one in which the language is made as easy and as precise as possible by creating a set of principles which will be employed without exceptions. The elements of the language should be regular and logical, regardless of the usages of any natural languages upon which it draws. The regularity of Esperanto word formation, pronunciation, word structure and syntax has already been discussed in the previous chapter. This regularity can result, however, in a language whose form is no longer familiar even to a speaker of one or more of those underlying natural languages. The naturalistic system, on the other hand, ensures that the language resembles as closely as possible the existing forms of natural languages, and in practice this has normally meant the Romanic group of languages. All elements in the language should be natural, even if this is achieved at the expense of regularity.

The predominance of *a posteriori* schemes in recent decades, however, does not signify the end of the *a priori* approach. A number of such schemes have been constructed, although they have proved less successful in attracting any substantial support. Nowadays, in marked contrast with earlier centuries, they tend to be viewed as the work of linguistic eccentrics, curiosities rather than serious attempts to promote international accord.

When considering twentieth-century rivals to Esperanto, it is impossible to ignore a different approach to the solution of the language problem. Modified natural languages, of which Basic English is the best example, are not strictly speaking artificial languages but natural languages simplified in grammatical structure or vocabulary. Nevertheless, the distinction between such a modified natural language and a naturalistic *a posteriori* language in practice is a fine one. It would be unwarrantable to include discussion of, say, Latino sine flexione but to exclude Basic English. In any case, both have the same objective: to serve as a means of international communication more effectively than any unmodified natural language.

A POSTERIORI CHALLENGERS

Of the many challengers to Esperanto, the most inveterate remains its old adversary, Ido, an autonomistic *a posteriori* language which in many respects closely resembles Esperanto. In 1901 a Délégation pour l'adoption d'une langue auxiliaire internationale had been set up on the initiative of Louis Couturat and Léopold Leau to choose an international language from a number of contenders, including Esperanto. The Délégation elected a Committee which finally decided to select Esperanto, but only on condition that some modifications be made 'along the lines defined by the report of the Secretaries [of the Committee] and by the project Ido'.[2] Ido was the pseudonym used by the author of a pamphlet which had been presented to the Committee at the last minute and which set out a language scheme similar to Esperanto. The story of how Zamenhof refused to accept the Committee's decision and broke with the Délégation in 1908 has already been recounted in chapter 4. The ensuing rift between Esperanto and Ido proved irreconcilable and a substantial part of the Esperanto leadership, though few of the rank-and-file members, subsequently became Idists. The new Ido movement established a monthly journal, *Progreso* (edited by Couturat) and a Union of Friends of the International Language (Uniono di la Amika de la Linguo Internaciona) which elected an Ido Academy in Zurich to direct day-to-day activities.

Couturat firmly led the growing Idist movement until his death in 1914, but his removal, together with the inhospitable atmosphere created by the First World War, decimated the Idist ranks and, perhaps more devastating, encouraged the growth of sectarianism, a danger ever-present in any artificial language movement. The Ido Academy had announced a period of stability in the language to extend for ten years from 1913, following the introduction of numerous changes in its early years. The extension of this breathing space until 1926 because of the war was not to the liking of all Idists. As Forster comments: 'Whereas the Esperanto movement was again "purged" of reformers by the Ido schism, and its control over fissiparous tendencies was now greater than ever, the opposite applied to Ido. As a schismatic movement of reformers, the Idists were themselves fissiparous.'[3] Interestingly, the creators of a number of subsequent language projects — Jespersen, Peano and de Wahl are good examples — where Idists whose restless quest after a more perfect auxiliary language eventually tore them from the Idist fold (de Wahl in fact had earlier been both a Volapükist and an Esperantist).

Despite these sectarian tendencies, the Idists organised their first World Congress in 1921, held in Vienna. The movement increased in strength during the inter-war period, only to be set back again by the Second World War. Today it manages to maintain a tenuous foothold in several European countries, North America, and a few other scattered outposts. In Britain the International Language (Ido) Society of Great Britain promotes the language in various ways. It organises courses, particularly of the correspondence variety, publishes a journal, *Ido-Vivo* three times per year and convenes annual meetings. Nevertheless, membership remains very small. Such national associations in turn are affiliated to La Uniono por la Linguo Internaciona (Ido), which publishes its own journal, *Progreso,* and organises international conferences.

The Idists are generally less vitriolic in their comments on Esperanto than are the Esperantists in their attacks on Ido. As one Idist expressed it, 'Every Esperantist is looked upon as a possible adherent to Ido, if he can be reached later through an exposition of the relative merits of the two rival languages.'[4] On the other hand, few Esperantists have shown interest in drawing the Idists back into the flock, and the Esperantist leadership remains implacable in its hostility to Ido. According to Forster, the Idists have claimed to be willing to re-enter negotiations with the Esperantists at any time, and have expressed their dislike of the term 'schism', widely used by Esperantists to describe the birth of the Ido movement.[5] Esperantist reluctance to allow old wounds to heal may be based partly upon a position of strength; the adherence of a small number of Idists would not greatly enhance their movement, although it would obviate the currently felt need to dissipate energy in internecine conflict. An additional reason for Esperantist reluctance, however, is the perpetual dread of linguistic anarchy. The admission of Idists to the Esperanto ranks would inevitably require not only initial reform of Esperanto but would also raise the spectre of further uncertainty and even dispute over the structure of the language. Esperanto has chosen the path of stability and order, resisting from its earliest days any calls for reform which threatened to split the movement. Ido has charted a different route, seeking perfection in the language even at the expense of linguistic stability. Proposals to reform Ido are still emerging; the pages of *Ido-vivo,* for example, as recently as 1984 included suggestions for simplifying the language. The Idists, though few in number, may well prove persistent and active in reformist proposals if admitted to the Esperantist ranks.

Ido uses an alphabet containing the same letters as English, although in some cases with pronunciation differences ('c' is always pronounced as 'ts', 'g' is always hard, and so on). Stress falls on the penultimate syllable (except for infinitives where it is on the final syllable). Nouns end in -o in the singular and -i in the plural (*libro,* book; *libri,* books), adjectives end in -a and adverbs in -e (*vera,* true; *vere,* truly). All verbs are regular, infinitives ending in -ar, the present tense in -as, past tense in -is, future in -os, conditional in -us and imperative in -ez:

dormar	to sleep
me dormas	I am sleeping
vu dormis	you slept
ilu dormos	he will sleep
ni dormus	we should sleep
dormez	sleep

Ido has no indefinite article, but the definite article is always *la.* An accusative case is used for the direct object (-n is added) *but* only if the object is placed in the sentence before the subject. For a flavour of the Ido numerals:

0	zero	7	sep
1	un	8	ok
2	du	9	non
3	tri	10	dek
4	quar	100	cent
5	kin	1000	mil
6	sis		

A quick comparison of this Ido outline with the brief summary of Esperanto in the previous chapter reveals the many similarities between the two languages. The pamphlet entitled 'How Ido works', issued by the International Language (Ido) Society of Great Britain, points out that Ido 'is, of course, based on Esperanto', adding 'but the crudities of Esperanto have been cleared away: the result is a beautiful, euphonic language similar to Italian, fully equal to all the demands made upon it'.

The major areas of linguistic divergence between Ido and Esperanto can be highlighted by listing the conditions which the Idists stipulated in 1925 for their reintegration into the Esperantist movement.[6] These were as shown below.

1   The immediate suppression of accented letters (ĉ, ĝ, ħ, ĵ, ŝ and ŭ) and the adoption of the Ido alphabet (the principal other difference being that the Ido alphabet employs the consonants w, x and y which occur in many internationally recognisable words).
2   Suppression of the table of correlatives and its replacement by the corresponding Ido words: words such as (in English) 'which', 'that', 'what', 'something', 'nothing', 'nowhere', 'everywhere'.
3   Suppression of agreement between an adjective and its noun (in Ido the adjective is invariable).
4   Suppression of the accusative case (in Ido it is only retained in instances where the normal word order of subject-verb-object is inverted).
5   Replacement of the prefix mal- (which gives the opposite meaning to the word to which it is attached) by des-.
6   Authorisation to use temporarily Ido vocabulary parallel with Esperanto vocabulary (Ido vocabulary was thoroughly reformed from its Esperanto antecedents, restoring the international spelling of many words and revising the system of word derivation).

According to the Frenchman, Monnerot-Dumaine, Ido is 'pleasant to speak' and easier for Europeans to translate than Esperanto.[7] Otto Jespersen considered it a most flexible and rich language, superior to Esperanto in a great many respects,[8] while for Dyer:

On a fair competitive basis, Ido is bound to win out over Esperanto because it is a more efficient form of IL . . . No Idist supposes that every jot and tittle of the language as it now stands is absolutely perfect and final. But I do assert that taking the language as a whole we have no reason to expect far reaching improvements, such as were made by Ido over Esperanto.[9]

The ease with which Ido can be understood without any prior knowledge of the language can be gauged by glancing at the text by Professor Jespersen and comparing it with the accompanying English translation (figure 6.1). A short text in both Ido and Esperanto can be compared in Appendix II.

Idists appear to have been more concerned with their language as a practical means of international communication than as a medium for creative writing, although some original literature has been published in Ido. Furthermore, the value-oriented ideals of world peace and universal solidarity so commonly encountered in the Esperanto movement are much less apparent amongst Idists, perhaps reflecting the difference between a (relatively speaking) mass movement and a small group of universal language enthusiasts. Anyone seeking the way to an ideal world through a shared language is likely to be attracted by the more successful Esperantist movement; Ido is likely to appeal only to those who believe that a real or supposed linguistic superiority over Esperanto outweighs its numerical insignificance in terms of supporters.

Ido is far from being the only language based upon a reform of Esperanto, or derived from Esperanto. Monnerot-Dumaine provides the following list of exotically named languages (together with their date of creation) derived from or inspired by Zamenhof's scheme, and even this collection is not complete:[10]

Perio	1904
Lingua internacional	1905
Ekselsioro	1906
Ulla	1906
Mondlingvo	1906
Ido	1907
Lingwo internaciona (Antido)	1907
Mez-Voio	1908
Romanizat	1908
Romanal	1909
Reform-Esperanto de Rodet	1910
Reform-Esperanto de Hugon	1910
Latin-Esperanto	1911
lingw Adelfenzal	1911
Esperanto de Stelzner	1912
Europeo	1914
Nepo	1915
Hom Idyomo	1921
Espido	1923
Néo	1937
Esperantuisho	1955
Globaqo	1956
Modern Esperanto	1958

HISTORIO DI NIA LINGUO

da

PROFESORO OTTO JESPERSEN

ORIGINAL TEXT WRITTEN IN IDO, THE LANGUAGE OF THE DELEGATION

EN JUNIO 1907 la Delegitaro por adopto di internaciona helpolinguo segun sua statuti elektis la komitato, qua devis decidar, qua linguo artificala esas la maxim konvenanta por introduktesar en internaciona komuniki.

La konto di la vot-folii kontrolesis da la konocata Franca generalo Sebert. En oktobro di la sama yaro la tale elektita komitato kunvenis en Paris, ube eventis sume 18 kunsidi longa e fatiganta. Ne omna elektiti aparis; kelki uzabis la yuro grantita a li da la statuti sendar supleanto kun prokuraco. La membri asistanta havis la sequanta patrala lingui: Franca, Germana, Angla, Dana, Italiana, Polona (Rusa). La sequanta cienci esis reprezentata: Linguistiko, astronomio, matematiko, kemio, medicino, filozofio.

Kom honor-prezidanto elektesis la astronomo Förster de Berlin, qua tamen povis partoprenar nur poka kunsidi; kom prezidanto la kemiisto Ostwald de Leipzig (Nobel-premiizita); kom vice-prezidanti la du profesori di linguistiko, Badouin de Courtenay de St. Petersburg e me. Kun la maxim granda zelo e persistemeso partoprenis la diskuti ultre la jus mencionita linguisti la sekretario profesoro Couturat de Paris, rektoro Boirac de Dijon (prezidanto di la Esperantistala *Lingva Komitato*), la supleanto di ica, sro Gaston Moch (a qua on permisis partoprenar anke ta kunsidi, en qui sro Boirac ipsa povis asistar), sro P. Hugon (reprezentanto di W. T. Stead) e la matematikisto profesoro Peano de Torino. La diskuti duktesis preske la tota tempo en Franca; kelkafoye tamen prof. Baudouin de Courtenay preferis parolar Germane e poka foyi sro Peano parolis en sua *Latina sen flexiono*. La dikuti pri *Parla* di sro Spitzer (videz infre) duktesis segun sua deziro tote en Germana. La debati direktesis

Figure 6.1   An Ido text with its English translation
Source: H. Jacob, *Otto Jesperson: his work for an international auxiliary language.* Loughton: International Language (Ido) Society of Great Britain, 1943, pp. 16—17.

HISTORY OF OUR LANGUAGE

by

PROF. OTTO JESPERSEN

Translated from the Ido Original by Gilbert H. Richardson

In June 1907 the Delegation for the adoption of an international auxiliary language, in accordance with its statutes, elected the committee which had to decide which artificial language was the most suitable to be introduced in international communications.

The counting of the voting papers was checked by the well-known French General Sebert. In October of the same year the committee thus elected met in Paris where altogether 18 long and fatiguing sittings took place. Not all those who were elected came; some had availed themselves of the right granted them by the statutes to send a deputy with power to act for them. The members who attended had the following native languages: French, German, English, Danish, Italian, Polish (Russian). The following sciences were represented: Philology, Astronomy, Mathematics, Chemistry, Medicine, Philosophy.

As Honorary President was elected the astronomer Förster of Berlin, who however was able to take part in only a few sessions; as President the Chemist Prof. Ostwald of Leipzig (Nobel Prizeman); as Vice Presidents the two professors of Philology, Baudouin de Courtenay of St. Petersburg and myself. Besides the linguists just mentioned the following took part' in the discussions with the greatest zeal and persistance: the Secretary Prof. Couturat of Paris, Rector Boirac of Dijon (President of the Esperantist *Lingva Komitato*), his deputy Mr. Gaston Moch (who was also allowed to take part in the sessions at which Mr. Boirac himself was able to be present), Mr. P. Hugon (representative of W. T. Stead) and the mathematician Prof. Peano of Turin. The discussions were conducted almost all the time in French; sometimes, however, Prof. Baudouin de Courtenay preferred to speak German, and once or twice Mr. Peano spoke in his *Latina sen flexiono*. The discussions on Mr. Spitzer's

Lest this list seems insufficient, Monnerot-Dumaine also provides the equally exotic names of a further 20 or so schemes which, this time, are derived from Ido.[11] Alas, not a single language from either list (with the exception of Ido itself) has achieved any greater measure of success than publication of its structure in some obscure treatise, and none deserves our further attention.

It would be erroneous to conclude from these failures, however, that no *a posteriori* language other than Esperanto and Ido has achieved any support during this century. A number of such languages have attracted the short-lived loyalty of ardent supporters, only to fade after a few years of bloom. The majority belong to the naturalistic category, whose structures closely resemble the forms found in natural languages.

An early example of such a naturalistic language had been published by an Austrian, Julius Lott, as long ago as 1888. Mundo-lingue included an international vocabulary of 7,000 terms, mostly derived from Latin roots. Although Lott gained little recognition in his own day, and his family burnt all his papers on his death in 1905, he was fortunate enough to acquire an excellent, if posthumous, disciple in Edgar de Wahl, who later made good use of his work.

Edgar von Wahl (or de Wahl as he is often known), a German-Estonian professor, was a passionate interlinguist who had shown an early interest in Volapük before switching to Esperanto in 1888. He collaborated with Zamenhof in a consideration of possible reforms to Esperanto, but his ideas were thrust aside by the Esperantist movement. Subsequently, he worked alongside Rosenberger to reform the Volapük offshoot, Idiom Neutral. Reform Neutral, as the new language was called, included natural forms at the expense of more regular forms and moved away from an autonomistic system towards a naturalistic, neo-Latin system. Later still, de Wahl changed sides once again, this time joining the Idists. He found Ido no more satisfactory than his earlier enthusiasms, however, and in 1922 he published his own scheme, Occidental, causing a schism in the Idist movement. He wanted to construct a language for use in the occidental (western) world, with no thought of catering for the remainder of the globe. De Wahl himself stated that the essential principle is not ease of use for *everyone* but 'for the majority of people who have international relationships'.[12] He therefore based his scheme on the western languages, and chiefly the Romance languages. The product was a very naturalistic language which is easy to understand at first sight, at least for the educated elite of Western Europe (although active use of the language is likely to prove much more difficult than passive use). De Wahl tried to find the most natural forms and features in both his vocabulary and grammar. Unfortunately, the naturalistic elements can only be purchased at the expense of numerous irregularities since natural languages themselves are characterised by such irregularities. Hitherto, these very irregularities had been the special targets of the language constructors, whether contemplating *a posteriori* or *a priori* schemes, on the assumption that a regular language was easier to learn and in some cases more logical in structure. Perfect regularity and perfect naturalness cannot be combined. Occidental exhibited irregularities in pronunciation (for example, 'y' can be used both as a consonant and a vowel, 'c' can be pronounced either as 'ts' or 'k'), in word endings (nouns, adjectives and adverbs do not have characteristic endings) and in the use of affixes (certain affixes have more than one meaning, and there may be more than one affix to express a certain relation between stem and derivative).

The most interesting characteristic of Occidental is that its vocabulary is largely made up from 'international' roots found in the chief Romance languages of Western Europe, or from Latin roots when no such common form could be found. The consequence is that 'Occidental presents such a natural appearance that it might almost pass as a dialect spoken somewhere on the shores of the Mediterranean'[13] (this same technique has been taken even further in the case of Interlingua, discussed below). Occidental is now only of historical interest, but a text in the language can be found in Appendix II.

Otto Jespersen, Professor of philology at the University of Copenhagen, and also for many years a lecturer at London University, was one of the few professional linguists who took an early interest in the movement for a constructed language, an interest which he maintained until his death in 1943. He had been a member of the Committee of the Délégation pour l'adoption d'une langue auxiliaire internationale, after earlier rejecting Volapük as impractical. Jespersen had also shown a close interest in Esperanto, but after the Ido schism he was elected as President of the Ido Academy, a post he held from 1907 until 1910.[14] He played an active part in the Idist movement and wrote *The history of our language* as well as contributing the preface to the Ido-Deutsch dictionary published in 1918, where he formulated his premise modelled on Bentham's famous dictum: 'that international language is best which in every point offers the greatest facility to the greatest number.' He also believed that an auxiliary language, to be useful, must be easy not only for the reader in passive usage, but also for the writer and speaker in active use. This necessitated a regular language with general rules which once learned could be easily applied in most instances. He was practical enough to concede, however, that some exceptions to regularity could be included if they were well-justified and easily remembered, saying that no constructed language is totally free from exceptions. Jespersen's search for regularity put him at odds with de Wahl and his naturalistic Occidental. At the same time, Jespersen agreed with de Wahl that an easy language must include words and forms already known to the greatest number of people. Roots which are wholly or partly international should therefore form the major basis of the vocabulary.

The product of Jespersen's thinking on the nature of an ideal artificial language was a break with Ido and the publication in 1928 of his own scheme, Novial (Nov = New, IAL = International Auxiliary Language). The former Ido journal, *Mondo*, became the *Novialiste* in 1934 and acted as the organ for linguistic discussion amongst the supporters of Novial. The main features of Novial differed in detail only from a number of earlier schemes. The vocabulary was chiefly from Ido (which itself had adopted many more international roots than Esperanto) whilst the grammatical structure included several features from Occidental. Although Novial was the first language ever to be constructed by a professional philologist, Jespersen modestly conceded that 'I have found the problem an extremely complicated one, and cannot pretend in every detail to have hit upon the best solution.'[15] In 1934 he suggested a number of improvements to Novial, but despite them the language made little impact in the long run. In his study of Jespersen, Henry Jacob confidently asserted in 1943 that 'The differences between Ido and Novial are small and we may justifiably hold the belief that the final auxiliary language cannot be far from either and is likely to incorporate the best points of both languages.'[16] Such a language is still awaited.

Somewhat earlier than Jespersen, another professor, this time of mathematics and from the University of Turin, had become intrigued by the possibility of constructing an artificial language on naturalistic principles.[17] Giuseppe Peano published his proposal for an international auxiliary language in the journal *Rivista* in October 1903; he called his language Latino sine flexione (Latin without inflections). The article in *Rivista* describing the language began in classical Latin and, as suggestions were made for simplifications, they were incorporated into the text so that the article finally ended in Latino sine flexione.

Peano's interest in artificial languages had been stimulated by a number of factors. As a mathematician he was familiar with the writings of Leibniz, and had read and quoted Louis Couturat's work, *La logique de Leibniz,* published in Paris in 1901, which included the seventeenth-century philosopher's suggestions for an artificial language. Peano had in fact met Couturat in the previous year at the International Congress of Philosophy, where the latter raised the question of an international language and argued for its acceptance. In a letter also written in 1900, Zamenhof had described Peano as 'a very able Esperantist', though it is not clear how accurate is this assessment.[18] Turin was a centre for Volapük rather than Esperanto, and a Volapük club had been established in the city since 1888. Peano may therefore have been more familiar with Volapük than Esperanto.

At the beginning of 1904, Peano read a paper to the Italian Academy of Sciences on 'Latin as an international auxiliary language'. In it he distinguished Latino sine flexione, which he had already essentially achieved, from Latino minimo, which still had to be constructed. Peano had already demonstrated that grammar could be minimised. He now proceeded to the second stage: to establish the minimum vocabulary for his language. He sought an international vocabulary, at least as far as Western Europe was concerned, by making a comparative study of the European languages to find out which Latin words were in use. This study resulted in a pamphlet containing 'A vocabulary of international Latin, compared with English, French, German, Spanish, Italian, Russian, Greek and Sanskrit', which extended to 40 pages. By 1908 Peano had expanded this *Vocabulario Commune* to 87 pages, and by 1915 it required a volume of 352 pages. He also managed in 1908 to publish the fifth edition of his *Formulario Mathematico* entirely in Latino sine flexione (the previous edition having appeared in French). According to his biographer, however, Peano's decision to use his new language was not a great success: 'Most mathematicians were put off by the strange appearance of the language and made no attempt to read it.'[19]

Peano attended the Second Esperanto World Congress held in Geneva in August 1906; all authors of artificial language projects had been invited. There he met Zamenhof for the first time. Zamenhof reputedly said with a smile, 'If my disciples see me now, they will excommunicate me', to which Peano replied, 'I have few disciples, but they are all tolerant: it is one compensation.'[20] The following year Peano attended the

Délégation pour l'adoption d'une langue auxiliaire internationale, and his commitment to the international language movement became stronger. By now he was convinced that the solution to the problem of an international auxiliary language would be found through scientific cooperation. He believed that the vocabulary for an international language already existed; it only need be discovered. He also thought that people could be more easily persuaded to accept an existing international vocabulary rather than an artificially created vocabulary. At the same time, he recognised that some kind of organisation was necessary to make his ideas effective. He could have founded a new academy, but then it would have seemed as if he was deliberately promoting his own Latino sine flexione. He therefore decided to use the old Volapük Academy, now called the Akademi internasional de lingu universal. Peano's application for the directorship of the Academy was unanimously accepted in December 1908 and he immediately began the task of reconstruction. He gained the approval of the Academy that its director might publish a journal in its name and that every academician may adopt that form of 'interlingua' in the journal or in any circulars that he prefers. Henceforward, Peano's statements in the *Discussiones* were written in Latino sine flexione. Within a year he had changed another Academy rule: membership of the Academy would henceforward be open to all. This radical step was accompanied by a change of name; it now became the Academia pro Interlingua, which Peano continued to direct until his death in 1932. At first he used the term 'interlingua' generically, but soon began to limit its use to the language (Latino sine flexione) evolving from the Academy. These changes, unsurprisingly, were not to the liking of all members, and many resigned from the Academy in protest.

By 1910, the Academy had adopted three rules for Interlingua which formed its grammatical basis.

1   It used every word common to English, French, Spanish, Italian, Portuguese, German and Russian, as well as every Latin word with English derivatives.
2   Every word which also existed in Latin used the form of its Latin root.
3   The suffix -s indicated plural.

The 1915 edition of Peano's *Vocabulario Commune* included some 14,000 common roots. Peano cut away any terminations for number, gender, tense and mood, and even the plural inflection was suppressed if an attribute expressed plurality (for example, in the phrase 'patre habe tres filio' the numeral expresses plurality and therefore there is no need to add an 's' to 'filio'). Peano by now was devoting all his energy to the project. As he wrote to Bertrand Russell: 'Thank you for the book *Principia Mathematica,* which I mean to read carefully. At present, the time I have free from school is occupied with the question of Interlingua, which I do not believe so absurd as the majority of people tend to believe. I am sending you some of my articles on this subject.'[21] The work of the Academy, like that of other artificial language movements, was badly disrupted by the First World War, and Peano published nothing in Latino sine flexione from 1915 until 1922 when he began to produce the *Academia pro Interlingua Circulare* (which changed its name in 1925 simply to *Academia pro Interlingua*).

Although a number of works were published in Latino sine flexione, it never gained mass support. It represents the most extreme end of the naturalistic spectrum, with a minimum of grammatical rules and little or no modification to existing scientific nomenclature. Indeed, it could almost be classified as a modified version of Latin. Jespersen accepted that it 'may be useful to express the abstract truths dealt with in mathematical treatises, but when it was claimed that it can be used also in other sciences and in practical everyday life, the matter is much more doubtful'.[22] Like Occidental, it may be easy to use passively in reading, but an active use is much more difficult. The very absence of rules and fixed vocabulary creates complexity as well as simplicity. In any case, a knowledge of Latin is highly desirable for correct expression in the language (a short text in Latino sine flexione is reproduced in Appendix II).

As a language constructor, then, Giuseppe Peano was not entirely successful, despite his investment in time and effort. As a mathematician, also, his best work was accomplished by the end of the nineteenth century and he never quite fulfilled the brilliant career promised by his early work. Yet as a man he has succeeded in winning the kind of appraisal from his biographer we all might envy: 'I am fascinated by his gentle personality, his ability to attract lifelong disciples, his tolerance of human weakness, his perennial optimism.'[23]

The work of individual language projectors — Jespersen, de Wahl, Peano, and so on — was given added impetus by the establishment in 1924 of the International Auxiliary Language Association (IALA). The

IALA was founded in New York on the initiative of three Americans, and was handsomely supported financially by the Rockefeller Foundation and the Vanderbilt family (one of whose members was among the three founders). The aim of the IALA was to establish through scientific research and experimentation 'the form of auxiliary language best fitted to serve as the international medium of communication for the contemporary world' and then to promote its adoption, especially in schools.[24] Its original objective was to assess the merits of a number of existing languages. At a conference organised by the IALA in Copenhagen in 1936 it chose as candidates Esperanto, Ido, Occidental, Novial, Latino sine flexione and Esperanto II (as its name suggests, a revised version of Esperanto). These six were considered 'existing, constructed languages of demonstrated usefulness', that is, they were already well-developed with a vocabulary, grammar and system of word formation rather than being mere paper projects.[25] Work began in Liverpool under the direction of William Collinson, who was Professor of German at Liverpool University but also held a unique chair of Esperanto. War brought this research to a halt, but a new team was later assembled in New York, including Alexander Gode, subsequently a key figure in the project. The *General report* of the IALA for 1945 made it clear that the idea of selecting one of the six existing artificial languages had by now been broadened. It was considered more practical to start from the common base which underlay all six of the 'candidate languages' rather than from any one of them: and by a common base was meant their international vocabulary of words common to the greatest number of widely distributed 'cultural' languages. The IALA's work was summed up by one of its members:

Our aim is not to 'make' a new international language, but to present the international vocabulary standardised in its most general form with only such complements of words as are supported by natural languages. We believe that this auxiliary language will be a language the passive use of which (reading and listening) should hardly require any previous learning on the part of educated speakers of the European languages in any part of the world.[26]

When considering an international vocabulary it is possible to distinguish two kinds of international words.[27] First, a word may occur in several languages (though in slightly different forms) because the languages are related. These cognates can be traced back to the same parent word. Thus the word 'maximum' is found in English, French and Spanish with the same meaning and can be traced back to its common Latin root. Second, a word may occur in unrelated languages (again, with modified spelling and/or pronunciation) due to the transition of words from one language to another. This transition can either reflect cultural influences (so, from Arabic has come 'alcohol', from Eskimo 'igloo' and from Finnish 'sauna') or the internationalisation of science and technology (telephone, terminal, radar, etc.). The greatest number of such scientific or technical words are of Latin or Greek origin.

In order to identify this international vocabulary, the IALA looked at the chief members of the Anglo-Romanic group: English, French, Italian and Spanish-Portuguese. If a word occurred in three of these four 'control languages' it was adopted at once. Most Interlingua words are in fact found in all four control languages; for example:

English:	chocolate	document
French:	chocolat	document
Spanish:	chocolate	documento
Italian:	cioccolata	documento
Interlingua:	chocolate	documento

Nearly all the remaining words are found in three of the control languages; for example:

English:	horse	table
French:	cheval	table
Spanish:	caballo	mesa
Italian:	cavallo	tavola
Interlingua:	cavallo	tabula

If a word could not be found in at least three of the control languages then German and Russian were also consulted. In fixing the precise form of the word, the method was to identify the common denominator of the cognates in the various languages, which often meant going back to a Latin word. In the case of a modern international word with no historical prototype, 'scientific imagination' had to be applied to deduce a 'parent word' by analogy. Additionally, the meaning or meanings of a word had to be established, as cognates may have different meanings in different languages; 'éditeur' in French does not mean 'editor' but 'publisher'. Finally, this international vocabulary inevitably had to be supplemented by national words when no common international root could be identified. Even here, a word containing an international element was chosen wherever possible. Less than 100 such indispensable structural terms were needed, examples of which are:

English:	also	almost	but
French:	aussi	presque	mais
Spanish:	también	casi	pero
Italian:	anche	quasi	ma
Interlingua:	anque	quasi	ma

A further extract from the Interlingua vocabulary can be found in figure 6.2.

As others before it, the IALA had to choose between a language which appeared natural but thereby included irregularities, or a language which was regular but no longer included so many natural features. Its decision was to be based upon experimentation. Specimen texts of two naturalistic variants and two autonomistic variants were sent in 1946 to linguists in a number of countries together with a detailed questionnaire in which they could express their reactions. The outcome of this procedure was a naturalistic language which was simply called Interlingua. It finally emerged in 1951 in the form of an *Interlingua-English dictionary* listing 27,000 terms, published under the direction of Alexander Gode (and republished in 1971), as well as a grammar of the language prepared by Gode and Hugh Blair.[28]

Alexander Gode, by birth a German but resident in the United States since 1927, subsequently played the key role in developing and publicising this new artificial language. He preferred to call Interlingua a planned rather than a constructed language as it is nothing more than the exploitation (or extraction) of existing interlingual (or international) word material:

It was visualised as a historical reality, and the laboratory work which led to its eventual formulation consisted in objective research in comparative and historical linguistics. The problem was to work out criteria for the collection and standardisation of verbal material already known, in the guise of multiple national variants, to a large segment of mankind. The ideal to be realised was a pan-Occidental and, beyond that, a pan-scientific language immediately

INTERLINGUA	ANGLESE	ESPANIOL	FRANCESE	GERMANO	ITALIANO
nonobstante	nevertheless	no obstante	nonobstant	trotzdem	nonostante
nos	we,us;ourselves	nosotros;nos	nous	wir;uns	noi;ci
nostre	our	nuestro(s)	notre,nos;nôtre	unser(e)	nostro,nostri
nove	new;nine	nuevo;nueve	nouveau;neuf	neu;neun	nuovo;nove
de nove	again	de nuevo	de nouveau	wider	di nuovo
nove(m)	nine	nueve	neuf	neun	nove
nulle	no,none	ninguno	nul	kein	nessuno
nunc	now	ahora	maintenant	nun,jetzt	adesso
nunquam	never	nunca	jamais	nie	mai,giammai
o	either,or	o	ou	oder,entweder	o
o ... o	either...or	o ... o	ou ... ou	entweder,,oder	o ... o
oblidar	forget	olvidar	oublier	vergessen	dimenticare
obra	work	obra	oeuvre	Arbeit,Werk	opera
obtener	obtain	obtener	obtenir	erlangen	ottenere
octo	eight	ocho	huit	acht	otto
oculo	eye	ojo	oeil	Auge	occhio
olim	once	antes	autrefois	früher	altre volte
omne	all,every	todo	tout	alle	tutto,ogni
on	one,you,they	uno	on	man	uno,si
ora	now	ahora	maintenant	nun,jetzt	adesso
pagar	pay	pagar	payer	bezahlen	pagare
pais	country	país	pays	Land	paese
parer	appear,seem	parecer	paraître	erscheinen	parere
parlar	speak,tell	hablar	parler	sprechen	parlare
parola	word	palabra	parole	Wort	parola
parve	small,little	pequeño	petit	klein	piccolo
passato	past (noun)	pasado	passé	Vergangenheit	passato
pauc	few	poco(s)	peu de	wenig(e)	poco,pochi
pauco	little	poco	peu	wenig	poco
paupere	poor	pobre	pauvre	arm, dürftig	povero
pede	foot	pie	pied	Fuss	piede
pena	difficulty	pena	peine	Mühe,Kummer	pena
a pena	hardly,scarcely	apenas	à peine	kaum	appena
pensar	think	pensar	penser	denken	pensare
per	by,through	por	par	durch,von	per
periculo	danger	peligro	danger	Gefahr	pericolo
perque	because;why	porqué;porque	pourquoi;parce	warum;weil	perchè
pertiner	belong	pertenecer	appartenir /que	gehören	appartenere
pesante	heavy	pesado	pesant	schwer	pesante
placer	please;pleasure	placer;agradar	plaire;plaisir	gefallen;Vergnü-	piacere
plen	full	lleno	plein	voll /gen	pieno
plure	several	varios	plusieurs	mehrere	parecchi
plus	more;plus	más	plus	mehr;plus	più
al plus	at most	por lo más	tout au plus	höchstens	tutt'al più
de plus	furthermore	por añadidura	de plus	dazu,obendrein	di più
in plus	furthermore	ademas	en plus	ausserdem	in più,inoltre
poc(o)	few	poco(s)	peu de	wenig(e)	poco,pochi
poner	place,put	poner	poser	stellen,legen	porre
populo	people	pueblo	peuple	Volk	popolo
portar	carry,wear	llevar	porter	tragen	portare
post	after,behind	detrás de	derrière,après	hinter,nach	dietro,dopo
postea	afterwards	después	ensuite	nachher	dopo
postmeridie	afternoon	tarde	après-midi	Nachmittag	pomeriggio
poter	be able,can	poder	pouvoir	können,dürfen	potere
povre	poor	pobre	pauvre	arm,dürftig	povero
prender	take	tomar	prendre	nehmen	prendere
presso (a)	near	cerca de	près de	bei,nahe	presso
presto	quickly	pronto	vite	schnell	presto
preter	beyond,besides	más allá de	au-delà de	ausser,über	oltre
prime	first	primero	premier	erst	primo
pro	for;in order to	por;para	pour	für;um...zu	per
probar	prove,test	probar	prouver	prüfen	provare
proponer	propose	proponer	proposer	vorschlagen	proporre
proprie	own	proprio	propre /que	eigen	proprio
proque	why;because	porqué;porque	pourquoi;parce	warum;weil	perchè
qua	like,as	como,en calidad	comme,en quali-	als	quale
qual	what,which	cuál,cual /de	quel /té de	welch-	quale
le qual	which,that,who	que,el cual	qui,que	welch-	che,il quale
qualque	some	algun	quelque	einige	qualche

Figure 6.2   Extract from the *Breve grammatica e vocabulario de Interlingua*
Source: Issued by the Union Mundial pro Interlingua, Beverwijk,
The Netherlands, 1984.

comprehensible to anyone conversant, either through his native language or by virtue of his linguistic training, with at least part of the 'international' vocabulary.[29]

For Gode, the only truly international language today is the language of science, and the language of science is West European. The international terminologies of science, Gode argues, form an integral part of 'Standard Average European', a term coined by the American linguist, Benjamin Lee Whorf, to describe the common European language which he believed was a correlate of the common occidental civilisation. Gode thought that the languages of Western Europe, by origin or by historical influence, are so close to one another that they can be considered variants of this one Standard Average European: 'Interlingua is to date the most satisfactory formulation' of Standard Average European.[30]

The grammar of Interlingua is essentially romanic, and not unlike Edgar de Wahl's Occidental. It is intended to be as simple as possible whilst still remaining compatible with pan-occidental usage. Any grammatical feature which one of Interlingua's contributing languages has eliminated should not be included; neither should any grammatical feature be excluded which is to be found in all the contributing languages, 'even if it seems logically and rationally superfluous'.[31] Interlingua has no genders, personal endings for verbs or declensions of nouns. It does include, however, a definite and indefinite article, a distinctive plural form for nouns, and different endings to distinguish between different verbal tenses. A part of the Interlingua conjugation is included in figure 6.3. As regards pronunciation, it is virtually that of ecclesiastical Latin.

Interlingua, then, is seen by its supporters as a means of enabling anyone familiar with English, French, Spanish, German, and so on, to expand the interlingual portion of that language into a fully-fledged language for international communication. Although active use would require some training, passive comprehension 'could be taken for granted on the part of all those whose educational equipment could serve them in their preoccupation with matters of supranational import'.[32] According to 'Interlingua is so easy', a leaflet published by the British Interlingua Society, all but 1,000 of the 27,000 words in the *Interlingua-English dictionary* are immediately intelligible to anyone who knows English. A smattering of either French, Spanish or Italian will make, it is claimed, all Interlingua words except a few grammatical terms intelligible, and an Interlingua text should therefore be comprehensible without any previous study.

Interlingua is primarily intended for scientific communication, although it could be (and is) used more extensively. It has particularly been encouraged as a language of secondary rather than primary publication: for abstracts of scientific articles, contents pages in journals, etc., rather than for the articles themselves. The first publication to include Interlingua abstracts was the *Quarterly bulletin of Sea View Hospital,* a relatively obscure scientific publication, but it was followed by more prestigious periodicals such as the *Journal of dental medicine,* the *Journal of the American Medical Association* and the *Danish medical bulletin.* The official programme of the Second World Congress of Cardiology, held in Washington in 1954, contained summaries in English and Interlingua of all papers presented, and marked the first mass trial of the language.

Interlingua is also recommended by its supporters as a wider language of international communication. A broadsheet on 'Using Interlingua: some suggestions', supplied by the British Interlingua Society, assures readers that: 'When you have mastered Interlingua, you will find it useful abroad in Italy, Spain and Latin America. If you speak it clearly, correctly,

Infinitive
crear   **vider**   **audir**
to create, see, hear

Present Participle		Past Participle
creante **vidente** **audiente**		**create** **vidite** **audite**
creating, seeing, hearing		created, seen, heard

Figure 6.3   An extract from the Interlingua conjugation
Source: Alexander Gode and Hugh E. Blair, *Interlingua: a grammar of the international language,* 2nd edn. New York: Storm, 1951, pp. 38—9.

Imperative
crea!   **vide!**   **audi!**
create!, see!, hear!

ACTIVE

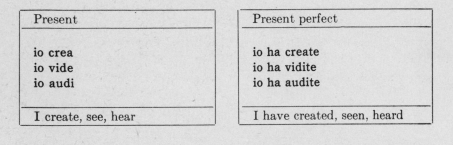

Present
io crea   **io vide**   **io audi**
I create, see, hear

Present perfect
io ha create   **io ha vidite**   **io ha audite**
I have created, seen, heard

Imperfect (Past)
io creava   **io videva**   **io audiva**
I created, saw, heard

Past Perfect (Pluperfect)
io habeva create   **io habeva vidite**   **io habeva audite**
I had created, seen, heard

Future
io creara   **io videra**   **io audira**
I will create, see, hear

Future Perfect
io habera create   **io habera vidite**   **io habera audite**
I will have created, etc.

Figure 6.3 *continued*

simply and confidently, you will be understood by all, given good will and reasonable intelligence on the other side.' A correspondent to the Interlingua journal, *Lingua e vita,* seems to confirm this when recounting his experiences on holiday in Andorra:

Obviously, in France I used French . . . but for the rest of the time, as my Spanish is more limited than the locals' command of English and as I am totally ignorant of Catalan and Aranese, I used Interlingua repeatedly and was understood about 90% of the time, though there were of course problems in understanding the various replies to my Interlingua. Only once — in a village restaurant — did I have to resort to my Spanish phrase book because of the non-international names of certain local dishes.[33]

The broadsheet also suggests that 'letters written in good Interlingua and clearly typed will be understood in countries where a romance language . . . is spoken.' Furthermore, 'if you subsequently decide to learn a romance language, Interlingua will give you a head start over other students.'

Gode himself acknowledged that there are areas where Interlingua is 'useless' and 'other areas where it can play but a minor role'.[34] Unlike, say, Esperanto, it was not primarily intended as a language for literary works nor for oral communication. Indeed, the effectiveness of Interlingua even in scientific and technical communication is related to the extent to which the terminology in a particular branch of science or technology is already linked to the Standard Average European tradition. Medicine and chemistry, for example, are therefore likely to fare better than, say, civil engineering. Nevertheless, literary works such as Molière's *Le misanthrope* as well as various books of the Old Testament have been translated into Interlingua, and some original poetry has even been composed in the language.

Within its chosen and limited remit — scientific abstracts — Interlingua for a time appeared to be making considerable headway. The extent of its challenge to Esperanto can perhaps be gauged by the bitter and frequent attacks and counter-attacks between supporters of the two rivals in the pages of journals such as *Eco-logos*.[35] The Esperanto League in Pennsylvania even considered it worthwhile to publish a brochure entitled *The structure of Interlingua compared with Esperanto's structure* in which the latter's advantages are hammered out point by grammatical point. Interlingua still has its faithful supporters. The British Interlingua Society (BIS), for example, is actively engaged in promoting the language, and together with the Interlingua Institute of New York publishes *Lingua e vita,* a journal which appears three or four times per year. The BIS works to tell people in Britain about Interlingua and its uses, to help them to learn the language and to provide easy access to its literature. Its membership, however, is tiny: less than 50. At the international level, the Union Mundial pro Interlingua, located in Beverwijk in the Netherlands and Odense in Denmark, has about 200 members and publishes its own quarterly journal, *Currero,* edited in Odense. Despite continued work in Western Europe and North America, the Interlingua star may now have waned. This can partly be explained, ironically, by the limited and practical goals at which the language has aimed. The case for Interlingua has been heavily based upon its use as a language of science, especially in abstracts, yet this is the area in which English has made greatest inroads as a language of international communication (see chapter 7). Increasingly, English itself is used for abstracts and contents pages in journals otherwise published in another language. Additionally, Interlingua is quite deliberately and explicitly drawn from a few West European languages without even the pretence of neutrality. This may reduce its acceptability in other parts of the world. True, English is one of the four control languages used for Interlingua, and English is widely known as a first or subsequent language in many parts of the globe. Yet it is by no means certain that Interlingua is quite so easy to understand from a knowledge of English alone as Gode and his followers would have us believe. How intelligible is the text reproduced in figure 6.4 (although it must be conceded that a scientist familiar with the subject matter would find this extract easier to read than the layperson)?

Like the alchemists of old, artificial language projectors are not easily deterred by others' failures. They doggedly cling to the belief that success can be achieved if only the right mixture of ingredients can be blended in the correct proportions. The favourite recipe today remains a naturalistic *a posteriori* language, though the precise constituents are endlessly varied. A recent example is Eurolengo, intended as a practical tool for business and tourism. Like Occidental and Interlingua, it is based upon West European languages, although in this case primarily on just two of these languages: 'Assuming that it is a fact that English is the most used Western European language throughout the world, with Spanish second, I have concentrated on these two languages as the base for Eurolengo.' Furthermore, it concentrates on the Latin component of English rather

Le administration de recercas scientific

L. Sprague de Camp

*SCIENTISTAS VARIA JUSTO COMO NOS ALTEROS. HA SAPIENTES E FATUOS, sobrios e dissipatos, solitarios e gregarios, corteses e inciviles, puritanos e licentiosos, industriosos e pigros, et cetera. Como genere iles exhibi certe tendentias. Per exemplo, iles son totos de alte inteligentia. Le scientista pote essere stupide re certe cosas, ma il debe haver le basic potentia mental que es requisit pro devenir scientista; il non pote essere moron in le stricte senso psicometric.

Essente plus inteligente que le homines medie, forsan le scientistas tende anque a essere plus judiciose, ma isto non impedi alcunos inter iles de cadere in dificultates amorose, de essere decepte per obvie mistificationes e fraudes, o de imbraciar doctrinas pseudoscientific.

Le psicologo Sheldon pensa que le scientistas tende verso su tipo ectomorfic in lor fisico e cerebrotonic in lor temperamento. De lo que io ha viste de scientistas io so inclinat a concurere. Le ectomorfo es le homine magre, e le cerebrotonico es le individualista pensative, introvertite, nervose, quiet, e maestro de se mesme. Il ama laborar solo, prefere ideas a homines, e invetera ben, deveniente arugat e coriacee in vice de grasse de pancia e de gena.

De tot le homines, le scientistas son, in general, le individualistas le plus obstinat e refractori del mundo, comunmente inofensive ma capace de persequere lor fines con le intensitat fanatic de un mania. Si non era assi, iles non vel jamais submitere se al longe e intense processo educational requisit a facere un scientista.

Ubi e como labora le scientistas? Un minoritat bastante parve — geologos, meteorologos, biologos, archeologos, et cetera — va via in expeditiones inter le quales iles labora in lor oficios o instrue in scolas e universitates. Le resto labora in laboratorios governamental o privat. Le privates son los de companias manufacturari, de universitates, e de altere

---

* Traducte del texto original anglese (*Astounding Science Fiction*, julio 1951, pp. 128 et seq.) per Hugh E. Blair, ilustrante le uso del ortografia regularizat, del participios passat iregular, e del distinction de infinitivos in -er e -ere. Vide §§ 15, 57, 79, 116, 134, 148.

Figure 6.4   An extract from an Interlingua translation of an English text
Source: Alexander Gode and Hugh E. Blair, *Interlingua: a grammar of the international language,* 2nd edn. New York: Storm, 1951, p. 112.

than its Anglo-Saxon aspect. This is intended to produce a more homogeneous language which can therefore be assimilated more easily. It is not considered a disadvantage to the North Europeans — the Scandinavians, Dutch and Germans — because they already have a good grasp of English from school. The author of Eurolengo, Leslie Jones, believes that a conversation can be conducted in the language after three weeks, or at the outside, one month.[36] Whether or not this claim can be justified, there is no denying that its grammar is presented in just three pages. Eurolengo has 20 consonants (it differs from the English alphabet in having no letter 'c', for which either 's' or 'k' are used, but including a letter 'ch') and six vowels. The author claims that all the difficult sounds in West European languages have been avoided, such as the English sounds indicated by 'th', 'ough', 'ph'; the Spanish 'll'; the French nasals and the Dutch guttural 'g' and 'sch'. The definite article is 'le' and indefinite article 'un'. Adjectives occur before their noun and adverbs are formed from adjectives by adding the suffix -lik (or -ik if the adjective already ends in 'l'). So, *rapid* means 'quick' and *rapidlik* is 'quickly'; *total* is 'total' and *totalik* is 'totally'. The nouns have no genders (except some genuine feminine nouns which add a final 'a', so *le hund* is 'the dog'; *le hunda,* 'the bitch'). Plurals are formed by adding 's' or 'es'. Verbs are regular, tenses and moods being indicated by suffixes, whilst person is indicated by the preceeding noun or pronoun:

Infinitive	-ar
Past Participle	-ado
Present Tense	-o
Past Imperfect	-ad
Past Perfect	-an
Present Participle	-ant
Imperatives	-a
	-amos
Future	Infinitive + a
Conditional	Infinitive + al

There are no other tenses; compound tenses can be formed, however, by using the verb *haber* with the equivalent participle. So, *Y habaral irado* means 'I would have gone'.

The *Eurolengo manual* includes a vocabulary of around 20,000 words, and it is claimed that an International Society of Eurolengo has been formed with English, French, German, Spanish and Dutch members. Leslie Jones says that the language has been tried with 'complete success' in seven European countries. Its 'Spanglish' flavour can be sampled in the following passage: 'Internasional komerse isto un vast subjekt ké no isto posabel aratar in un kort leson. Al le paroles employado in industrie and komerse istan konservado so simpel as posabel in eurolengo. Medikal and teknikal terms isto spelado fonetikalik para akordar kon le pronunsiasion de le lengo.' Like other naturalistic languages of its kind, Eurolengo is much easier to read than to write, and even reading is only straightforward if the requisite natural languages (in this case English and Spanish) are already familiar.

Another recent example (1981) of a naturalistic language, Glosa, has a central vocabulary of about 1,000 words 'with which any kind of information can be given or received; and this includes advanced technical information'.[37] The words have been 'carefully selected from the already long-established International Scientific Vocabulary, and are so generally useful that any kind of intelligent conversation can be carried on by means of them.'[38] An excerpt from this vocabulary is included in figure 6.5. An extended vocabulary of more than 100,000 words, it seems, is available for 'literature, poetry and stylistic variety'. In the case of Glosa, its vocabulary largely comprises Latin roots, supplemented by Greek roots 'which are already familiar to all Europeans and in all languages into which scientific terminology is penetrating (the name Glosa itself comes from the Greek word for language, 'glossa'). Those intending to learn Glosa will be delighted to find that it apparently has no grammar 'exactly like Chinese', although by this its authors seem to mean that it has no inflections. Nor, indeed, does it even require a textbook as 'you speak straight from the Glosa dictionary.'

Like Interlingua, Glosa attempts to identify and utilise internationally recognisable roots. In the following list, taken from the Glosa brochure, G = Greek, L = Latin, capitals indicate Glosa roots:

G	BI-CYCLe	two-wheels
G	GYNA-ecoLOGy	woman-study
L	SEDentary	sit
G	EPI-DERMis	on-skin
L	GRAMINiVOROus	grass-eating

L	CARNI-VORo-us	meat-eating
L	imBIBe	drink
G	TELE-SCOP-e	far-look
L	PLUral	more than one
G	PAED-IATR-ist	child-doctor
G	HIPPO-DROM-e	horse-race
L	INTER	among, between
G	POLY-TECHN-ic	many-skills
G	RHODO-DENDR-on	red-tree

When this list is written horizontally, it produces a Glosa sentence: BI GYNA SEDE EPI U GRAMINA, VOR E BIBE E SCOPO PLU PAEDA DROMO INTER POLY DENDRO, or, in English, 'Two women are sitting on the grass, eating and drinking, and watching the children running about amongst a lot of trees.'

Glosa is in fact a modified version of an earlier language, Interglossa, devised by an Englishman, Lancelot Hogben, and published in 1943. Hogben intended his book as a first draft of the language rather than as a full-scale linguistic exposition:

The author of *Interglossa* does not flatter himself with the hope that it will ever become the common language of international communication. A good enough reason for publishing this draft is that the post-war world may be ripe, as never before, for recognition of need for a remedy which so many others have sought. When need becomes articulate, it will be relatively simple for an international committee to draw on a common pool of effort, seemingly spent with little result.[39]

The authors of Glosa, W. Ashby and R. Clark, have now resuscitated Hogben's language, with considerable modification, for contemporary employment as an international auxiliary language. They belong firmly within the idealistic category of language projectors; in their own words, 'Glosa is not an end in itself, but a means of helping to rid the world of poverty and ignorance.' The language is intended to enable ordinary people in the developing world to 'receive and understand the appropriate technology information now so abundantly available from the industrialised nations'. Any peasant or artisan in the Third World should be able to memorise 1,000 words of Glosa for this purpose. Additionally, Glosa is

Glosa		English
A.AD		to,at,in
ABSTRACTO		abstract
ACIDE		happen,event
ADAPTA	G.	adapt,fit
AERO	G.	air
AGE	G.	drive,lead
ACIDO		acid,sour
AKORDA	G	agree;accord
AKRO	G	top,tip,summit
AKT.O		do;behave
AKU		needle,nail
AKUSTI	G.	hear,listen
AKUTE		sharp,acute
ALO	G.	each other
ALGO		G.pain;ache
ALI/ALIMENTA		any/ to feed
ALTERNO		strange
ALO...ALO		either...or
ALTO		high,tall
AMI/AMIKO		friend-/ly
-AM /ANA		he,him,his/up
AMBIENTA		environment
ANDRO	G.	man,husband
ANEMO	G.	wind(weather)
ANTI	G.	against;although
ANU	G.	year,annual
APO	G.	away;remove
AP(E)RI		open
ARCA;ARKA	G.	arch,arc
ARCHO	G.	authority
AREA		area
ARENA		sand
ARGENTO	G.	silver,Ag.
ARGILA		clay
ARGUE		argue
ARMA	G.	weapon
AROGA		arrogant
ARTHRO	G.	joint
ARTIKLA	G.	article
ARTI		art
ASPEKTO	G.	aspect
ASTRO	G.	star
ASYLO	G.	safe place
ATTENDE		wait
ATTITUDO	G.	attitude,mood
AUSTRO	G.	south
AUTO	G.	self;ones own
CHLORO	G.	green
CHARITA		compassion
CHOLERO	G.	angry,choleric
CHOREO	G.	dance
CHROMO	G.	colour;paint
CHRYSO	G.	golden
*DATA		data,facts
DE		of;about;than
DEBE/DEBTYO		should/ see
DEFENDE		defend
DECIDE		decide
DEFINI		define
DEMO/DEFEKT		people/defect
DENDRO	G.	tree
DENSO		dense
DENTI	G.	tooth
DERMA	G.	skin
DESERTA		desert
DETEKTO		find,discover
DEXTRO		right(hand)
DI		day;diurnal
DIA		through
DIFERE		differ...ent
DIFUSO		broadcast
DIGITO	G.	finger,digit
DICE	G.	speak,say,tell
DILUTO		dilute
DISKO		plate,disk
DIPLO		double
DISIPA		waste,dissipate
DISPUTA		quarrel
DISTA		be far;distant
DIVINA		guess;bet
DIVIDE		divide,share
-DO;DOMO		house,building
DOMINA		dominate
DONA	G.	give,donate
DORSO	G.	back;dorsal
DOXO	G.	opinion,spine
DRAMA	G.	act(theatre)
DROMO	G.	run,race
DULO	G.	slave
DU;DURA		continue
DUCK	G.	to lead;chief
DURANYO	G.	during,while
DYNO	G.	force,power
PISI		crack;fissure
FILA		fix,tighten
PLACIDO		limp,flaccid
FLEXO		bend;flexible
FLA./FLU		blow/flow;current
FLORA		flake
FLORI		flower
FLUVIA		river
.FO; FORTI		very;intense
POLIO		leaf;folio
FONTI		spring,origin
FORMULA		recipe;formula
FORTUNA		chance,fortune
FOSO/FORA		dig/hole
FRAKTO		fracture,break
FREQUE		frequent
FRIGE		rub,friction
FRIGO		cold,frigid
FRUKTO		fruit
FRUSTRA	G.	frustrate
FU		shall;future
FUGE/FUGIMINA		flee/to store
FULMO		smoke
FUNDA		bottom..;to found,
FUNGUS		fungus
FUNKTIO		function;for
FUEKA		fork
FURNA		stove,oven
FUSO		pour
FUSILA		gun,shoot
*GALA;GEO	G.	Earth
GAMO	G.	marry
GANIA		win,gain
GAS.		gas
	G.	got-
GELA/GENU		freeze/knee
GENNTO	G.	inherit
GDNE		get;become
CLABRO	G.	smooth
GLACIA		ice
GLANDI		acorn;gland
GLOSA	G.	tongue;language
GLU		glue;stick
GLUKO	G.	sweet;pleasant
CONGO		angle,corner
GRAMINA		grass
INVOLVE		wrap up
ISO	G.	equal;identical
ITERA	G.	again (iterate)
ITINERA		travel
*JA		yes
JACE	G.	lying;-jacent
JUDIKA		judge,decide
JUGA		join;joint
JURA		swear on oath
JUSTI		justice;fair
JU-VE;JU-AN		girl;boy
JUVENI		young,juvenile
*KA; KAISA		(be)cause
KARINETA		cupboard
KADE		fall
KAFA		coffee
KAKO	G.	horrible;bad
KALO	G.	beautiful
KAMBIA		exchange
KAMERA;-RA		room
KAMP O;		field;camp
KAMPANA		bell
KANALI		canal;channel
KANCELA		lattice;cancel
KANIS		dog
KANTA		sing;song
KAPILA		hair
KAPITALA		capital
KAPITULA		chapter
KAPSA		packet,parcel
KAPTI		seize,capture
KARO.....		Bear:....
KARNA		coal
KARBONA		carbon
KARCERA		prison
KARDIA	G.	heart;cardiac
KARDINA		hinge;cardinal
KARGA		load;charge
KARNI		flesh,meat
KARPE		pluck;harvest
KARTA		card
KARTONA		cardboard
KASA		cheese
KASO		in (the) case of
KATA		commands
KATENA		chain
KAUDA		tail,caudal
KOPULA		link; to mate
KONOMA		crown;breath
KORTEKI		bark,cortex
KOSMO	G.	ordered universe
KOSTA		rib,side,coast
KULA		hip,thigh
KRATO	G.	govern
KREDE	G.	believe,creed
KRENA		notch
KRESKE		grow
KRESTA		crest
KRETA		chalk
KRIBRO		sieve
KRISIS		crisis
KRITIKO	G.	criticise
KRUCI		cross
KRUDO		raw
KRUELO	G.	cruel
KRYPTO	G.	hide,secret
KRISTA		frost
KRYSTALA	G.	crystal
KUBO		cube
KUKO		cook
KULPA		guilty;accuse
KULTIVA		cultivate;rear
KUMULA		heap
KURNA		wedge
KURA		barrel,tub
KURA		care;careful
KUPRA		copper,Cu
KURVA		curve
KUSPI		cusp,point
KYANO	G.	blue
KYKLO	G.	circle,wheel
KYLINDRO	G.	cylinder
KYTO	G.	living cell
* LA		that one
U-LA		there
LANI/LACERA		lip/tear
LAPVO		left hand
LACHIMA		tear;weep
LANTI		silk
LAMINA		blade,slice
LAMPA;LAMPI		lamp; shine
LANA		wool
LANA		a country
LAPSO		slide

Figure 6.5   An excerpt from the Glosa vocabulary

Source: W. Ashby and R. Clark, *Glosa 1000*. London: Glosa, 1983.

intended to provide a language for the European Communities and for 'scientists, technicians, computers and view data, around the world'. Finally; 'Glosa is the language of nature, of gardens and the outdoor world. It is the ideal language for the essential inevitable world cooperation'[40]

A short article in Glosa is included in figure 6.6. It is unlikely that many peasants and artisans in developing countries are already familiar with Latin and Greek roots, so much depends upon the skill of the writer in expressing ideas within the constraints of the 1,000 words available in the basic Glosa vocabulary, and the willingness of people to learn these words. Ashby and Clark claim to have 'an enthusiastic nucleus of Glosa speakers in every continent and we are continually receiving enquiries from influential organisations'.[41] Dictionaries containing the basic 1,000 word Glosa vocabulary have now been compiled in French, Spanish and German as well as English. They now intend to concentrate on publicity and on forming a centre together with local groups. Any artificial language movement must grow from small beginnings, and certainly the enthusiasm of those who create and support such languages as Glosa cannot be doubted. Nevertheless, it is hard to imagine how such a language might prove successful where a relatively well-organised and long-standing movement like Esperanto has hitherto failed.

MODIFIED NATURAL LANGUAGES

Proposals for the adoption of a natural language as an international auxiliary language have been numerous, but such a solution to the problem of international communication lies outside the scope of a work on artificial languages. The idea of modifying a natural language — simplifying its grammar, vocabulary, or both — in order to make it practical and acceptable as an international language is a rather different matter. It is not quite the same, of course, as constructing a truly artificial language, but it has many similarities both in approach and objective. In practice, the distinction between a naturalistic artificial language like Latino sine flexione and a modified natural language is relatively minor.

Irregularities of grammar, spelling and pronunciation, coupled with a rich and extensive vocabulary, are features of natural languages which make them hard to learn and difficult to use proficiently. On the other

TRANSMIGRATIO INTRA INDONESIA

Indonesia es u mega landa ge-face de 13,000 nesia. Id demo, ordina penta de u geo, habe eko epi solo tetra intra-nesia; qui, syn-alelo tegu solo 7% de Indonesia. Proxi 2/3 de u demo de 154 miliona pe habe eko epi solo bi nesia...Java e Madura. Ne poly pe habe eko epi plu extra nesia ad u nu-pe tem. Plu-ci es ge-lysi grega qui pa casa, kapti piski,e pe vaga kultiva intra foresta. Nu es cirka 70 persona epi singu quadra kilometra de Sumatra, mei de deka epi Kalimantan e mei de tri epi Irian Jaya; intra plu mero Java es ma de 2,000.!

92 m. persona habita Java, 4/5 de plu-ci in plu rura area, 40% habe zero suela e u pluso 35% habe no-sati suela te dona phago mu familia. Mono ra qui stimula u-ci excesi densi de plu-pe es u no-justi divide de u suela. 1% de u demo habe 1/3 de u landa.

Singu familia gene u quarto-hektara suela syn u tetra-kamera domi, mono hektara de ge-prepara suela pro plu phago phyto, e bi hektar de agrio ge-dendro suela. Mo ex deka persona gene u fe- bovi, e singu faski de 15 (mo-penta) domi gene u manu hydro-pumpa. Plu persona suri ergo de face plu via, plu kanali,fluvi-puerta e phrea.

Kaso oligo demo-lo plu -pe gene bi pluso hektara de agrio suela pro plu valuta-dendro. Mu gene valuta duranto plu prima penta anua pro prepara u suela, e pro kultiva plu dendro, qui dona latici, plu koko-nuci, plu Anas alo banana; e mu gene permito de tena plu profito tem plu-ci penta anua. Anti- cio, kausa plu-ci persona utili solo plu manu-ru, freque mu spende penta e six anua prepara u suela.

Figure 6.6   An excerpt from an article in Glosa
Source: Plu Glosa nota 16, n.d., p. 7.

hand, such languages are 'natural' to use, at least for those who speak them or are familiar with other related languages in the same linguistic family. It is therefore argued that by eliminating the more 'difficult' features, by modifying a natural language in one or more respects, the advantages of naturalness (and an existing body of speakers, especially if a major world language is chosen) can be combined with ease of acquisition and use. On this basis, a number of proposals have been made to modify such languages as English, German, French, Spanish, Italian, Latin and Greek. In 1915, for example, a Professor Baumann of Munich worked out a scheme called WEDE (Welt-Deutsch) which was a simplified German with phonetic spelling. Baumann thought that WEDE could be employed as the universal language in a German-dominated post-war world.

Just as English has been proposed for the role of world language more frequently than any other natural language, it has also played a central role in the language modification movement. In some cases, of course, modifications have been suggested as a means of improving the language for the benefit of its native speakers rather than with a world language in mind. Reform of English spelling, for example, has often been urged to help schoolchildren struggling with words like 'through' and 'occasion' which seem to abound in the language. Many such proposals have come, not surprisingly, from Britain and North America. In the late nineteenth century the American librarian, Melvil Dewey, was interested in phonetic spelling and actually included some reformed spellings in several editions of his famous Decimal Classification scheme, including the words Jeology, filosofy and helth (as well as spelling his own name Dui). American English, indeed, has adopted certain spelling reforms such as 'thru' and 'theater'. Foreigners have also lent their efforts to the cause of a phonetic spelling system for English In 1889 a Russian, Starchevsky, urged the use of phonetised English as an international language and around 1930 a Swedish professor proposed a semi-phonetic spelling which he called Anglic. Unfortunately, such spellings as 'internashonal asoesiaeshon' are not easily recognised by existing users of the language and may not greatly help the learner. Mario Pei may be right when he says that a pre-condition for using English as an international auxiliary language must be a spelling reform, but he is equally correct when he points out that there is little evidence to indicate that a phonetically-spelled English would prove any more acceptable to the rest of the world as an official international language than present-day English.[42]

The most famous proposal to modify English was made by C.K. Ogden in 1930 when he first published his *Basic English* (BASIC being an acronym for British American Scientific International Commercial, as well as suggesting a simplified version of English pared down to its fundamentals). Ogden described Basic English as 'a careful and systematic selection of 850 English words which will cover those needs of everyday life for which a vocabulary of 20,000 words is frequently employed'. These 850 words were made up of 400 general nouns, 100 adjectives, 100 verb-forms (which Ogden called operators), particles, etc., a supplementary list of 200 'picturable objects' and 50 adjectival opposites (for a full list see figure 6.7). According to Ogden, 'with this vocabulary the style of Swift, Tolstoi, Stevenson and Franklin can be attained', whilst below this minimum 'only Pidgin English or travellers' enquiries can emerge'.[43] He stressed that the 850 words were not necessarily the most commonly used as determined by word counts but those words needed to cover everything of general interest that can be talked about. Such word economy was gained by removing everything unnecessary to meaning. Thus, instead of the word 'disembark', the phrase 'get off a ship' would be employed, instead of 'difficult', Basic uses 'hard', and so on. Economy was particularly gained by putting together the names of simple operations — get, give, come, go, put, take, etc. — with words of direction like 'in', 'over', 'through'. In this way two or three thousand complex ideas could be formed from a small number of simple concepts. According to its author, once the functions of the different parts of speech were understood and the meanings of the 850 words memorised, it was only necessary to learn the conjugations of the operators (see figure 6.8), to learn the pronouns (see figure 6.9) and the five simple rules covering the formation of plurals, compounds, derivatives, comparatives and adverbs. Compounds could be formed by combining together two nouns (coal and mine into coalmine, milk and man into milkman); derivatives were formed, for example, by adding -er to a noun to indicate a thing or person performing the operation indicated by the noun, or by adding -ing to the noun to indicate the operation itself. Using these rules, then, a large number of words could be formed from the Basic 850 words.

Ogden intended Basic English to serve as a spoken and written international auxiliary language as well as providing a rational introduction to standard English. It is interesting to note that Ogden was also preoccupied with the same concerns as his seventeenth-century predecessors. He envisaged Basic English as something more than a mere language of international communication: 'The divisions for which

BASIC ENGLISH

OPERATIONS 300 ETC.	THINGS — 400 General				THINGS — 200 Pictured		QUALITIES — 100 General	QUALITIES — 50 Opposites
COME	ACCOUNT	EDUCATION	METAL	SENSE	ANGLE	KNEE	ABLE	AWAKE
GET	ACT	EFFECT	MIDDLE	SERVANT	ANT	KNIFE	ACID	BAD
GIVE	ADDITION	END	MILK	SEX	APPLE	KNOT	ANGRY	BENT
GO	ADJUSTMENT	ERROR	MIND	SHADE	ARCH	LEAF	AUTOMATIC	BITTER
KEEP	ADVERTISEMENT	EVENT	MINE	SHAKE	ARM	LEG	BEAUTIFUL	BLUE
LET	AGREEMENT	EXAMPLE	MINUTE	SHAME	ARMY	LIBRARY	BLACK	CERTAIN
MAKE	AIR	EXCHANGE	MIST	SHOCK	BABY	LINE	BOILING	COLD
PUT	AMOUNT	EXISTENCE	MONEY	SIDE	BAG	LIP	BRIGHT	COMPLETE
SEEM	AMUSEMENT	EXPANSION	MONTH	SIGN	BALL	LOCK	BROKEN	CRUEL
TAKE	ANIMAL	EXPERIENCE	MORNING	SILK	BAND	MAP	BROWN	DARK
BE	ANSWER	EXPERT	MOTHER	SILVER	BASIN	MATCH	CHEAP	DEAD
DO	APPARATUS	FACT	MOTION	SISTER	BASKET	MONKEY	CHIEF	DEAR
HAVE	APPROVAL	FALL	MOUNTAIN	SIZE	BATH	MOON	CHEMICAL	DELICATE
SAY	ARGUMENT	FAMILY	MOVE	SKY	BED	MOUTH	CLEAN	DIFERENT
SEE	ART	FATHER	MUSIC	SLEEP	BEE	MUSCLE	CLEAR	DIRTY
SEND	ATTACK	FEAR	NAME	SLIP	BELL	NAIL	COMMON	DRY
MAY	ATTEMPT	FEELING	NATION	SLOPE	BERRY	NECK	COMPLEX	FALSE
WILL	ATTENTION	FICTION	NEED	SMASH	BIRD	NEEDLE	CONCIOUS	FEEBLE
ABOUT	ATTRACTION	FIELD	NEWS	SMELL	BLADE	NERVE	CUT	FEMALE
ACROSS	AUTHORITY	FIGHT	NIGHT	SMILE	BOARD	NET	DEEP	FOOLISH
AFTER	BACK	FIRE	NOISE	SMOKE	BOAT	NOSE	DEPENDENT	FUTURE
AGAINST	BALANCE	FLAME	NOTE	SNEEZE	BONE	NUT	EARLY	GREEN
AMONG	BASE	FLIGHT	NUMBER	SNOW	BOOK	OFFICE	ELASTIC	ILL
AT	BEHAVIOUR	FLOWER	OBSERVATION	SOAP	BOOT	ORANGE	ELECTRIC	LAST
BEFORE	BELIEF	FOLD	OFFER	SOCIETY	BOTTLE	OVEN	EQUAL	LATE
BETWEEN	BIRTH	FOOD	OIL	SON	BOX	PARCEL	FAT	LEFT
BY	BIT	FORCE	OPERATION	SONG	BOY	PEN	FERTILE	LOOSE
DOWN	BITE	FORM	OPINION	SORT	BRAIN	PENCIL	FIRST	LOUD
FROM	BLOOD	FRIEND	ORDER	SOUND	BRAKE	PICTURE	FIXED	LOW
IN	BLOW	FRONT	ORGANIZATION	SOUP	BRANCH	PIG	FLAT	MIXED
OF	BODY	FRUIT	ORNAMENT	SPACE	BRICK	PIN	FREE	NARROW
ON	BRASS	GLASS	OWNER	STAGE	BRIDGE	PIPE	FREQUENT	OLD
OVER	BREAD	GOLD	PAGE	START	BRUSH	PLANE	FULL	OPPOSITE
THROUGH	BREATH	GOVERNMENT	PAIN	STATEMENT	BUCKET	PLATE	GENERAL	PUBLIC
TO	BROTHER	GRAIN	PAINT	STEAM	BULB	PLOUGH	GOOD	ROUGH
UNDER	BUILDING	GRASS	PAPER	STEEL	BUTTON	POCKET	GREAT	SAD
UP	BURN	GRIP	PART	STEP	CAKE	POT	GREY	SAFE
WITH	BURST	GROUP	PASTE	STITCH	CAMERA	POTATO	HANGING	SECRET
AS	BUSINESS	GROWTH	PAYMENT	STONE	CARD	PRISON	HAPPY	SHORT
FOR	BUTTER	GUIDE	PEACE	STOP	CART	PUMP	HARD	SHUT
OF	CANVAS	HARBOUR	PERSON	STORY	CARRIAGE	RAIL	HEALTHY	SIMPLE
TILL	CARE	HARMONY	PLACE	STRETCH	CAT	RAT	HIGH	SLOW
THAN	CAUSE	HATE	PLANT	STRUCTURE	CHAIN	RECEIPT	HOLLOW	SMALL
A	CHALK	HEARING	PLAY	SUBSTANCE	CHEESE	RING	IMPORTANT	SOFT
THE	CHANCE	HEAT	PLEASURE	SUGAR	CHEST	ROD	KIND	SOLID
ALL	CHANGE	HELP	POINT	SUGGESTION	CHIN	ROOF	LIKE	SPECIAL
ANY	CLOTH	HISTORY	POISON	SUMMER	CHURCH	ROOT	LIVING	STRANGE
EVERY	COAL	HOLE	POLISH	SUPPORT	CIRCLE	SAIL	LONG	THIN
NO	COLOUR	HOPE	PORTER	SURPRISE	CLOCK	SCHOOL	MALE	WHITE
OTHER	COMFORT	HOUR	POSITION	SWIM	CLOUD	SCISSORS	MARRIED	WRONG
SOME	COMMITTEE	HUMOUR	POWDER	SYSTEM	COAT	SCREW	MATERIAL	
SUCH	COMPANY	ICE	POWER	TALK	COLLAR	SEED	MEDICAL	
THAT	COMPARISON	IDEA	PRICE	TASTE	COMB	SHEEP	MILITARY	
THIS	COMPETITION	IMPULSE	PRINT	TAX	CORD	SHELF	NATURAL	SUMMARY OF RULES
I	CONDITION	INCREASE	PROCESS	TEACHING	COW	SHIP	NECESSARY	
HE	CONNECTION	INDUSTRY	PRODUCE	TENDENCY	CUP	SHIRT	NEW	PLURALS IN 'S.'
YOU	CONTROL	INK	PROFIT	TEST	CURTAIN	SHOE	NORMAL	
WHO	COOK	INSECT	PROPERTY	THEORY	CUSHION	SKIN	OPEN	
AND	COPPER	INSTRUMENT	PROSE	THING	DOG	SKIRT	PARALLEL	DERIVATIVES IN 'ER,' 'ING,' FROM 300 NOUN
BECAUSE	COPY	INSURANCE	PROTEST	THOUGHT	DOOR	SNAKE	PAST	
BUT	CORK	INTEREST	PULL	THUNDER	DRAIN	SOCK	PHYSICAL	
OR	COTTON	INVENTION	PUNISHMENT	TIME	DRAWER	SPADE	POLITICAL	
IF	COUGH	IRON	PURPOSE	TIN	DRESS	SPONGE	POOR	ADVERBS IN 'LY' FROM QUALIFIERS.
THOUGH	COUNTRY	JELLY	PUSH	TOP	DROP	SPOON	POSSIBLE	
WHILE	COVER	JOIN	QUALITY	TOUCH	EAR	SPRING	PRESENT	
HOW	CRACK	JOURNEY	QUESTION	TRADE	EGG	SQUARE	PRIVATE	
WHEN	CREDIT	JUDGE	RAIN	TRANSPORT	ENGINE	STAMP	PROBABLE	DEGREE WITH 'MORE' AND 'MO
WHERE	CRIME	JUMP	RANGE	TRICK	EYE	STAR	QUICK	
WHY	CRUSH	KICK	RATE	TROUBLE	FACE	STATION	QUIET	
AGAIN	CRY	KISS	RAY	TURN	FARM	STEM	READY	QUESTIONS BY INVERSION AND 'DO.'
EVER	CURRENT	KNOWLEDGE	REACTION	TWIST	FEATHER	STICK	RED	
FAR	CURVE	LAND	READING	UNIT	FINGER	STOCKING	REGULAR	
FORWARD	DAMAGE	LANGAUGE	REASON	USE	FISH	STOMACH	RESPONSIBLE	
HERE	DANGER	LAUGH	RECORD	VALUE	FLAG	STORE	RIGHT	OPERATORS AND PRONOUNS CONJUGATE IN FULL
NEAR	DAUGHTER	LAW	REGRET	VESSEL	FLOOR	STREET	ROUND	
NOW	DAY	LEAD	RELATION	VIEW	FLY	SUN	SAME	
OUT	DEATH	LEARNING	RELIGION	VOICE	FOOT	TABLE	SECOND	MEASUREMENT NUMERALS, CURRENCY CALENDAR, AND INTERNATIONA TERMS IN ENGLISH FORM
STILL	DEBT	LEATHER	REPRESENTATIVE	WALK	FORK	TAIL	SEPARATE	
THEN	DECISION	LETTER	REQUEST	WAR	FOWL	THREAD	SERIOUS	
THERE	DEGREE	LEVEL	RESPECT	WASH	FRAME	THROAT	SHARP	
TOGETHER	DESIGN	LIFT	REST	WASTE	GARDEN	THUMB	SMOOTH	
WELL	DESIRE	LIGHT	REWARD	WATER	GIRL	TICKET	STICKY	
ALMOST	DESTRUCTION	LIMIT	RHYTHM	WAVE	GLOVE	TOE	STIFF	
ENOUGH	DETAIL	LINEN	RICE	WAX	GOAT	TONGUE	STRAIGHT	
EVEN	DEVELOPMENT	LIQUID	RIVER	WAY	GUN	TOOTH	STRONG	
LITTLE	DIGESTION	LIST	ROAD	WEATHER	HAIR	TOWN	SUDDEN	THE ORTHOLOGICA INSTITUTE 10 KING'S PARADI CAMBRIDGE ENGLAND.
MUCH	DIRECTION	LOOK	ROLL	WEEK	HAMMER	TRAIN	SWEET	
NOT	DISCOVERY	LOSS	ROOM	WEIGHT	HAND	TRAY	TALL	
ONLY	DISCUSSION	LOVE	RUB	WIND	HAT	TREE	THICK	
QUITE	DISEASE	MACHINE	RULE	WINE	HEAD	TROUSERS	TIGHT	
SO	DISGUST	MAN	RUN	WINTER	HEART	UMBRELLA	TIRED	
VERY	DISTANCE	MANAGER	SALT	WOMAN	HOOK	WALL	TRUE	
TOMORROW	DISTRIBUTION	MARK	SAND	WOOD	HORN	WATCH	VIOLENT	
YESTERDAY	DIVISION	MARKET	SCALE	WOOL	HORSE	WHEEL	WAITING	
NORTH	DOUBT	MASS	SCIENCE	WORD	HOSPITAL	WHIP	WARM	
SOUTH	DRINK	MEAL	SEA	WORK	HOUSE	WHISTLE	WET	
EAST	DRIVING	MEASURE	SEAT	WOUND	ISLAND	WINDOW	WIDE	
WEST	DUST	MEAT	SECRETARY	WRITING	JEWEL	WING	WISE	
PLEASE	EARTH	MEETING	SELECTION	YEAR	KETTLE	WIRE	YELLOW	
YES	EDGE	MEMORY	SELF		KEY	WORM	YOUNG	

Figure 6.7   The 850 words of the Basic English vocabulary
Source: C. K. Ogden, *A short guide to Basic English.* Cambridge:
The Orthological Institute, n.d., p. 41.

FORMS OF 'OPERATORS'

PRESENT		PAST	ING-FORM	SPECIAL PAST FORM
ONE	MORE THAN ONE			
1,2 COME	COME	CAME	COMING	COME
1,2 GET	GET	GOT	GETTING	GOT
1,2 GIVE	GIVE	GAVE	GIVING	GIVEN
1,2 GO	GO	WENT	GOING	GONE
1,2 KEEP	KEEP	KEPT	KEEPING	KEPT
1,2 LET	LET	LET	LETTING	LET
1,2 MAKE	MAKE	MADE	MAKING	MADE
1,2 PUT	PUT	PUT	PUTTING	PUT
1,2 SEEM	SEEM	SEEMED	SEEMING	SEEMED
1,2 TAKE	TAKE	TOOK	TAKING	TAKEN
1 AM* 2 ARE 3 IS	ARE	WERE I } was he }	BEING	BEEN
1,2 DO*	DO	DID	DOING	DONE
1,2 HAVE*	HAVE	HAD	HAVING	HAD
1,2 SAY	SAY	SAID	SAYING	SAID
1,2 SEE	SEE	SAW	SEEING	SEEN
1,2 SEND	SEND	SENT	SENDING	SENT

* Has a use as a helping word.

The form with *he, she, it* is made by the addition of 's '. *Go* and *do* take *es* ; *have* becomes *has*.

Figure 6.8   Operators in Basic English
Source: C. K. Ogden, *A short guide to Basic English.* Cambridge: The Orthological Institute, n.d., p. 42.

FORMS OF 'PRONOUNS'

NUMBER	SEX	FORM FOR DOER OF ACT	FORM FOR THING TO WHICH ACT IS DONE	FORM FOR OWNER
One More than one	M. F. N.	THIS THESE	THIS THESE	
One More than one	M. F. N.	THAT THOSE	THAT THOSE	
One More than one	M. F. N.	WHO WHICH	WHOM WHICH	WHOSE
One More than one	N.	WHAT	WHAT	
One More than one	M. F.	I WE	ME US	MY OUR
One More than one	M. F. N. M. F. N.	HE SHE IT THEY	HIM HER IT THEM	HIS HER ITS THEIR
One More than one	M. F.	YOU	YOU	YOUR

M = Male.   F = Female.   N = No sex.

One, though part of the number system (p. 170), has a use as a 'pronoun'.

For *this is my* (*book*) and so on, we may say *this is mine* (*yours, ours, theirs, his, hers*).

Figure 6.9   Pronouns in Basic English
Source: C. K. Ogden, *A short guide to Basic English.* Cambridge: The Orthological Institute, n.d., p. 43.

language is responsible are not limited to those between nations using different tongues. There is a more deeply-rooted language trouble which comes up even between those using the same tongue, and has been the cause of more waste of man's powers than, possibly, any other one thing.' A common language was needed, he believed, 'this time for bridging the divisions not between the science of different countries but between science and the public, and even between one science and another'.[44] It was necessary for his language to be 'basic' not just in the sense of being 'simple' but also in the sense of getting to the roots of the language. He wanted the words in Basic to be, as far as possible, lacking any subjective connotations. It would then be possible to use them unambiguously and, furthermore, to construct from these simple words the most complex ideas, just as Wilkins and Leibniz had intended.

On his assumption that the average rate of learning words in a foreign language is about 30 per hour, Ogden thought that the typical learner whose natural language was not too remote from English should be able to read anything written in Basic English in less than 30 hours' study. He estimated that over 35 per cent of the words would be recognisable to French speakers and a slightly lower percentage to Germans. In Ogden's opinion, no other existing language could be simplified to anything like the same extent.

Its author certainly held high hopes for his modified language. As he wrote, possibly rather tongue-in-cheek:

when once Basic is established as a universal linguistic foundation, its technique of expansion is chiefly the acquisition of further invariable names, and since such names can be added at an average rate of one every two minutes, a few hundred addenda could at any time be acquired over the week-end. In other words, the time may not be far distant when Governments will initiate special Language Weeks to focus attention on the benefits accruing to a community through any extension of its power of communicating with other communities; when the public prints will feature the year's most plausible guess at the next most useful word; and when philanthropists will solace their retiring years by watching Basic Institutes rise around them for the diffusion of defter definitions and dumpier dictionaries.[45]

Some idea of Basic English can be gained from the text in figure 6.10, the left-hand side of which is in standard English, with its Basic English 'translation' on the right. The use of an asterisk indicates an international term.

CXXXI.—THE DETERMINATION OF UNSATURATED AND AROMATIC HYDROCARBONS IN LIGHT OILS AND MOTOR SPIRITS[1]

By ALEXANDER BERNARD MANNING

In the course of a systematic examination of the various products of carbonization of coal at different temperatures and in different types of retort, the problem arose of determining the composition of the light oils obtained. The study of these light oils, which have a boiling range of ca. 30–170°, throws considerable light on the processes occurring during carbonization, and is of importance also as affecting the utilization of the refined oils as motor spirits. In analysing light hydrocarbon oils of this character, it is sufficient for most purposes to determine the relative proportions of unsaturated, aromatic, naphthene, and paraffin hydrocarbons. It is evident that, if a method for such a determination is once established, a more complete knowledge of the composition of the oil is readily attained by applying the method to suitably chosen fractions of the original oil.

Details of typical methods which have been used for the analysis of light oils will be found in papers by, e.g. Egloff and Morrell (J. Ind. Eng. Chem., 1926, 18, 354), Kattwinkel (Brennstoff-Chem., 1927, 8, 353), and Brame (J. Inst. Pet. Tech., 1926, 12, 48; Brame and Hunter, ibid., 1927, 13, 794). Such methods usually depend on observing the successive losses in volume when the oil is shaken (a) with a reagent which absorbs the unsaturated but not the aromatic hydrocarbons, and (b) with a second reagent which absorbs the aromatic but not the saturated

[1] Printed from the Journal of the Chemical Society, 1929.

40

CXXXI.—PROCESS FOR GETTING THE AMOUNTS OF UNSATURATED[1] AND AROMATIC* HYDROCARBONS IN LOW-BOILING AND MOTOR PETROLS.

In the process of working on the different substances formed when coal is coked* at different temperatures* and in different sorts of heating apparatus, it became necessary to get an analysis* of the low-boiling petrols present. A knowledge of these liquids, which have a boiling range of about 30–170°, is of great help in the discovery of the processes taking place in coking, and is important in connection with their use as motor petrols after fraction-distillation.* To get an analysis of low-boiling petrols of this sort, it is only necessary, for most purposes, to have the ratio of unsaturated, aromatic, naphthene* and paraffin* hydrocarbons. It is clear that when we have a process for doing this, it will be possible to get a more complete knowledge of the make-up of a petrol by using the process on a selection of fractions from it.

Details of the chief processes which have been used for the analysis of low-boiling petrols are given in papers by, for example, Egloff and Morrell (J. Ind. Eng. Chem., 1926, 18, 354), Kattwinkel (Brennstoff-chem., 1927, 8, 353), and Brame (J. Inst. Pet. Tech., 1926, 12, 48; Brame and Hunter, ibid., 1927, 13, 794). Such processes are commonly dependent on observation of the series of losses in volume when the petrol is well mixed (a) with a reagent for the absorption* of unsaturated but not aromatic hydrocarbons, and (b) with a second chemical for the absorption of the aromatic but not of the saturated hydrocarbons. In order not to have

[1] Negative qualifier from 'Saturation.'

41

Figure 6.10 A standard English text (on the left) with its Basic English equivalent (on the right)
Source: C. K. Ogden, Basic English applied (science). London: Kegan Paul, Trench, Trubner, 1931, pp. 40–1.

Basic English has not been well received by its many critics. In the first place, it has been pointed out that the claim to have reduced the vocabulary to just 850 words is simply not true. Ogden himself says that many words in both general and especially scientific English are in fact international and universally understood, and cites as examples 'radio' and 'alcohol'. Such words are included in Basic English in addition to the original 850 words, although critics are not always unanimous about their international status. A further increase of vocabulary is permitted in the case of scientific writings; 100 words were added to cover the general language of science, plus 50 more for the needs of any special branch of science. Together with accepted measurements, numerals, currency terms, names of countries, etc., which were also allowed, the vocabulary had by now mushroomed to several thousand words. Ogden himself did not see this as a valid criticism, and in particular defended the use of international terms: 'Quite apart from the pertinent fact that Basic would be unable to cope with scientific requirements without these international aids, it would be a disastrous policy for any proposed world language to ignore these tendencies, and impose a closed system of its own which left current internationalisms outside.'[46] It must be conceded that even taking into account these additional words, the Basic English vocabulary is far smaller than that of any standard language. Nevertheless, it is somewhat misleading to emphasise constantly, as Ogden and his supporters did, the limit of 850 words in Basic English.

A second major criticism is that the morphology, syntax and idiomatic use of language present the biggest problems to the learner, rather than the vocabulary, which can always be looked up in a dictionary. But Basic English, in its attempt to restrict the vocabulary, has probably increased irregularities and idiomatic usage and has certainly retained spelling anomalies. Ogden himself considered that with such a small vocabulary to learn, each word could be treated individually, and phonetic irregularities do not therefore pose any great problem. In fact, he thought they might even be a help to memory.

It does seem a little harsh of critics to deny that a restricted vocabulary will facilitate language learning, but certainly a distinction must be made between reading and writing in Basic English. The limited vocabulary enables texts to be read after relatively little word learning, and a reduction in dictionary consultation is surely a considerable benefit to the reader in terms of time and temper. It is in writing that more fundamental problems arise. Compensation must be made for the small vocabulary at hand and considerable ingenuity is demanded of the writer; in practice the memory may be less taxed but the intellect is called upon to a greater degree. It is probably unfair to cite examples like 'this watermelon tastes good', which in Basic English is said to read 'this large green fruit with the form of an egg and a sweet red inside has a good taste'. Nevertheless, less extreme examples from the Basic dictionary can still tax the imagination: 'man who goes round with cart for house waste' instead of dustman, 'ornament for ear' instead of earring, and 'earth walls put up in war' for earthwork (included in the excerpt reproduced in figure 6.11). Such constructions presume a considerable command of the English language, and it is far from certain that the rest of the world finds this scheme particularly basic. The formation of compound words from two Basic words is likely in particular to cause difficulty to users unfamiliar with standard English. Compounds such as 'birthday' and 'schoolroom' should not pose problems, but what of other examples such as 'sweetheart', 'hairdresser', 'bookkeeper', 'box office' and 'cupboard'? In these cases the meaning of the idiomatic compounds cannot readily be deduced from the individual meanings of the constituent words. Further, Ogden treated homonyms in a rather cavalier fashion, including them as single entries in his list of 850 words even though their meanings might be very different. As Sack points out, 'a babe in arms' and 'a nation in arms' are two widely different concepts. It is hard to disagree with his assertion that what Ogden calls words are really phonetic units.[47] At the same time, writers already familiar with English may encounter great difficulties in adjusting to the rigours of the Basic variety.

Ogden himself was not unaware of certain difficulties, at least in the case of scientific texts. He recognised that two kinds of technical terms could prove awkward to render in Basic English: first, those which are so specialised that they can only be defined satisfactorily with the help of other technical terms. He cited as an example the term 'common genital duct', for which a general description such as 'reproduction organ' would be too vague. In such cases, either the term or its constituent parts must be included in the special scientific vocabularies allowed by Basic English or else international expressions must be found in which the terms could be defined. Second, those terms which are a distortion of some common word used in ordinary speech. Here, the only solution might be to include the original term within inverted commas rather than attempt to convert drain (-er, -ing, -ed), n. drein: *égout, tuyau d'écoulement, drain; Abflussleitung, Entwässerungs-graben.* -ing, (c) Process of making less or feebler; *affaiblissement: Verbrauchen.* Put water down the d.; draining a bit of land. Draining away his power.

drawer, n. drɔː*: *tiroir: Schublade.* Put away in a d.

dress (dresses, -er, -ing, -ed), n. dres; *robe; Kleid.* (c) Clothing; *habit, habillement: Kleidung.* -ing, (e) Cover put on wound: substance put on food; *pansement: assaisonnement, sauce; Verband: Sauce.* She had a beautiful d.; their dresses were blue. A new form of d.: dressing oneself (the baby). Put a dressing on the leg: dressing the leg. A thick dressing on the meat. *(Dressing up).

drink, n. driŋk; *boisson; Getränk* (s) Alcohol d.; *liqueurs fortes; (geistige) Getränk.* (c) (D. for) one act of taking d.; *coup de boire; Schluck.* Tea is a good d. They had some d.; d. is his trouble. Have a d. of water; have a d. to him; give me another d. *(The worse for d.).

driving (driver), n., a. draiviŋ; *action de conduire; fahren, Führen.* (c) Forcing; *action de pousser; Treiben.* D. an automobile (cart); a good driver. Put the nail in by d. it with a hammer; the wind was d. the ship forward; a d. rain; you are d. me to drink.

drop (-per, -ping, -ped), n. drɔp; *goutte; Tropfen.* (c) Fall; *chute; Fall.* Dd. of rain on the window; a d. of blood from the wound. It is a long d. from the top of the wall; a d. in prices; dropping the plate.

dry (-er, -ing), a. drai; *sec arid; trocken.* (c) Not interesting; *ennuyeux.* A d. field (tongue, day); get d. in front of the fire; drying the linen. A d. discussion (book).

dust (-er, -ing, -ed), n. dast; *poussière; Staub.* (c) Powder; *poudre.* -er, (s) Cloth for taking off dust; *torchon; Staubtuch.* D. on the books; get d. in his eyes; dusting the table (room). Chalk d. Cleaning with a duster.

dustman, n. *Basic words.* Man who goes round with cart for house waste.

dynamic*, dainəmait. *International word.*

ear, n. iə*: *oreille; Ohr.* He put his e. to the key-hole; news comes to one's ee. **An e. for music; playing by e.

early, a., adv. əːli; *de bonne heure, premier; früh.* (c) Before the time; *prématuré*, (za) früh.* It is e. in the day; the e. years. E. for the meal. Get up e.

ear-ring, n. *Basic words.* Ornament for ear.

earth, n. əːθ: *terre, sol; Erde.* (c) The ball on which we are living; *terre.* Put a seed in the e. The e. goes round the sun. ** Nothing on e.

earthwork, n. *Basic words.* Earth walls put up in war.

east, a., adv., s., iːst; *est; östlich: Osten.* The e. side; an e. wind. Going e.; Germany is e. of France. The sun comes up in the e.: religions of the E.

edge (-er, -ing, -ed), n. edʒ; *bord, tranchant; Rand, Schneide.* The e. of the sea (dress); the knife has a sharp e.; the collar is edged with blue.

education, n. edju(:)ˈkeiʃən; *éducation, instruction; Erziehung, Bildung.* Give a boy a good e.; the e. of the young; the experience will be a good e. for you.

effect (-er, -ing, -ed), n. iˈfekt; *effet, résultat: Wirkung.* A strange e. of light; his statement had no e.; get a snow e. by dropping paper; effecting a change. *(Have an e. on). **In e.; he of no e.; put into e.; take e.

egg, n. eg: *œuf; Ei.* This e. comes from the farm.

egg-cup, n. *Basic words.* Sort of cup used at table for eg.

elastic (un-, -ally), a., n. iˈlæstik; *élastique; elastisch, dehnbar; Gummiband.* (c) Readily stretched, changed. An e. material. Very e. views. A. bit of e.

electric (-ally), a., iˈlektrik; *électrique; elektrisch.* E. light (current); get an e. shock; the house is electrically heated.

embassy, 'embəsi. *International name.*
empire, 'empaiə*. *International word.*
encyclopaedia*, en.saiklo'piːdiə. *International word.*

end (-er, -ing, -ed), n. end; *fin, bout; Ende.* -ing, (e) The end part of a story (word); *fin, terminaison; Endung, Ende.* Come (get) to the e.; the e. of the street (story, work); a loose e. of thread; the day is ending. The ending '-ing. *In the e. (Put an e. (a stop) to).

Figure 6.11 Excerpt from the Basic dictionary

Source: C. K. Ogden, *The Basic words: a detailed account of their uses.* London: The Orthological Institute, 1964, pp. 26—7.

it into Basic; for example, 'Theory of relativity' cannot be accommodated by 'Theory of comparative relations'. The lay translator must be especially careful to avoid misunderstandings. 'Steam', for example, cannot be called 'water gas' because for the chemist, water gas has a special meaning: the mixture of gases produced by passing steam over coal. Ogden advised that where there was difficulty in supplying an accurate definition of a technical term that is not accepted as international, the original term should always be included in brackets after its Basic equivalent.[48]

Otto Jespersen, commenting upon Basic English, said that 'it would be too much of a parody of English, laughed at and mocked at, and all those millions who know and love the old English language would not consider it a serious attempt to solve an important problem, but would turn away with horror.'[49] The fundamental fallacy which lies at the heart of all such schemes for the modification of a natural language, however, is that objections to the use of any natural language as an international language lie in the realm of linguistics rather than politics. No doubt the world would rather learn a simplified language than a difficult, irregular language, but it is naive to think that modification alone will remove the deep-rooted political suspicions of giving any natural language such a powerful role. In *The shape of things to come,* published in 1933, H.G. Wells prophesied:

One of the unanticipated achievements of the twenty-first century was the rapid diffusion of Basic English as the lingua franca of the world . . . It was made the official medium of communication throughout the world by the Air and Sea Control, and by 2020 there was hardly anyone in the world who could not talk and understand it.[50]

It is unlikely that any science fiction writer today would hold out such a bright future for Ogden's Basic English.

Before leaving Basic English, it is worth mentioning its connection with the work of Otto Neurath in the field of visual communication. Ogden had asked Neurath to design an illustrated primer to outline Basic English. Neurath agreed, but in turn asked if Ogden would publish at the same time his book, which he would write in Basic English, to explain the principles of his visual work. The outcome was Ogden's *Basic by Isotype,* published in 1937, and Neurath's *International picture language,* which had appeared in the previous year.[51] ISOTYPE (International System Of TYpographic Picture Education) was intended as a 'helping language' into which statements could be 'translated' from any normal language rather than as a complete language in itself. (As it happens, the idea of using pictures for educational purposes had been pioneered by Comenius in the seventeenth century, one of his many interests beyond the construction of a universal language; see p. 8). As Neurath described his plans:

Education by pictures in harmony with the ISOTYPE system, advertisement by ISOTYPE signs, will do much to give the different nations a common outlook. If the schools give teaching through the eye in harmony with this international picture language, they will be servants of a common education all over the earth, and will give a new impulse to all other questions of international education.[52]

He argued that the signs must be clear in themselves and convey meaning, as far as possible, without the help of words; they must be simple; and they must make good use of colours (seven colours were used). The signs should also be designed so that two or more could be combined to form a new sign. An example of this is provided in figure 6.12. The sign for shoe can be combined with the sign for works to represent a shoe factory. The signs showing where luggage could be deposited and collected are good examples of ISOTYPE and could easily be mistaken for designs of the 1980s rather than the 1930s (note how the terms 'works', 'boxes', 'put' and 'get' are used instead of the more suitable 'factory', 'luggage', 'deposit' and 'collect' because Neurath was writing his captions in Basic English).

A PRIORI CHALLENGERS

A priori schemes have not greatly appealed to language constructors in this century and *relatively* few have been designed. Ours is a practical rather than a speculative age and the attraction of inventing an artificial language for everyday international communication is now more compelling than a philosophical device for structuring thought more logically. The history of the artificial language movement appears to demonstrate that *a posteriori* schemes which bear some resemblance to the natural languages already spoken have more chance of attracting and retaining popular support.

Despite such an unpromising atmosphere, however, *a priori* languages continue to emerge, and Mario Pei has listed a number of them.[53] A numerical scheme (not unlike Dewey's Decimal Classification scheme which is used to arrange documents in libraries and entries in catalogues and bibliographies) was designed by a Berlin architect called Tiemer in 1921. The phrase 'I love you' in Timerio was thereby reduced to 1-80-17, with some inevitable loss of romantic appeal. Another numerical project

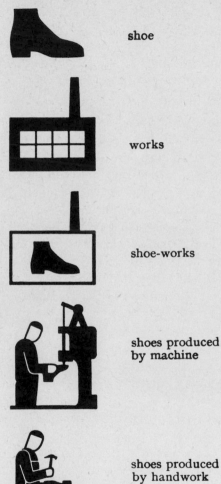

shoe

works

shoe-works

shoes produced by machine

shoes produced by handwork

Figure 6.12   Examples of ISOTYPE

Source: Otto Neurath, *International picture language: a facsimile reprint of the [1936] English edition*. Reading: University of Reading, 1980, pp. 18, 35.

Where to put your boxes

Where to get your boxes

Figure 6.12 *continued*

was devised by an American artillery officer. Nouns always began with the numerals 1, 2 or 3; verbs with 4; adjectives with 5; adverbs with 6; pronouns with 7; conjunctions with 8; and prepositions with 9. The suffixes 10, 20 and 30 were used respectively to indicate the present, past and future tenses of verbs. So 'The boy eats the red apple' was translated as 5-111-409-10-5-516-2013. Such numerical structures can only really be used in a written language and are therefore not fully-fledged artificial languages with a phonemic as well as a graphic aspect. In this respect they resemble the polygraphic schemes of the sixteenth and seventeenth centuries, of which Cave Beck's project is an example (see chapter 2). Another scheme reminiscent of those earlier times was constructed by the Reverend Foster of Ohio at the beginning of this century. In this case, Ro resembles the philosophical languages of Wilkins and Dalgarno in being based upon a classification of ideas. Knowledge was divided into 25 main divisions, with further subdivisions. In class b, for example, *bod* is universe, *bodak* is comet, *bodam* is moon, *bodas* sun and *bodar* means star. In other words, related concepts are indicated by alphabetically related words. Apart from the difficulty of agreeing upon what are related concepts, the task of memorising a language like Ro is formidable. The phonetic likeness of semantically related words also enhances the probability of mis-hearing the spoken language. To take the first ten numerals in Ro, only a very slight distortion in the message would cause misinterpretation:

1	zab	6	zal
2	zac	7	zam
3	zad	8	zaq
4	zaf	9	zar
5	zag	10	zax

Despite such potential difficulties, Ro did attract a group of supporters for a time.[54]

7

Prospects for an International Language

The history of artificial languages is one of earnest endeavour with long hours spent in painstaking labour, but also of frustration and failure. Several hundred language schemes, many of great ingenuity, have been constructed since the seventeenth century, and some at least have proved their worth as media of written and spoken communication. Yet the adoption of any one project as an international auxiliary language for use throughout the world seems as distant as when John Wilkins pored over his manuscript of *An essay towards a real character* some 300 years ago. The repeated disappointments experienced by generations of language projectors have obviously not deterred newcomers from testing their linguistic wits. Why are people so attracted by the prospect of constructing an artificial language?

All kinds of motives have impelled people (mostly men, in fact) to tackle the many problems involved in planning and constructing an artificial language. An intrinsic interest in language itself is an essential requirement if months and years are to be devoted to the task. Yet an intellectual fascination with language is not enough. Indeed, very few language constructors have been professional linguists: there spring to mind the Abbess Hildegarde, Bishop Wilkins, the merchant Lodwick, the schoolmaster Beck, the philosopher Condorcet, the financial expert Faiguet, the priest Schleyer, the oculist Zamenhof, the mathematician Peano, the architect Tiemer, and so on. Such individuals as these, and many more, have been driven to their toil by a stronger urge than mere love of languages or fascination with morphemes and phonemes. Quite specific motivating forces can often be detected behind the fancies and follies of artificial language projectors.

The early schemes of the seventeenth century were prompted by philosophical, religious, scientific and commercial considerations, and often a mixture of all four. As trading and missionary activity spread beyond the boundaries of Europe to the Far East and the Americas, European merchants and missionaries needed a language which could be taught to the heathen without difficulty, in order better to barter goods and save souls. Further, they required a common language for use amongst themselves if they were to collaborate in the material and spiritual exploitation of overseas territories. The lively exchange of scientific theories across linguistic frontiers also could be facilitated by a language of international communication. For various reasons (see chapter 1) Latin was no longer the obvious choice for such a language, and scholars began to look elsewhere for a solution.

These practical benefits to be expected from an international language were complemented by a growing desire on the part of seventeenth-century thinkers to create a language which would 'mirror' the natural order of things in the universe: a philosophical language whose structure and vocabulary would reflect the ideas represented. Such a philosophical language, it was confidently believed, would facilitate logical thought and outlaw ambiguity of expression. Instead of contributing towards confusion and discord, language would work in favour of clarity and harmony. The likes of Descartes, Leibniz and Wilkins were attracted to the idea of an artificial language by the prospect of establishing a rational language in which rational men could think and communicate.

The idea of constructing philosophical languages continued to attract attention in the following century, though it never again played such an important role in intellectual life. By the second half of the nineteenth century, however, the desire to construct a practical language for international communication had become the primary motive behind artificial language projects. The increasing number of international contacts at governmental, institutional and personal levels highlighted the barrier created by the diversity of natural languages and emphasised the advantages to be gained from the introduction of an international auxiliary language. As long ago as 1903, Couturat could write:

These international relations, which are continually extending and multi-plying, are making the absence of some one common medium of communication, familiar to all the diverse peoples speaking different languages, more and more keenly felt . . . The means of intellectual communication have not progressed at an equal pace with the other means of communication; they are in a most extraordinary degree behind the times.[1]

How much more is this true today.

Such practical considerations alone, however, were frequently insufficient to motivate the language constructors, but by now they were reinforced by idealistic rather than philosophical forces in the artificial language movement. Schleyer envisaged Volapük as contributing to the unity of mankind and working towards a universal peace. Zamenhof was haunted by the memory of hatred and conflict between hostile ethnic populations, in which he believed linguistic differences had played a crucial role. His linguistic creation would reconcile people of different nations, breaking down the barriers of distrust and replacing them by mutual understanding. Zamenhof even conceived the idea of a world religion to reconcile existing religions which so often were at odds with one another. Such idealistic strains are by no means extinct; contemporary language schemes like Glosa emphasise their humanitarian and pacific aims.

The supporters of artificial language movements are impelled, of course, by similar motives as the constructors. Those who actively participate in these movements are prepared to invest significant reserves of time, energy and money; in return, however, they often hope to reap the satisfaction which derives from idealistic actions but cannot easily accrue from the more pragmatic search for a practical means of international communication. People will make great sacrifices for a cause, but that cause must be judged worthy of them. Many Esperantists, for example, are attracted by the ideals of world peace and universal brotherhood, what Forster has called the value-oriented interpretation, rather than the norm-oriented interpretation (appeals for official recognition of the language by those in power in economic, cultural and political life), which the Esperanto leadership tends to stress.[2] The psychologist, Flugel, writing some years ago, observed: 'One of the most immediately striking aspects of the Esperanto movement, an aspect which often proves astonishing, and sometimes disconcerting, to those who happen to come across any considerable body of Esperantists without previous acquaintance with the movement, is its enthusiastic and quasi-religious character.'[3] One Esperantist has in fact compared a language constructor with the founder of a monastic order or a Christian-philanthropic organisation like the Salvation Army. He must above all show by his deeds that he takes seriously the ideals he preaches to others. In this way he will 'stimulate his followers to complete identification with his language'.[4] Ironically, the value-oriented approach is likely to attract and retain a minority of dedicated enthusiasts but may well deter the mass support which must be won if any artificial language is to attain its goal, at least by democratic means. The person who is not wedded to the ideas (and ideals) of an international auxiliary language is more likely to respond positively to the practical, norm-oriented approach.

Calls for the adoption of a world language as a panacea are especially widespread in times of war, and H.W. Harrison's plea during the Second World War is typical (although Harrison proposed the adoption of a natural language — English — rather than an artificial language): 'There is only one way by which permanent peace can be brought to the peoples of Europe, and that is, through a common speech.'[5] A more cautious but not dissimilar conclusion was reached by Guérard:

It would be a crude simplification to say that the disease of Europe is first of all a linguistic one . . . I do not believe in single magic keys . . . most of all no single language could efface an immemorial tradition of strife and purify our hearts from primitive instincts . . . Yet it is impossible not to be struck with the extreme importance of language problems in modern Europe. The main cause of war, now that dynasties have ceased to count, is jealous nationalism. And nationalism has a tendency to translate itself into linguistic terms.[6]

Another supporter of the quest for an international language, Mario Pei, believes that 'short of a foolproof system for preventing war and ensuring perpetual peace, coupled with freedom for the individual, the adoption of an international language is the greatest gift with which we could collectively endow our children and their descendents.'[7]

Flugel offered his own Freudian explanations for the 'ultimate psychological appeal' of artificial languages. Linguistic activities, he argued, are to some extent sublimations of sexual activities. He went on to explain the story of the Tower of Babel. It belonged to a class of story concerned with the storming of heaven, a theme which represents a cosmic projection of father hatred connected with the Oedipus complex. The high tower motif is a symbolic expression of erection, whilst the successful storming of heaven is the defiance of the father and the gratification of sexual desires. The failure of the enterprise represents the revenge of the threatened father: castration. The destruction of the tower, the diversity of speech, the scattering of man and the discord sown between men are all forms of dismemberment or castration. Flugel then went on to offer an explanation for the activities of language constructors: 'In view of the connection between speech, impregnation and flatus . . . we can scarcely doubt that displaced anal effects (ultimately derived from the satisfaction gained by the production of faeces or flatus) play a part in the joy of *creating* an artificial language.' One of the features of certain well-marked types of anal character is dogged perseverance in the face of obstacles; Flugel believed that this might explain the number of international language schemes devised. Further, he suggested that the frequent schisms in artificial language movements afford satisfaction at two levels. At the Oedipus level they signify defiance of the father and incest with the mother (taking forbidden liberties); at the anal-erotic level, they signify defiance of the nursery authorities by indulgence in the tabooed anal activities (playing with or touching faeces).[8]

To many people, of course, the attractions of artificial languages are beyond rational comprehension. A leading information scientist wrote in obvious exasperation: 'The urge has also been powerful to spawn numerous 'artificial' languages like Volapük, Esperanto, Interlingua, Novial, etc. In retrospect, it may seem remarkable that people of so many nations grasped so eagerly at the 'linguistic' monstrosities frankensteined by idealist inventors.'[9]

FEATURES OF ARTIFICIAL LANGUAGES

The designers of artificial languages have attempted to include all kinds of features in their projects, some of which have been discussed in earlier chapters. It is possible, however, to identify a number of general features which have assumed prominence in a large proportion of constructed languages, and which can be said to characterise many, if not all, such languages.

Artificial languages tend to be easier to learn than a second natural language, or at any rate their designers intend and believe that they can be learnt more easily. Excepting the tiny handful of children who have learnt a language like Esperanto as their first tongue, artificial languages can only be acquired through personal or group study. Furthermore, most language projectors are realistic enough to accept that the hardest but most crucial part of their enterprise is to persuade large numbers of people actually to learn their language. It is therefore usually considered an important feature that it can be learnt with as little effort and time as possible. Fortunately, constructed languages can avoid the irregularities of syntax, morphology and phonology which so often plague their natural cousins, and which so handicap second-language learning.

The *a posteriori* schemes have attempted to facilitate learning and use by incorporating syntactic and morphological features found in natural languages. Unfortunately, natural languages include irregularities, and therefore it has not proved possible to make a language completely natural *and* completely logical: both characteristics which simplify learning. Some schemes have opted to be more regular but less natural, others to suffer some irregularities as the price of naturalness. A general criticism of all *a posteriori* schemes, of course, is that they only appear familiar to those people who already know the natural language from which they have drawn grammatical structure and/or vocabulary (see below). *A priori* schemes look much less familiar to potential learners, and may indeed seem unlike any natural langauge known to them. A criticism frequently made of such schemes is just that they are difficult to learn and then to use. Yet their creators often assert confidently that they can be mastered with little trouble. John Wilkins claimed for his Real Character, for example, that a student could learn more of it in one month than of Latin in 40 months (see above p. 37).

A second feature commonly sought in an artificial language is clarity. The language is intended to provide a more precise and logical medium of expression than any natural equivalent. *A priori* seventeenth-century philosophical languages in particular were expressly designed to facilitate the logical analysis of nature and to provide a more accurate and unambiguous means of communication. The taxonomic structure through which this analysis was expressed, however, not only complicated such languages but also introduced a rigidity which was ultimately restricting. The classification of concepts enabled relationships to be established between a word and its meaning, as well as between words whose meanings were related. Yet the classification itself could only reflect the language constructor's own image of reality; a universal and unchanging image did not and does not exist. Furthermore, the classification tables and the symbols used in the language to represent concepts in the tables often provided little room for manoeuvre in case of new developments in knowledge.

An artificial language should also be capable of conveying the range and wealth of concepts that men and women are likely to use in international communication. In some cases a language has been specifically or primarily intended for use in a limited sphere, as for example Interlingua was meant particularly for scientific communication. Mostly, however, a constructed language is designed to cope both with the needs of specialists in their own fields (which may employ their own terminologies or even syntax) and the needs of ordinary citizens in the pursuit of their everyday lives. To succeed in this task the language must be able to change and develop as new demands are put upon it, in much the same way as natural languages constantly evolve. The supporters of Esperanto, for example, stress its receptivity to new words and the fact that it is a genuinely living language. It is just this flexibility, of course, which the philosophical *a priori* schemes tended to lack.

There has been no shortage of blue-prints for a successful artificial language. The 'Memorandum on the problem of an international auxiliary language'[10] had a particularly illustrious authorship, including Edward Sapir and Leonard Bloomfield, both eminent figures in linguistics, and the anthropologist, Franz Boas. It proposed that any international auxiliary language should include the following general principles.

1   It should have no sounds that cause serious difficulty to large bodies of speakers.
2   It should have the simplest grammatical structure that is compatible with effectiveness.
3   It should be easily convertible into and from any of the major languages now in use.
4   It should have considerable flexibility of structure, 'so that any speaker may not too greatly impair its intelligibility if he bends it involuntarily to constructions familiar to him or his own language'.
5   It should be built as far as is possible from materials which are familiar to speakers of West European languages.
6   It should be, as far as possible, a logical development of international linguistic habits that have been formed in the past.

7   It should be easily expressed in shorthand.
8   Its phonetic system should make it intelligible with a minimum of ambiguity on the telephone, records or radio.

The authors of the Memorandum suggested a series of experiments to test such things as the relative ease with which various sounds are heard and sound differences perceived, ease of pronouncing various sounds by different nationalities, and so on. This particular blue-print shows its vintage by such things as references to shorthand, no longer commonly employed even by secretaries. Nevertheless, it is typical of the sort of features which were ideally sought in an international auxiliary language.

To what extent can existing artificial language schemes match up with such ideal blue-prints? It is worth our while to consider the *linguistic* suitability of constructed languages for their intended role. Some schemes for an artificial language have been little more than outlines of their creators' intentions, never actually realised in a fully developed and usable language. Although both Descartes and Leibniz gave considerable thought to the construction of a philosophical language, for example, neither succeeded in constructing a completed structure of grammar and vocabulary which could express graphically or orally human thoughts. Similarly, Faiguet's early proposal for an *a posteriori* language was little more than an outline of a grammar.

Nevertheless, many other schemes have been formulated into fully-fledged languages which could and did work. These artificial languages varied widely in design, of course, ranging from the strange looking *a priori* schemes like Sudre's musical Solresol to easily recognisable (to the West European, at any rate) naturalistic *a posteriori* schemes like Occidental. In some cases the language has been little more than tested in application by its creator or his sympathisers (for example, Robert Hooke's use of Wilkins' Real Character for a description of pocket watches; see above p. 37); in other instances it has been extensively and successfully employed for a wide variety of tasks. Above all, Esperanto has by now proved its capability to convey information on all kinds of topics in speech as well as writing, between individuals from the most diverse natural language backgrounds. In particular, it has been successfully employed as a medium for original literary and poetic works.

Despite the proven workability of many artificial languages, criticism has been readily forthcoming, and the most vitriolic barbs have been concentrated upon the linguistic fine print of many schemes. Those interested enough in artificial languages to play an active part in the movement are often those who also have the most dogmatic opinions on the linguistic structure of artificial languages. Consequently, intense controversies have raged around points such as the use of a circumflexed letter, often the most bitter conflicts being conducted between supporters supposedly of the same scheme. Edward Sapir observed:

As to the theoretical desirability of an international auxiliary language there can be little difference of opinion. As to just what factors in the solution of the problem should be allowed to weigh most heavily there is room for every possible difference of opinion, and so it is not surprising that interlinguists are far from having reached complete agreement as to either method or content.[11]

Some of the criticisms directed against individual artificial languages have already been identified in earlier chapters. It is worth considering here, however, several general reservations which have been expressed. The classificatory *a priori* languages try to isolate a relatively small number of simple concepts which can be categorised by specific characteristics into classes of concepts. In order to express the myriad complex concepts which must be accommodated in any effective language, the schemes also provide a way of combining two or more simple concepts to form a complex idea. This is all very well as long as the basic ingredients — the simple concepts — can be isolated. But as Louis Couturat concluded after his study of Leibniz's work in this field, such schemes are 'absolutely chimerical' because the postulate that all our ideas are homogeneous and uniform combinations of a limited number of simple ideas is itself too simplistic: 'the greatest defect of these systems, and the gravest error of their authors, consists in supposing that the simple elements of our ideas are limited in number, and can be represented by a collection of letters or syllables so restricted as to be easily remembered.'[12] The consequence is that such a language may prove difficult to memorise and use, inhospitable to new concepts and logical and rational only to those who accept its designer's identification and classification of simple concepts.

A posteriori languages may be easier to memorise than many *a priori* schemes, but they are likely to prove easier for some people to learn than others. The property of neutrality is frequently cited as an argument for using an artificial language as an international auxiliary language rather than any natural equivalent. The choice of a natural language will inevitably give some nationalities an advantage over others, whilst an artificial language will be alien to all users. Yet *a posteriori* schemes, and especially those of the naturalistic variety, closely resemble in grammar and/or vocabulary one or more natural languages, whose speakers will thereby gain an advantage. In practice, of course, most *a posteriori* schemes, and certainly the more successful, have been largely drawn from West European languages; they are rather less naturalistic to those who only know, say, Turkish or Thai. In responding to such criticism of a particularly naturalistic and overtly West European scheme — Interlingua — Alexander Gode pointed out that if proportional representation were to be given to the major oriental tongues, for example, the end product would be a language that no-one found easy to understand. It would no longer be readily intelligible to Westerners, yet the great discrepancies between individual oriental languages would mean that the Chinese or Japanese would be little or no better placed to understand it than Interlingua as presently constituted.[13] Gode was surely right in this contention; natural languages differ so greatly in structure and vocabulary that it would be impossible to construct an artificial language which is equally accessible to all peoples regardless of mother tongue. *A priori* languages are much more likely to offer an equal appeal regardless of natural language, but here equality is based upon a shared lack of comprehension until they have been mastered by hard work.

Even this last contention would not necessarily receive unanimous approval. The most fundamental criticism of artificial languages of any kind is that they presuppose a common perception of the world by people everywhere, when such a shared perception does not exist. The exponents of this theory argue that there is no universal human system of concepts; perception itself is influenced by language. The authors of constructed languages, then, have attempted to provide a means of expressing universal concepts, but in reality people use the conceptual systems of their various natural languages. According to Benjamin Lee Whorf, the leading representative of this school of thought, linguistic patterns determine an individual's view of reality, and because languages differ widely in syntax and lexical structure, the perceptions and thoughts expressed in one natural language are incapable of uniform expression in any international language. At best, the conceptual system of an artificial language can only be that of the natural language or languages on which it is based, which in practice is often European. As Whorf himself stated:

the forms of a person's thoughts are controlled by inexorable laws of pattern of which he is unconscious. These patterns are the unperceived intricate systematisations of his own language — shown readily enough by a candid comparison and contrast with other languages, especially those of a different linguistic family. His thinking itself is in a language — in English, in Sanskrit, in Chinese. And every language is a vast pattern system, different from others, in which are culturally ordained the forms and categories by which the personality not only communicates, but also analyses nature, notices or neglects types of relationship and phenomena, channels his reasoning and builds the house of his consciousness.[14]

If Whorf's argument be accepted then it is only possible to use a constructed language between peoples whose natural languages, and therefore conceptual systems, are similar. In the case of Interlingua, Gode explicitly accepted Whorf's theory:

we must emphasise the observation that no linguistic community is imaginable that is not at the same time a cultural community. The supranational linguistic community referred to in the present [Interlingua] context is identical with the cultural community of the Occident. It is the Western world, the Latin or Greco-Latin tradition, or, if we wish, the civilisation of Judaeo-Christian-Mediterranean individualism.[15]

Gode argued that Interlingua would work between scientists of whatever natural language just because the scientific community shared common patterns of thought based upon European scientific traditions. A degree of cultural contiguity exists amongst scientists which is rarely encountered in other fields. Indeed, Whorf himself conceded that scientists describe the world in the same terms, be they Chinese or British, because 'they have taken over bodily the entire Western system of rationalisations.'[16]

Whorf's ideas are not widely acclaimed, at least in their more extreme interpretation, and attempts to verify his hypothesis that thought patterns are conditioned by language have mostly been inconclusive. As Cole and Scribner comment, 'evidence related to the Whorfian hypothesis indicates that language is a less powerful factor in its constraints on perception and thought than Whorf believed it to be.'[17]

The 'universality' of a universal language has been assailed on a related but narrower front: on the problem of idiom. In an article on 'Interlanguage', for example, Macaulay claimed that 'an artificial language cannot succeed', or at any rate, 'a real language, capable of expressing the infinite shades of meaning which the human mind desires to express'.[18] He pointed out that language is more than just vocabulary and grammar; it also includes idiom, 'the whole body of linguistic habits or convention belonging to each tongue'. Interlinguists must face the fact, according to Macaulay, that 'civilised man' requires probably 10,000 or more stereotyped forms of speech for expressing his thoughts, and that these forms vary enormously between languages. As an artificial language will have no idiomatic tradition of its own, it must confront the dilemma either of formulating a complete body of idiom and asking its pupils to learn it, or of allowing the use of national idiom by each speaker. As Macaulay thinks that the first option is impossible, then the second cannot be avoided. The consequence will be that speakers convert the idiomatic expressions of their own native language into the artificial language, even though the idiom may be unintelligible when 'translated' by others from that artificial language into their native languages. An artificial language may have the following words in its vocabulary: cat, chestnut, hoary, house, in, old, recount, some, tar, the. If an Englishman expressed the sentence 'The old tar recounted some hoary chestnuts in the cat house', but using the artificial language rather than English, is it probable that, say, a Japanese listener would extract the meaning from the sentence that his fellow conversationalist intended? This is a rather extreme example, it could be argued, but unless speakers (or writers) of an artificial language are very aware of idiomatic expressions in their native language then they may unwittingly transfer them to the artificial language, with confusing consequences.   *So ?*

Macaulay goes on to discuss the problem of polysemy: the fact that every word has many shades of meaning, but that words which are nominal equivalents in different languages do not have identical variations of meaning. He cites the example of 'leg' in English which extends to the legs of an insect, whereas in French one talks of the 'paws' of a centipede or lobster (and, incidentally, the 'paw' of a wine glass).

The author of one artificial language, Otto Jespersen, who also happened to be a professional linguist, disposed of the idiomatic problem by saying that 'It must be the task of an instructor to warn his pupils against those idiomatic terms and expressions which cannot be easily understood abroad.'

Easier said than done. How can the instructor even know all the terms and expressions which might cause problems, short of knowing every natural language? Grammatical structure as well as vocabulary can create confusion. Macaulay quotes a sentence from the preface to the *Chartreuse de Parme* by Stendhal: 'ce livre n'est rien moins que moral.' By this he means, of course, 'this book is anything but a moral one', but after being converted from French into an artificial language, and then re-converted into English, there is a danger that it would appear as 'this book is nothing less than moral.'

Words may also carry connotations in one language which are absent or different in another language. This is really approaching Whorf's theories of the relationship between language and culture. The concept 'red' in English and Russian provides a good example. In English the word 'red' conjures images of blood, fire and fierceness as in expressions such as 'red with anger', 'seeing red', 'red in tooth and claw', whereas in Russian the same colour, expressed by the word 'krasny' has a very different aura; it means 'beautiful' as well as 'red'. Thus 'krasota' is 'beauty', 'krasnoe zoloto' is 'pure gold', and 'krasny zver' a superior type of game animal. Red Square in Moscow should therefore trigger thoughts of beautiful architecture rather than bloodthirsty outrages. Again, such shades of meaning may be lost in passing through the filter of an artificial language.

All these criticisms of artificial languages have validity, yet the supporters of constructed languages reply to these theoretical harpings with the assertion that in practice such languages do work, and work well. Writing in 1930, Macaulay followed his critique of artificial languages by predicting the imminent disappearance of Esperanto. More than 50 years later his prediction has still not been realised.

THE SELECTION OF AN INTERNATIONAL AUXILIARY LANGUAGE

There can be little doubt that the foreign-language barrier, the barrier which prevents the exchange of information across linguistic frontiers, is a considerable problem in many fields of human endeavour. Scientific research, for example, is an international activity which ideally should accept no boundaries: political, economic or linguistic. The product of research — information — should be carried to those who can best use it regardless of whether this means to the laboratory down the corridor or on the far side of the globe. Yet up to 50 or so languages are currently used for scientific communication (some much more heavily than others, of course), far more than even the most linguistically gifted scientist can be expected to know.[19] Much of the information generated will inevitably be second rate, and the genuine nuggets may be mined in some scientifically rich countries more than others, but as Holmstrom has argued:

there is absolutely no justification for assuming *a priori* that the potentially most useful item of information to assist any given scientist in meeting any given purpose at any given moment is more likely to have been published in one language than in any other. The best item is no more likely to exist in the fraction of the world's literature which he happens to be able to read for himself than in the perhaps equal or larger fraction which, so far as he is concerned, is running to waste because it has not been translated and he cannot read it in the original.[20]

Translations can and do help to reduce the dimensions of this foreign-language barrier, but the introduction of an effective international auxiliary language in which scientists, along with everyone else, could publish their research findings and present papers at international conferences, would offer a much more comprehensive solution to the problem, if only such an international auxiliary language could be selected and implemented.

The literature on artificial languages abounds with polemics on the relative linguistic merits of one or another language. Debates are conducted with the intensity and often the ferocity of a tribal vendetta where the slightest compromise would be treachery. Points of syntax, phonetics or even orthography are disputed interminably, as if the success or failure of an artificial language depended solely upon its linguistic characteristics. Much less attention seems to have been devoted to the ways in which an international language might actually be adopted, yet there is scant evidence to suggest that the world still lacks an international auxiliary language because of any linguistic shortcomings in the contenders for this title.

An international auxiliary language might be adopted by one of two courses. It could be chosen by the leaders of the international community or their representatives *de jure* to serve from that day hence as the medium of communication in some or all spheres. One writer who has paid some attention to the problems of implementation, Mario Pei, concluded that a solution to the language problem must be found in the adoption of a language, any language, by international agreement in all countries at the same time. This language would become compulsory after a five-year period of teacher training, first in all primary schools and later also in secondary schools, so that it might be learnt 'easily, naturally and painlessly by the oncoming generations'. He emphasised that the international language of the future is for the future, not for the present generation. It therefore does not have to be made especially easy or logical; it only has to be taught at an age when children are receptive to language learning (whether such an age exists and if so what age, is itself a controversial topic). On the thorny issue of selection, he proposed that a commission of international linguists, possibly constituted proportionately to the number of literates in each state, should be established to select the most popular language from existing natural and artificial contenders by a series of run-off elections. Pei asserted that 'at the present moment, the chances of success of an international language are excellent, since at no time in history have people been more aware of its need and possible benefits.'[21]

It is difficult to decide whether Pei was serious when expressing these views. The most superficial familiarity with international relations would reveal beyond any doubt that the apparently logical answer to people's needs is often the most difficult to achieve. Presumably a good many people are more than ever aware of the need for, and the likely benefits from, universal nuclear disarmament, yet this goal still remains elusive. Is it really probable that every state, or even a majority of states, will be capable of accepting the decision of an international committee, however constituted, on the choice of an international auxiliary language? Is it even likely that such a committee could reach a decision? The committee of international experts elected by the Delegation for the Adoption of an International Auxiliary Language at the beginning of this century did, admittedly, reach such a decision eventually, only to find that the leadership of the language chosen, Esperanto, refused to accept the committee's prerequisite modifications. Instead of the introduction of an international auxiliary language, then, the committee only succeeded in provoking a schism in the strongest of the artificial language movements whose effects are still to be felt. In a world divided into scores of states and even more languages, a world in which nationalism is a rallying point, and political, economic and ideological conflict is more evident than harmonious cooperation, the prospects for agreement on an international language do not seem good.

There is another possibility, however; an international auxiliary language for limited purposes, let us say scientific communication, might emerge from amongst its rivals simply because people choose to use it in order to reach as wide an international audience as possible. Such *de facto* recognition of a language to act as a medium of international communication does seem a possibility in one case, but it is a natural rather than an artificial language: English.

Natural languages have evolved to meet the needs of human communication over many thousands of years, stretching back into the unexplored depths of prehistory, and it is not surprising that supporters of an international auxiliary language have looked to a natural language as the answer to their problems. Why try to create an artificial language when there are so many existing languages from which to choose? Languages have developed to facilitate the kind of communication that is required by the people using them, and have become closely linked with particular groups of people, often organised into stable societies, and more recently political entities: states. It is this close relationship between a language and its speakers which makes the selection of just one language to serve all so very difficult. Almost every language at present spoken in the world could probably be supported by one argument or another as a contender for the role of international auxiliary language. Some would argue that the language should be selected from those which already play a dominant role in the world. But how is this dominance to be measured: by number of speakers, number of literates, geographical diffusion, cultural or scientific importance? These are only some of the criteria which could be considered and not all of them can be quantified with any precision. It may be argued that the greater the number of people already able to read or speak a language, the easier it will be to achieve universal proficiency; but, on the other hand, linguistic hegemony may precede political hegemony. The selection of a language spoken in one of the more powerful states is unlikely to prove popular with its great power rivals. Such reasoning has led to the suggestion that a language spoken only by the citizens of a small and politically-insignificant state, or better still a language used only by a regional minority within a state, should be chosen. In contrast to such practical or political criteria, others have argued the case for an international language purely on linguistic grounds, seeking that language whose grammar, vocabulary, spelling and pronunciation make it easy to learn and sufficiently flexible to fulfil its role.

If English is considered first, this is not so much a matter of chauvinism (although there is no shortage of that in international language debates) as of recognition that a forceful case has been presented in its favour, mainly, but not exclusively, by its native speakers. The linguistic case for English is largely based upon its supposed relative simplicity compared with many other languages. It is argued that over the centuries many grammatical complexities have been discarded and its vocabulary, although large, combines the roots of Latin, German and French. In this sense it is more international (or more accurately European) than most of its leading contenders. George Steiner has asserted that:

There is ample evidence that English is regarded by native speakers of other languages whether in Asia, Africa or Latin America, as easier to acquire than any other second language. It is widely felt that some degree of competence can be achieved through mastery of fewer and simpler phonetic, lexical, and grammatical units than would be the case in North Chinese, Russian, Spanish, German or French (the natural rivals to world status).[22]

Ease of acquisition is undoubtedly an important characteristic for any competitor intending to be adopted as international auxiliary language, but it is by no means certain that English (or any other natural language) can claim such a quality. Word inflections may have disappeared, but problems such as word order and richness of vocabulary remain, and even the staunchest Anglophiles would probably not deny the quagmires of spelling and pronunciation which await the learner. Furthermore, ease of acquisition of any second language depends to a considerable extent upon the student's native language; English is likely to pose fewer problems for the German than the Hungarian, just as French is more readily assimilated by the English-speaker than the Japanese.

The linguistic case for selecting English as the international language is usually buttressed by more hard-headed considerations. Chinese alone has more native speakers than English but it is both far less standardised and geographically more concentrated. Approximately 250 million people around the world use English as their mother tongue and perhaps as many as 700 million have some working knowledge of the language. In 1975, English was the sole designated official language of 21 countries and the co-official language of 16 more. English is the foremost foreign language studied in school in a wide range of countries, and according to one estimate, 76 per cent of secondary school students in the non-English

speaking world, excluding China, are now studying it.[23] Furthermore, it is
the international language of aviation, the leading medium for international
broadcasting and it is estimated that it is used for 70 per cent of
international mail. In the scientific sphere, again, English is the most
important language of communication and, in most disciplines, upwards
of 50 per cent of the literature is published in this language. A Japanese
economist has recently written that:

Like it or not, even the most convinced ultra-nationalist, intent upon making
Japan a beacon for world culture, cannot ignore the economic need for the
general vehicle of verbal exchange that happens to be the English language,
unless he wishes to see Japan close its frontiers again and try to feed one
hundred million people under miserable conditions of autarky.[24]

In the light of this substantial evidence, it is pertinent to consider
whether English is fast becoming *de facto* an international auxiliary
language for broad areas of activity. In terms of its widespread use
throughout the world by non-native speakers as well as native speakers,
there is little doubt that at present English is closer to achieving this
status than any of its rivals. It has even been suggested that it is now
appropriate to call it EIAL (English as an International Auxiliary Language)
as it *is* already a world language.[25] In fact, it would seem more accurate to
categorise it as front-runner than victor. Certainly its growth has been
most impressive, and this can be explained more by British and later
American economic, political and cultural influence than by any supposed
linguistic qualities. Surely Steiner is right when he says that, 'In ways too
intricate, too diverse for socio-linguistics to formulate precisely, English
and American-English seem to embody for men and women throughout
the world — and particularly for the young — the "feel" of hope, of
material advance, of scientific and empirical procedures.'[26]

   The very success of English in the wake of British and American power,
however, threatens to provoke a backlash which could jeopardise its
dominant position. The relationship between language and nationalism,
surely one of the most potent forces in the contemporary world, is too well
known to require elaboration, and national sensitivity is already being
irritated in countries such as France by the role of the English language.
Any increase in English penetration may further exacerbate this condition.
It is significant that a Soviet author writing on the subject of an

international auxiliary language for science has outlined the following objections to any proposal to employ a natural language in this role. First, he argues that the country whose language is used would be in a privileged position because its scientists need not spend time in studying a foreign language but can devote more time to science: 'Hundreds of millions of hours of working time will be economised and this country will take the lead in the development of science.' Second, that country would gain great opportunities for economic and ideological expansion because scientific works would be followed by technical specifications, catalogues, advertisements and mass communication media which would give it an advantage in political relations. Although he does not name any language it is unlikely that English was far from his thoughts, and he concluded pointedly that 'it is amply clear that other countries will never agree to give a particular country such advantages.'[27]

It is easy to exaggerate the extent to which English already acts as an international language. Admittedly, highly visible 'jet-setting' travellers in the political, commercial, sporting and entertainment arenas may increasingly employ a kind of English in international gatherings. Yet it is equally hard to avoid the impression that whether writing or speaking the language, they are often at a grave disadvantage compared with the native user. But in any case, such people in fact represent a tiny minority of the world's population. As Matsumura has pointed out in the case of Japanese scientists, the number who can deliver papers in English at international meetings or publish in English is deceptive; they still comprise 'only a minor portion of the Japanese population'.[28] Resentment of English dominance may itself provoke a backlash. Michael McWhite, the delegate of Eire to the League of Nations, always used French in his Geneva speeches, allegedly explaining this by saying: 'I can't speak my own language, and I'll be damned if I'll speak English.'[29] Such an attitude would not seem out of place in the European Parliament today. On the other hand, it must be admitted that the French themselves, for so long at the forefront of the battle against English hegemony, now seem to be faltering, precisely because a refusal to use English is isolating them from international developments. A recent survey revealed that about two-thirds of the papers published by French scientists were in a language other than their own, and in practically all cases, that other language was English.[30]

English is not the only major world language to be proposed as an international auxiliary language; French, German, Spanish and Russian, amongst others, each have their supporters. In every case, however, they suffer from the same main disadvantage as English: they are linked to one or more states and can therefore be perceived as the vehicle of political, economic and cultural expansionism. At the same time, these languages lack the most important asset of English: its dominant role in contemporary international communication. French has a long and honourable history of international usage, especially in the realm of diplomacy where it reigned supreme from the end of the seventeenth century until after the First World War, when English was accepted as an equal language in the peace negotiations and later in the newly formed League of Nations. Its influence now, however, is considerably reduced. Russian is widely used as an international language in Eastern Europe and is said to be taught in the schools of 34 countries and the universities of over 60 countries. Yet its geographical confinement as well as its perceived linguistic difficulties (at least as far as many English speakers are concerned) and ideological associations reduce its prospects of either expanding its influence 'organically' or gaining support in any international gathering to select an international auxiliary language. From time to time Spanish is suggested as an international language, but support is usually confined to the Iberian peninsula or South America, although Spanish certainly has geographical and linguistic credentials as well as being an official language of the United Nations and its specialised agencies. Italian and German are handicapped by their identification with specific European states and the relatively small number of speakers, while Hindi is too localised and quite unintelligible to outsiders, Arabic probably too closely linked with Mohammedism and Chinese too daunting for serious consideration.

When contemplating the selection of a natural language to act as an international auxiliary language it is tempting to turn to one of the great languages, but the more minor tongues, in terms of political and demographic influence, could certainly avoid some of the more awkward associations discussed above. The selection of Basque or Breton, for example, should provoke little international suspicion, but their major advantage is also their major weakness. It seems improbable that every person in the world except those born in northern Spain, let us say, would be willing to learn a new language of considerable difficulty even for the sake of improved international communication. From time to time one of the classical languages is suggested as an international auxiliary language:

neither Greek nor Latin is connected to any particular state. In the late nineteenth century a French Hellenist, Gustave d'Eichthal, suggested classical Greek and his idea was adopted by a group of German scholars, but the complexity of the language and its decline as a language of study even in Europe makes it an unlikely choice. Latin seems to have a better chance and in the scientific field, at any rate, its influence on terminology has been very marked. As long ago as 1922, however, a report adopted by the League of Nations Assembly summed up the shortcomings of Latin as a possible international language: 'Latin has at least the advantage of being a neutral language from a political if not from a religious point of view, but it is difficult to learn, and is, therefore, not very accessible to the masses; its vocabulary, too, has long ceased to meet the needs of modern life.'[31] The revival of Hebrew as the official language of Israel shows that a moribund language can be resuscitated (Wood in fact draws a number of interesting parallels between the restoration of modern Hebrew as a spoken language and the development of Esperanto[32]). Yet Latin, for all its political neutrality, is hardly linguistically international and may well appeal less to the Japanese or even British citizen than to the Italian or Rumanian.

THE FUTURE

The total number of people who have ever spoken any artificial language during the last 500 years is only the merest fraction of the English-speakers distributed around the world today. What chance does any constructed language really have of being chosen to act as an international auxiliary language, an objective which still must seem as remote now as in Shakespeare's days? In general terms, of course, many people will express support for the concept of a universal language. Opinion polls on this subject have been conducted from time to time in various countries, often with very encouraging results for those committed to the artificial language movement. When confronted with a question such as 'Do you believe a universal or common language which all countries could understand is practical and should be encouraged?', a majority may well answer affirmatively. In response to this very question in a poll conducted in Minnesota, for example, 74 per cent answered 'yes'. It is more doubtful, of course, to conclude (as do Connor et al.) that 'such figures prove that the

American people — just like people elsewhere in the world — have become language-conscious and that the time is ripe for decisive action in favour of Esperanto as a means of communication and understanding.'[33] Alas, the gap between vague sympathy and determined action seems yawning, as any statistics on active support for specific artificial languages quickly reveal.

Alexander Gode believed that 'An international language can subsist only as the speech instrument of an expansive supranational dynamism of which it is both vanguard and adequate expression.' He thought it unlikely that an artificial language could ever fulfil these requirements. Further, he argued that the only supranational dynamism at work today is a product of scientific activity. The language of science alone is truly an international language, and this language is conceptually Western European (which is why Gode thought that his Interlingua, not an artificial language as such in his opinion, based upon 'Standard Average European' was the only international language which could prove workable).[34]

Languages have been spread by political and military power (Latin throughout the Roman Empire, Spanish and Portuguese in Central and South America, Russian in Eastern Europe), by economic activity (English throughout the world in the present and previous centuries), by religion (Arabic in the Middle East and North Africa), by the arts and sciences (Latin, Greek, English and many more) and more recently, by tourism (especially English). Such powerful vehicles of dissemination are not available to any artificial language. It begins with the initial disadvantage that it is *artificial:* it is not the first language of any group of people (other than those few who may have learnt it in the cradle from enthusiastic parents). It cannot therefore build upon a homogeneous body of speakers; rather its speech community is scattered throughout the world. Second, there are no political, economic or cultural pressures emanating from one or more states to learn the language. As Forster has argued, using Esperanto as an example, 'the fact which is crucial to the sociological understanding of Esperanto is that the speech-community of the language is a social movement.'[35] An artificial language depends for its promotion on a social group for whom it is only an occasional language, largely used for the activities of the group. Proselytising therefore becomes very difficult as most effort is expended 'converting the converted'. The task of winning large-scale support around the world is formidable. Even a language such as Esperanto, which has achieved some modest success, has failed to attract people who are primarily looking for an international language to use. According to Forster's study, the members of the Esperanto movement, in Britain at any rate, are 'still more interested in the utopian communitarian aspects . . . of earlier times and the Gemeinschaft social relations of the movement' than acting as a pressure group for the widespread adoption of the language.[36] Many of their activities centre upon the group at local, national or international level, as in any other kind of social movement.

The difficulties in attracting a mass following for Esperanto have not eluded Esperantists. Bernard Cavanagh, then President of the BEA, admitted that although 'the spontaneous dissemination of Esperanto on its own merits has been continuous', it is 'too slow to establish a functioning universal second language within a useful time'. In his opinion, 'success, therefore, can only come by the joint action of several governments in introducing Esperanto into their schools, thus giving a common second language to their younger people in one generation.'[37] This view was expressed even more forcibly in the first issue of the Association's *Newsletter:* 'until children have had it in the schools for a generation Esperanto *cannot* be a universal language.'[38] It is interesting to note, however, that this view was not shared by Zamenhof himself. As he expressed it at the Sixth International Esperanto Congress in 1910:

The end for which we are working can be attained in two ways — either by the work of private individuals, that is, by the masses of the people, or by decree of the Governments. Our purpose is most likely to be attained by the first method; for to a cause like ours the governments generally come with their sanction and help only when everything is already quite prepared.[39]

There is little sign of any real international willingness to adopt an artificial language, despite some collaboration between the UEA and Unesco. Indeed, international organisations like the United Nations and the European Communities have chosen a very different path. Even before the entry of Greece into the European Communities, it was estimated that a third of all the staff employed by the Commission and over half the Parliament's staff were attributable to its multilingual policy. Almost 50 per cent of the administrative expenditure incurred by Communities' institutions are related to language costs. A visit of a European Parliamentary delegation to Columbia in 1980 created a furore:

of the 90 administrative staff taken to support just 39 MEPs, 47 were interpreters, 12 translating staff and four technicians for the interpreting equipment.[40] The effect of the introduction of Greek, and probably Spanish and Portuguese before long, can only be imagined. Yet there are few signs of any linguistic rationalisation, and even less of an artificial language being adopted as the official language of the Communities.

Experience suggests that a commission of linguists may well be the worst group to choose an international auxiliary language, for linguists are the very people most likely to stumble over the linguistic subtleties of individual competitors, losing track of the final goal. Ultimately, the success of any artificial language must surely be determined by the willingness of people to devote time (no matter how little is required) to its acquisition. For some, language exerts a powerful fascination, but for most of us a second language is something learnt slowly and painfully either under the compulsion of a school curriculum or through necessity in order to communicate with those of a different language group. I.A. Richards summed up the dilemma (admittedly as part of an argument against an artificial language but in favour of a modified natural language):

The root criticism of any revived or artificial language, however well designed, is that the immediate incentive which would make enough people learn and use one is lacking . . . We may all wish that everyone would learn such a language. But these wishes, however strong they might be, will never be strong enough to make enough people put enough time into learning an artificial language as a speculative investment. If you are going to the trouble of learning a language you need to feel that you will get a return for your toil this very year. A man may plant an orchard and wait six years for his apples; but six months is long enough to wait for verbs and prepositions to bear fruit. You do not want access merely to a limited and artificial literature, or to a few other speakers and correspondents. You want a vast and undelayed expansion of your contacts. The feeling that you are contributing in your small way to an idealistic but doubtful future is an inadequate motive. It is sad, but it is so. The realisation that the speakers of any artificial language are unlikely to increase as rapidly as the inhabitants, say, of Madagascar is a fatal damper.[41]

The widespread suspicion that those active in the artificial language movement are eccentrics, a source of ridicule and amusement, certainly of amazement, rather than figures to be emulated, does not help. As one jaundiced observer commented of artificial languages: 'such a language can serve only language cranks and language maniacs who want to speak merely for the sake of speaking, quite regardless of what or with whom they are speaking.'[42] Furthermore, although an international auxiliary language may offer a better solution to the problems of the foreign-language barrier than, say, the cheaper and faster production and distribution of translations, these other approaches are already working and are seen to be more practical and realisable. As a leading Esperantist conceded, 'Every Esperanto propagandist knows by experience that outsiders hardly ever reject Esperanto for its linguistic defects, but mostly because it is of little use due to small numbers of users, and less often for its alleged cultural inferiority to the natural languages.'[43] The continued construction of linguistically more perfect (whatever this might mean) schemes is unlikely to impress the large numbers of 'non-believers' who must be reached somehow if any artificial language is to succeed. Zamenhof's first publication of his language scheme in 1887 contained detachable 'promise forms' with the words: 'I, the undersigned, promise to learn the international language proposed by Dr Esperanto, if it appears that ten million people have publicly given the same promise.' How to get that promise *and* believe it was always the catch; without it the ideal will not become reality.

APPENDIX I

The Sixteen Rules of Esperanto Grammar

(A) THE ALPHABET

Aa, a as in 'last'
Bb, b as in 'be'
Cc, ts as in 'wits'
Ĉĉ, ch as in 'church'
Dd, d as in 'do'
Ee, a as in 'make'
Ff, f as in 'fly'
Gg, g as in 'gun'
Ĝĝ, j as in 'join'
Hh, h as in 'half'
Ĥĥ, strongly aspirated h, 'ch' in 'loch' (Scotch)
Ii, i as in 'marine'
Jj, y as in 'yoke'
Ĵĵ, z as in 'azure'
Kk, k as in 'key'
Ll, l as in 'line'
Mm, m as in 'make'
Nn, n as in 'now'
Oo, o as in 'not'
Pp, p as in 'pair'
Rr, r as in 'rare'
Ss, s as in 'see'
Ŝŝ, sh as in 'show'
Tt, t as in 'tea'
Uu, u as in 'bull'
Ŭŭ, u as in 'mount' (used in diphthongs)
Vv, v as in 'very'
Zz, z as in 'zeal'

Remark: If it be found impracticable to print works with the diacritical signs (ˆ , ˇ), the letter *h* may be substituted for the sign (ˆ), and the sign (ˇ), may be altogether omitted.

(B) PARTS OF SPEECH

1 There is no indefinite, and only one definite, article, *la* for all genders, numbers, and cases.

These rules are taken from *Fundamento de Esperanto*, pp. 57–61. Marmande: Esperantaj Francaj Eldonoj, 1905. Translated and reprinted in Peter G. Forster, *The Esperanto movement*. The Hague: Mouton, 1982, pp. 375–8.

2   Substantives are formed by adding *o* to the root. For the plural, the letter *j* must be added to the singular. There are two cases: the nominative and the objective (accusative). The root with the added *o* is the nominative, the objective adds an *n* after the *o*. Other cases are formed by prepositions; thus, the possessive (genitive) by *de*, 'of'; the dative by *al*, 'to'; the instrumental (ablative) by *kun*, 'with'; or other prepositions as the sense demands. E.g. root *patr*, 'father'; *la patr'o*, 'the father'; *la patr'o'n*, 'the father' (objective); *de la patr'o*, 'of the father'; *al la patr'o*, 'to the father'; *kun la patr'o*, 'with the father'; *la patr'o'j*, 'the fathers'; *la patr'o'j'n*, 'the fathers' (obj); *por la patr'o'j*, 'for the fathers'.

3   Adjectives are formed by adding *a* to the root. The numbers and cases are the same as in substantives. The comparative degree is formed by prefixing *pli* (more); the superlative by *plej* (most). The word 'than' is rendered by *ol*, e.g. *pli blank'a ol neĝ'o*, 'whiter than snow'.

4   The cardinal numerals do not change their forms for the different cases. They are:

unu (1), *du* (2), *tri* (3), *kvar* (4), *kvin* (5), *ses* (6), *sep* (7), *ok* (8), *naŭ* (9) *dek* (10), *cent* (100), *mil* (1,000).

The tens and hundreds are formed by simple junction of the numerals, e.g. 583 = *kvin'cent ok'dek tri*.

Ordinals are formed by adding the adjectival *a* to the cardinals, e.g. *unu'a*, 'first'; *du'a*, 'second', etc.

Multiplicatives (as 'threefold', 'fourfold', etc.) add *obl*, e.g. *tri'obl'a*, 'threefold'.

Fractionals add *on*, as *du'on'o*, 'a half'; *kvar'on'o*, 'a quarter'. Collective numerals add *op*, as *kvar'op'e*, 'four together'.

Distributive prefix *po*, e.g., *po kvin*, 'five apiece'.

Adverbials take *e*, e.g., *unu'e*, 'firstly', etc.

5   The personal pronouns are: *mi*, 'I'; *vi*, 'thou', 'you'; *li*, 'he'; *ŝi*, 'she'; *ĝi*, 'it'; *si*, 'self'; *ni*, 'we'; *ili*, 'they'; *oni*, 'one', 'people', (French 'on').

Possessive pronouns are formed by suffixing to the required personal, the adjectival termination. The declension of the pronouns is identical with that of substantives. E.g. *mi*, 'I'; *mi'n*, 'me' (obj.); *mi'a*, 'my', 'mine'.

6   The verb does not change its form for numbers or persons, e.g. *mi far'as*, 'I do'; *la patr'o far'as*, 'the father does'; *ili far'as*, 'they do'.

Forms of the verb

(a) The present tense ends in *as*, e.g. *mi far'as*, 'I do'.

(b) The past tense ends in *is*, e.g. *li far'is*, 'he did'.

(c) The future tense ends in *os*, e.g. *ili far'os*; 'they will do'.

(c) The subjunctive mood ends in *us* e.g. *ŝi far'us*, 'she may do'.

(d) The imperative mood ends in *u*, e.g. *ni far'u* 'let us do'.

(e) The infinitive mood ends in *i*, e.g. *fari*, 'to do'.

There are two forms of the participle in the international language, the changeable or adjectival, and the unchangeable or adverbial.

(f) The present participle active ends in *ant*, e.g. *far'ant'a*, 'he who is doing'; *far'ant'e*, 'doing'.

(g) The past participle active ends in *int*, e.g. *far'int'a*, 'he who has done'; *far'int'e*, 'having done'.

(g) The future participle active ends in *ont*, e.g. *far'ont'a*, 'he who will do'; *far'ont'e*, 'about to do'.

(h) The present participle passive ends in *at*, e.g. *far'at'e*, 'being done'.

(h) The past participle passive ends in *it*, e.g. *far'it'a*, 'that which has been done'; *far'it'e*, 'having been done'.

(i) The future participle passive ends in *ot*, e.g. *far'ot'a*, 'that which will be done'; *far'ot'e*, 'about to be done'.

All forms of the passive are rendered by the respective forms of the verb *est* (to be) and the participle passive of the required verb; the preposition used is *de*, 'by'. E.g. *ŝi est'as am'at'a de ĉiu'j*, 'she is loved by every one'.

7   Adverbs are formed by adding *e* to the root. The degrees of comparison are the same as in adjectives, e.g., *mi'a frat'o kant'as pli bon'e ol mi,* 'my brother sings better than I'.

8   All prepositions govern the nominative case.

(C) GENERAL RULES

9   Every word is to be read exactly as written, there are no silent letters.

10   The accent falls on the last syllable but one (penultimate).

11   Compound words are formed by the simple junction of roots (the principal word standing last), which are written as a single word, but, in elementary works, separated by a small line ('). Grammatical terminations are considered as independent words. E.g. *vapor'ŝip'o*, 'steamboat' is composed of the roots *vapor*, 'steam', and *ŝip*, 'a boat', with the substantival termination *o*.

12   If there is one negative in a clause, a second is not admissible.

13   In phrases answering the question 'where?' (meaning direction), the words take the termination of the objective case; e.g. *kie'n vi ir'as*? 'where are you going?'; *dom'o'n,* 'home'; *London'o'n,* 'to London', etc.

14   Every preposition in the international language has a definite fixed meaning. If it be necessary to employ some preposition, and it is not quite evident from the sense which it should be, the word *je* is used,

which has no definite meaning; for example, *ĝoj'i je tio*, 'to rejoice *over* it'; *rid'i je tio*, 'to laugh *at* it'; *enu'o je la patr'uj'o*, 'a longing *for* one's fatherland'. In every language different prepositions, sanctioned by usage, are employed in these dubious cases, in the international language, one word, *je* suffices for all. Instead of *je*, the objective without a preposition may be used, when no confusion is to be feared.

15 The so-called 'foreign' words, i.e. words which the greater number of languages have derived from the same source, undergo no change in the international language, beyond conforming to its system of orthography. — Such is the rule with regard to primary words, derivatives are better formed (from the primary word) according to the rules of the international grammar, e.g. *teatr'o*, 'theatre', but *teatr'a*, 'theatrical' (not *teatrical'a*), etc.

16 The *a* of the article, and final *o* of substantives, may be sometimes dropped euphoniae gratia, e.g. *de l'mond'o* for *de la mond'o*; *Siller'* for *Siller'o*; in such cases an apostrophe should be substituted for the discarded vowel.

APPENDIX II

Comparative Texts in English, Esperanto, Ido, Novial, Occidental and Latino sine Flexione

1. ENGLISH

The idea of a world literature, which Herder and Goethe conceived essentially from the point of view of art, has now gained even greater importance from the point of view of science. For, of the things that mankind possesses in common, nothing is so truly universal and international as science. Now all communication and propagation of science uses the means supplied by language, and so the internationality of science irresistibly demands the internationality of language. If we consider that today numerous scientific works, particularly textbooks, are translated into twelve or more foreign languages, then we understand what an immense quantity of labour could be saved, if everywhere on the globe books could be as generally understood as, for example, musical notes or tables of logarithms.

2. ESPERANTO

La ideo pri mondliteraturo, kiun Herder kay Goethe konceptis chefe el la vidpunkto de la arto, akiris nun el la vidpunkto de la scienco multe pli gravan signifon. Char el la komunaj posedajhoj de la homaro, neniu estas tiel vere ghenerala kaj internacia kiel la scienco. Sed chiu komunikado kaj disvastigado de la scienco uzas la helpilon de la lingvo kaj tial la internacieco de la scienco nerezisteble postulas la internaciecon de la lingvo. Se ni konsideras, ke nuntempe kelkaj sciencaj verkoj, precipe lernolibroj, estas tradukitaj en dek du au pli da fremdaj lingvoj, tiam ni komprenas, kiom granda kvanto da laboro povus esti shparata, se libroj chie en la mondo povus esti tiel ghenerale komprenataj kiel ekzemple la muziknotoj au logaritmaj tabeloj.

As accents were unobtainable, the accented letter is followed by an ' h ' in this text.

From H. Jacob, *Otto Jespersen: his work for an international auxiliary language.*
Loughton: International Language (Ido) Society of Great Britain, 1943, pp. 30—1.

3. IDO

La ideo pri mondo-literaturo, quan Herder e Goethe konceptabis esence del vidpunto dil arto, ganis nun del vidpunto dil cienco mem plu granda importo. Nam del kozi, quin la homaro posedas komune, nula es tam vere universala ed internaciona kam la cienco. Or, omna komunikado e propagado dil cienco uzas la moyeno dil linguo, do la internacioneso dil cienco postulas nerezisteble la internacioneso dil Jinguo. Se ni konsideras, ke cadie sat multa ciencala verki, specale lernolibri, tradukesas aden dekedu o plu multa stranjera lingui, ni komprenas, qua enorma quanto de laboro povus sparesar, se libri omnaloke sur la terglobo povus komprenesar tam generale, kam exemple muzikal noti o logaritmala tabeli.

5. OCCIDENTAL

Li idé pri mund-literature, quel Herder e Goethe hat conceptet essentialmen ex li vidpunctu del arte, ha nu gan'at ancor mult plu grand importantie ex li vidpunctu del scientie. Nam de omni comun possedages del homanité niun es tam vermen general e international, quam scientie. Ma omni comunication e transmediation del scientie usa li medie del lingue. Do li internationalità del scientie inresistibilmen postula li internationalità del lingue. Si noi considera, que hodie pluri sciential ovres, specialmen libres de aprension, trova se traductet in decidu o plu foren lingues, tande noi comprende quel immens quantità de labor on vell economisar, si on vell posser comprender libres partú sur li glob sam generalmen quam por exemples notes o tabelles de logaritmes.

4. NOVIAL

Li idee pri mondo-literature, kel Herder e Goethe koncepted esentialim fro li vidpunctu del arte, ha nun ganat mem multim plu grand importanteso fro li vidpunctu del scientie. Den ek li còses kel li homaro posese comunim, nuli is tam verim general e international kam li scientie. Or omni comunico e mediatione del scientie usa li moyene del lingue, dunke li internationaleso del scientie demanda nonresistablim li internationaleso del lingue. Si nus considera ke disdi pluri sciential verkes, particularim lernolibres, es traductet en dekdu e plu multi lingues, tand nus comprenda qui imensi quanteso de laboro povud bli sparat, si libres povud omnilok sur li globe bli comprendat tam generalim kam exemplim musical notes o tabeles de logaritmes.

6. LATINO SINE FLEXIONE (INTERLINGUA)

Idea de literatura mundiale, que Herder et Goethe habe intellecto præcipue ex puncto de visu de arte, habe hodie acquisito, ex puncto de visu de scientia, sensu etiam majore. Nam, de commune possesiones de genere humano, nihil es tam generale et internationale quam scientia. Sed omne communicatione et propagatione de scientia ute auxilio de lingua, et ita internationalitate de scientia postula in modo irresistibile internationalitate de lingua. Si nos considera, que hodie plure opere scientifico, in particulare tractatus, es translato in duodecim vel plus lingua extero, tunc nos cognosce quale immane mole de labore pote es præservato, si libros, ubicumque in terra, pote es æqualiter intellecto in generale, sicut per exemplo notas musicale aut tabulas de logarithmos.

Notes

INTRODUCTION

1 Julius Balbin, Is Esperanto an artificial language?, *Geolinguistics* 8 (1982), 11; see also David L. Gold, What kind of language is Esperanto?, *Language problems and language planning* 6 (1982), 340—1.
2 Leszek Kolakowski, *Main currents of Marxism: its rise, growth and dissolution*, vol. 1. Oxford: Clarendon Press, 1978, p. v.

CHAPTER 1 ORIGINS

1 Susanne K. Langer, *Philosophy in a new key: a study in the symbolism of reason, rite and art.* Cambridge, Mass.: Harvard University Press, 1967, p. 103.
2 Mario Pei, *One language for the world.* New York: Devin-Adair, 1958, p. 142.
3 M. D. Barry, St. Hildegarde, *New Catholic encyclopedia,* vol. 6. New York: McGraw-Hill, 1967, p. 1117.
4 J. P. Cooper (ed.), *The new Cambridge modern history,* vol. 4. Cambridge: Cambridge University Press, 1970, p. 143.
5 Paolo Rossi, *Francis Bacon: from magic to science.* London: Routledge & Kegan Paul, 1968, pp. xii—xiii.
6 Vivian Salmon, Language-planning in seventeenth-century England: its context and aims. In Vivian Salmon, *The study of language in 17th-century England.* Amsterdam: Benjamins, 1979, p. 153.
7 In James R. Knowlson, *Universal language schemes in England and France 1600—1800.* Toronto: University of Toronto Press, 1975, pp. 40—1.
8 Marc Bloch, *Feudal society.* London: Routledge & Kegan Paul, 1961, p. 77.

9   Cave Beck, *The universal character, by which all the nations in the world may understand one anothers conceptions, reading out of one common writing their own mother tongues . . .* London: Printed by Tho. Maxey for William Weekley, 1657.

10 Juan Luis Vives, *On education.* Cambridge: Cambridge University Press, 1913, p. 93.

11 Vivian Salmon. *The works of Francis Lodwick: a study of his writings in the intellectual context of the seventeenth century.* London: Longman, 1972, pp. 59—60.

12 Knowlson, *Universal language schemes in England and France 1600—1800,* p. 31.

13 Richard Foster Jones, Science and language in England of the mid-seventeenth century. In his *The seventeenth century: studies in the history of English thought and literature from Bacon to Pope.* Stanford: Stanford University Press, 1951, pp. 147—8.

14 Richard Foster Jones, *Ancients and moderns: a study of the rise of the scientific movement in seventeenth-century England,* 2nd edn. Berkeley: University of California Press, 1965, p. 105.

15 Martha Ornstein, *The role of scientific societies in the seventeenth century.* Hamden: Archon, 1963, p. 45.

16 Richard Foster Jones, *The triumph of the English language: a survey of opinions concerning the vernacular from the introduction of printing to the Restoration.* London: Oxford University Press, 1953, pp. 7, 211.

17 Louis G. Kelly, *The true interpreter: a history of translation theory and practice in the West.* Oxford: Blackwell, 1979, pp. 86—7.

18 David S. Katz, The language of Adam in seventeenth-century England. In Hugh Lloyd-Jones, Valerie Pearl and Blair Worden (eds), *History and imagination.* London: Duckworth, 1981, pp. 132—45.

19 Knowlson, *Universal language schemes in England and France 1600—1800,* p. 13.

20 John Wilkins, *An essay towards a real character and a philosophical language.* London: Sa. Gellibrand and John Martin, 1668, p. 13.

21 In Jones, *Ancients and moderns,* p. 48.

22 Francis Bacon, *The philosophical works;* edited by J. M. Robertson. London: Routledge, 1905, p. 122.

23 Matthew Ricci, *China in the sixteenth century: the Journals of Matthew Ricci, 1583—1610.* New York: Random House, 1953, pp. 28—9.

24 Donald F. Lach. *China in the eyes of Europe: the sixteenth century.* Chicago: University of Chicago Press, 1968, pp. 806—8; Wilkins, *An essay towards a real character,* pp. 13, 450—2.

25 Salmon, *The works of Francis Lodwick,* pp. 145—7.

26 Frances A. Yates, *The art of memory.* London: Routledge & Kegan Paul, 1966, pp. 370—89.
27 In Charles E. Raven, *John Ray, naturalist: his life and works.* Cambridge: Cambridge University Press, 1942, p. 182.
28 Salmon, *The works of Francis Lodwick*, p. 23.
29 Wilkins, *An essay towards a real character,* [p. vi.]
30 Margaret M. Slaughter, *Universal languages and scientific taxonomy in the seventeenth century.* Cambridge: Cambridge University Press, 1982, p. vii.
31 Wilkins, *An essay towards a real character,* [p. v.]
32 George E. McCracken, Athanasius Kircher's universal polygraphy, *Isis* 39 (1948), 215—28.
33 Salmon, *The works of Francis Lodwick*, pp. 61—2.
34 Paul Cornelius, *Languages in seventeenth- and early eighteenth-century imaginary voyages.* Geneva: Librairie Droz, 1965, pp. 45—50; see also H. Neville Davies, Bishop Godwin's 'Lunatique language', *Journal of the Warburg and Courtauld Institutes* 30 (1967), 296—316; Knowlson, *Universal language schemes in England and France 1600—1800,* pp. 112—38.

CHAPTER 2   SEVENTEENTH-CENTURY LANGUAGE PROJECTS

1 Richard Boston (ed.), *The admirable Urquhart: selected writings.* London: Fraser, 1975, pp. 9—53; Kelsie B. Harder, Sir Thomas Urquhart's universal language, *Notes and queries* 201 (1956), 473—6.
2 James Knowlson, *Universal language schemes in England and France 1600—1800.* Toronto: University of Toronto Press, 1975, Appendix B.
3 For an extended discussion of his life and works see Vivian Salmon, *The works of Francis Lodwick: a study of his writings in the intellectual context of the seventeenth century.* London: Longman, 1972.
4 Francis Lodwick, *A common writing: whereby two, although not understanding one the others Language, yet by the helpe thereof, may communicate their minds one to another.* London: for the author, 1647. In Ibid., p. 167.
5 Knowlson, *Universal language schemes in England and France 1600—1800,* p. 59.
6 Francis Lodwick, The ground-work, or foundation laid, (or so intended) for the framing of a new perfect language: and an universall or common writing. London, 1652. In Salmon, *The works of Francis Lodwick*, p. 213.

7 For an extended biographical description see Vivian Salmon, Cave Beck: a seventeenth-century Ipswich schoolmaster and his 'Universal character'. In Vivian Salmon, *The study of language in 17th-century England.* Amsterdam: Benjamins, 1979, pp. 177—90.

8 Ibid., p. 188.

9 Barbara J. Shapiro, *John Wilkins 1614—1672: an intellectual biography.* Berkeley: University of California Press, 1969, p. 30.

10 R. Plot, *The natural history of Oxford-shire*, Oxford: Printed at the Theater, 1677, p. 235.

11 John Aubrey, *Aubrey's brief lives,* edited from the original by Oliver Lawson Dick. 3rd edn. London: Secker & Warburg, 1960, p. 320.

12 Shapiro, *John Wilkins 1614—1672,* pp. 35—9.

13 John Wilkins, *Mercury, or the secret and swift messenger.* 2nd. ed. London: Rich. Baldwin, 1694, p. 106.

14 Ibid., p. 145.

15 L. Couturat and L. Leau, *Histoire de la langue universelle.* Paris: Librairie Hachette, 1903, p. 13.

16 Seth Ward, *Vindiciae academiarum.* Oxford: by Leonard Lichfield for Thomas Robinson, 1654, pp. 21—5.

17 Margaret M. C. McIntosh, The phonetic and linguistic theory of the Royal Society School, from Wallis to Cooper. B.Litt. Thesis, Oxford University, 1956, p. 82.

18 M. M. Slaughter, *Universal languages and scientific taxonomy in the seventeenth century.* Cambridge: Cambridge University Press, 1982, pp. 152—3.

19 John Wallis, *A defence of the Royal Society and the Philosophical transactions in answer to the cavils of Dr. William Holder.* London: By T. S. for Thomas Moore, 1678, p. 16.

20 Salmon, *The Works of Francis Lodwick*, p. 29.

21 Vivian Salmon, 'Philosophical' grammar in John Wilkins's 'Essay'. In Vivian Salmon, *The study of languages in 17th-century England*, pp. 98—9.

22 Benjamin DeMott, Science versus mnemonics: notes on John Ray and on John Wilkins's *Essay towards a real character, and a philosophical language, Isis* 48 (1957), 4.

23 John Wilkins, *An essay towards a real character and a philosophical language.* London: Sa. Gellibrand and John Martin, 1668, [p. ii]

24 Ibid., p. 1.

25 Ibid., pp. vi, 453—4, 21.

26 Slaughter, *Universal languages and scientific taxonomy in the seventeenth century,* p. 173.

27 DeMott, *Isis* (1957), 3, 9.
28 Wilkins, *An essay towards a real character*, pp. 454, vi.
29 E. N. Da C. Andrade, The real character of Bishop Wilkins, *Annals of science* 1 (1936), 4—5.
30 A. J. Turner, Andrew Paschall's tables of plants for the universal language, *Bodleian Library record* 9 (1978), 346—50.
31 Aubrey, *Aubrey's brief lives*, p. 320.
32 Knowlson, *Universal language schemes in England and France 1600—1800*, pp. 103—7.
33 L. Couturat, *La logique de Leibniz: d'après des documents inédits.* Paris: Alcan, 1901, p. 54.
34 Couturat and Leau, *Histoire de la langue universelle*, pp. 23—8.
35 Slaughter, *Universal languages and scientific taxonomy in the seventeenth century*, pp. 189—94.
36 Shapiro, *John Wilkins 1614—1672*, p. 222.
37 Peter Mark Roget, *Roget's thesaurus of English words and phrases;* new edn. by Robert A. Dutch. London: Longman, 1962, pp. xxxv—xxxvi.
38 Shapiro, *John Wilkins 1614—1672*, pp. 221—2.
39 Salmon, Language-planning in seventeenth-century England: its context and aims. In Vivian Salmon, *The study of language in 17th-century England,* p. 130.

CHAPTER 3   THE ENLIGHTENMENT AND AFTER

1 M. S. Anderson, *Europe in the eighteenth century, 1713—1783.* Harlow: Longman, 1970, p. 364.
2 Quoted in Norman Hampson, *The Enlightment.* Harmondsworth: Penguin, 1968, p. 56.
3 Quoted in ibid., p. 53.
4 Peter Gay, *The Enlightenment: an interpretation*, vol. 2. London: Weidenfeld & Nicolson, 1970, p. 60.
5 Eric A. Blackall, *The emergence of German as a literary language, 1700—1775.* Cambridge: Cambridge University Press, 1959, p. 1.
6 James Knowlson, *Universal language schemes in England and France 1600—1800.* Toronto: University of Toronto Press, pp. 228—9.
7 Ibid., p. 141.
8 Ibid., pp. 142—9; Paul Kuehner, Theories on the origin and formation of language in the eighteenth century in France. Ph.D. Thesis, University of Philadelphia, 1944.
9 Knowlson, *Universal language schemes in England and France 1600—1800*, p. 162 (author's own translation).

10 L. Couturat and L. Leau, *Histoire de la langue universelle.* Paris: Librairie Hachette, 1903, pp. 29—32.

11 Knowlson, *Universal language schemes in England and France 1600—1800,* pp. 153—60.

12 Keith M. Baker, *Condorcet: from natural philosophy to social mathematics.* Chicago: University of Chicago Press, 1975, p. 112.

13 Quoted in H. B. Acton, The philosophy of language in Revolutionary France, *Proceedings of the British Academy* 45 (1959), 205.

14 Quoted in Baker, *Condorcet,* p. 122.

15 Magda Whitrow, An eighteenth-century faceted classification system, *Journal of documentation* 39 (1983), 88—94; Baker, *Condorcet,* p. 122.

16 Quoted in ibid., p. 127.

17 Ibid., p. 366.

18 Elémens d'idéologie. Quoted in Knowlson, *Universal language schemes in England and France 1600—1800,* p. 185 (author's own translation).

19 Ibid., p. 208.

20 Joachim Faiguet de Villeneuve, Langue nouvelle. In *Encyclopédie, ou dictionnaire raisonné des sciences, des arts et des métiers,* vol. 9. Paris: A. Neufchastel, 1765, pp. 268—71.

21 *News to the Whole World.* Quoted in Knowlson, *Universal language schemes in England and France 1600—1800,* pp. 95—6.

22 James R. Knowlson, The idea of gesture as a universal language in the XVIIth and XVIIIth centuries, *Journal of the history of ideas* 26 (1965), 495—508; Jules Paul Seigel, The Enlightenment and the evolution of a language of signs in France and England, *Journal of the history of ideas* 30 (1969), 96—115.

23 Quoted in Knowlson, *Universal language schemes in England and France 1600—1800,* pp. 217—18 (author's own translation).

24 James Burnet, *Of the origin and progress of language,* vol. 2. Edinburgh: J. Balfour, 1774, pp. 480, 441—2.

25 William Knight, *Lord Monboddo and some of his contemporaries.* London: Murray, 1900.

26 *A rhetorical grammar of the English language.* Quoted in Murray Cohen, *Sensible words: linguistic practice in England, 1640—1785.* Baltimore: Johns Hopkins University Press, 1977, pp. 123—4.

27 Quoted in ibid., p. 127.

28 Joshua A. Fishman, *Language and nationalism: two integrative essays.* Rowley, Mass.: Newbury House, 1972, p. 46.

29 Couturat and Leau, *Histoire de la langue universelle,* pp. 71—6; A. L. Guérard, *A short history of the international language movement.* London: Unwin, 1922, p. 85.

30 Couturat and Leau, *Histoire de la langue universelle*, pp. 59—70; M. Monnerot-Dumaine, *Précis d'interlinguistique générale et spéciale.* Paris: Librairie Maloine, 1960, p. 76.
31 Couturat and Leau, *Histoire de la langue universelle*, pp. 46—58; Monnerot-Dumaine, *Précis d'interlinguistique générale et spéciale*, pp. 76—7.
32 Couturat and Leau, *Histoire de la langue universelle*. pp. 33—9.
33 Ibid., p. 37.

CHAPTER 4   THE WIDENING OF APPEAL

1 Mario Pei, *One language for the world.* New York: Devin-Adair, 1958, p. 151.
2 E. D. Durrant, *The language problem: its history and solution.* Rickmansworth: Esperanto Publishing, 1943, p. 30.
3 L. Couturat and L. Leau, *Histoire de la langue universelle.* Paris: Librairie Hachette, 1903, pp. 128—62.
4 Albert L. Guérard, *A short history of the international language movement.* London: Unwin, 1922, p. 103.
5 Ibid., p. 97.
6 Charles E. Sprague, *Handbook of Volapük.* London: Trubner, 1888, p. v.
7 Couturat and Leau, *Histoire de la langue universelle*, pp. 152—63.
8 Otto Jespersen, *An international language.* London: Allen & Unwin, 1928, p. 33.
9 Guérard, *A short history of the international language movement,* p. 96.
10 Quoted in Marjorie Boulton, *Zamenhof, creator of Esperanto.* London: Routledge & Kegan Paul, 1960, pp. 6—7.
11 E. James Lieberman, Esperanto and trans-national identity: the case of Dr Zamenhof, *International journal of the sociology of language* 20 (1979), 91—2.
12 Quoted in Durrant, *The language problem*, p. 37.
13 Dr Esperanto, *An attempt towards an international language.* New York: Holt, 1889.
14 Durrant, *The language problem*, p. 51.
15 Boulton, *Zamenhof*, p. 53.
16 Dr Esperanto, *An attempt towards an international language*, pp. 21—2.
17 Boulton, *Zamenhof*, p. 60.
18 Guérard, *A short history of the international language movement,* pp. 116—17.
19 Edmond Privat, *The life of Zamenhof.* London: Allen & Unwin, 1931, p. 54.

20   Quoted in Boulton, *Zamenhof*, p. 81.
21   Quoted in Peter G. Forster, *The Esperanto movement*. The Hague: Mouton, 1982, p. 111.
22   Julius Balbin, Is Esperanto an artificial language? *Geolinguistics* 8 (1982), 22.
23   Boulton, *Zamenhof*, p. 93.
24   Durrant, *The language problem*, pp. 65—6.
25   *The British Esperantist* 1, no. 4 (April 1905), pp. 44—5.
26   Luther H. Dyer, *The problem of an international auxiliary language and its solution in Ido*. London: Pitman, 1923, p. 56.
27   Quoted in Forster, *The Esperanto movement*, p. 75.
28   Quoted in Privat, *The life of Zamenhof*, p. 73.
29   Pierre Janton, *L'Espéranto*, 2nd edn. Paris: Presses Universitaires de France, 1977, p. 39.
30   *The British Esperantist*, 2, no. 15 (March 1906), p. 22.
31   Reprinted in Louis Couturat, *A plea for an international language*. London: Henderson, 1903, pp. 31—2.
32   Couturat and Leau, *Histoire de la language universelle*, pp. 484—506.
33   Louis de Beaufront, *Complete manual of the auxiliary language Ido,* 3rd edn. London: Pitman, 1919.
34   Quoted in Boulton, *Zamenhof*, pp. 125—6.
35   Forster, *The Esperanto movement*, p. 122.
36   Ibid., pp. 129—30; Boulton, *Zamenhof*, pp. 129—31.
37   Forster, *The Esperanto movement*, pp. 130—1.
38   Louis Couturat et al., *International language and science: considerations on the introduction of an international language into science*. London: Constable, 1910, p. 23.
39   Bertrand Russell, *The autobiography of Bertrand Russell*. London: Unwin Paperbacks, 1975, pp. 135—6.
40   M. Monnerot-Dumaine, *Précis d'interlinguistique générale et spéciale*. Paris: Librairie Maloine, 1960, p. 106.
41   Quoted in Forster, *The Esperanto movement*, p. 136.
42   Max Talmey, *Ido: exhaustive text book of the International Language of the Delegation*. New York: Ido Press, 191, p. 3.
43   E. Drezen, *Osnovy yazykoznaniya: teorii i istorii mezhdunarodnogo yazyka*, vol. 3. Moscow: Ts.K. SESR, 1929, p. 4.
44   Durrant, *The language problem*, p. 82.
45   Privat, *The life of Zamenhof*, p. 21.
46   Boulton, *Zamenhof*, p. 3.
47   Durrant, *The language problem*, p. 33.
48   Louvan E. Nolting, The deficiency of Esperanto as a world language, *Federal linguist* 5 (1973), 18—22.

49 M. S. Anderson, *The ascendancy of Europe: aspects of European history, 1815—1914.* London: Longman, 1972, p. 166.

CHAPTER 5   ESPERANTO

1 Bernard Cavanagh, *Esperanto: a first foreign language for all mankind.* London: British Esperanto Association, 1971, p. 16.
2 Mario Pei, Wanted — a world language, *Public affairs pamphlets* 434 (1969), 13.
3 Peter G. Forster, *The Esperanto movement.* The Hague: Mouton, 1982, pp. 35—6.
4 Pierre Janton, *L'Espéranto*, 2nd edn. Paris: Presses Universitaires de France, 1977, p. 113.
5 Luther H. Dyer, *The problem of an international auxiliary language and its solution in Ido.* London: Pitman, 1923, p. 58.
6 Pei, *Public affairs pamphlets* (1969), 13; Cavanagh, *Esperanto*, p. 15.
7 Margaret Hagler, The Esperanto language as a literary medium: a historical discussion of Esperanto literature, 1887—1970, and a stylistic analysis of translated and original Esperanto poetry. Ph.D. Thesis, Indiana University, 1970, p. 85; see also W. A. Verloren van Themaat, Literature in a constructed language, *La monda lingvo-problemo* 4 (1972), 153—8.
8 Ivo Lapenna, *Esperanto en perspektivo: faktoj kaj analizoj pri la internacia lingvo.* London: Universala Esperanto-Asocio, 1974, p. 47.
9 Humphrey Tonkin, Equalising language, *Journal of communication* 29 (1979), 128.
10 League of Nations, *Esperanto as an International Auxiliary Language: Report of the General Secretariat of the League of Nations adopted by the Third Assembly, 1922.* Paris, 1922.
11 Forster, *The Esperanto movement*, p. 175.
12 Quoted in Centre for Research and Documentation on the Language Problem, Basic facts about the International Language (Esperanto), *La monda lingvo-problemo* 3 (1971), 173.
13 Victor Sadler and Ulrich Lins, Regardless of frontiers: a case study in linguistic persecution. In Samir K. Ghosh (ed.), *Man, language and society.* The Hague: Mouton, 1972, p. 207.
14 A. Hitler, *Mein Kampf.* Cambridge, Mass.: Riverside, 1943, p. 307.
15 Sadler and Lins, *Man, language and society*, pp. 209—10.
16 Marjorie Boulton, *Zamenhof, creator of Esperanto.* London: Routledge & Kegan Paul, 1960, pp. 213—14.

17   Forster, *The Esperanto movement*, p. 225.
18   George P. Springer, *Early Soviet theories in communication.* Cambridge, Mass.: MIT Press, 1956.
19   Lapenna, *Esperanto en perspektivo,* p. 721.
20   Alexander Barmine, *One who survived.* New York: Putnam, 1945, p. 260.
21   Lapenna, *Esperanto en perspektivo*, p. 732.
22   Alexander Solzhenitsyn, *The Gulag archipelago, 1918—1956.* Glasgow: Collins, 1974, pp. 58—9.
23   Stanley Nisbet, *Esperanto's time has come.* London: Esperanto-Asocio de Brituju, n.d., p. 10.
24   Forster, *The Esperanto movement*, p. 206.
25   M. I. Isayev, *National languages in the USSR: problems and solutions.* Moscow: Progress, 1977, pp. 399—400.
26   Richard E. Wood, A voluntary non-ethnic, non-territorial speech community. In William Francis Mackey and Jacob Ornstein, eds, *Sociolinguistic studies in language contact: methods and cases.* The Hague: Mouton, 1979, pp. 436—7.
27   *Esperanto news*, 8, no. 2 (March/April 1982).
28   *BEA Newsletter* 0, no. a (Nov. 1972), 4.
29   *Esperanto news* 1, no. 2 (March/April 1975); ibid., 8, no. 1 (Jan/Feb 1982), 3.
30   Forster, *The Esperanto movement*, p. 280.
31   Ibid., pp. 285—6.
32   Ibid., pp. 265—6.
33   Ibid., pp. 299—346.
34   Peter G. Forster, Esperanto as a social and linguistic movement, *Thought and language in operation* 2 (1971), 213.
35   *Esperanto news* 8, no. 1 (Jan/Feb 1982), p. 7.
36   Quoted in Forster, *The Esperanto movement*, pp. 233—4.
37   Quoted in ibid., p. 248.
38   John Cresswell and John Hartley, *Esperanto*, 2nd edn. London: Hodder & Stoughton, 1968.
39   Hagler, The Esperanto language as a literary medium, 54.
40   Cresswell and Hartley, *Esperanto*, p. 10.
41   Pierre Burney, *Les langues internationales.* Paris: Presses Universitaires de France, 1962, p. 89.
42   *The British Esperantist* 2, no. 8 (June 1906), p. 67.
43   Centre for Research and Documentation on the Language Problem, *La monda lingvo-problemo* 3 (1971), 165, 167.

44   Pei, *Public affairs pamphlets* (1969), 12.
45   In L. Couturat et al., *International language and science: considerations on the introduction of an international language into science.* London: Constable, 1910, pp. 38—41.
46   Burney, *Les langues internationales*, pp. 90—1.
47   Louvan E. Nolting, The deficiency of Esperanto as a world language, *Federal linguist* 5, nos 1—2 (1973), 20—2.
48   *Esperanto news* 6, no. 1 (Jan/Feb 1980), pp. 8—9.
49   Bernard Long, *Esperanto: aims and claims: a discussion of the language problem and its solution.* London: Esperanto Publishing, 1930, p. 13.
50   Humphrey Tonkin and Thomas Hoeksema, *Esperanto and literary translation.* Rotterdam: Universal Esperanto Association, 1982, pp. 8—9.
51   Richard G. Lillie, Asia and the world language, *Eco-logos* 20 (1974), 2.
52   Tonkin, *Journal of communication* 29 (1979), 128.
53   Mario Pei, *The story of language*, 2nd edn. London: Allen & Unwin, 1966, p. 421.
54   Quoted in *The British Esperantist* 6, no. 71 (Nov. 1910), 204.
55   In Couturat, *International language and science*, p. 41.
56   Stanley Rundle, *Language as a social and political factor in Europe.* London: Faber & Faber, 1946, p. 179.
57   In Richard E. Wood, Proceedings of the Symposium on the Teaching of Esperanto at United States Universities and Colleges, *La monda lingvo-problemo* 4 (1972), 168.
58   Ivo Lapenna, Reply to Mr Macmillan's report: the case for Esperanto. *La monda lingvo-problemo* 3 (1971), 157.
59   Norman Williams, A plea for Esperanto, *Head teachers' review* (Oct. 1952), 138.
60   D. Vallon, Teaching the universal language, *California Teachers Association journal* (May 1968), pp. 21—4.
61   Bruce Arne Sherwood and Chin-Chuan Cheng, A linguistics course on international communication and constructed languages, *Studies in the linguistic sciences* 10 (1980), 192.
62   See, for example, A. Fisher, Modern languages by way of Esperanto, *Modern languages* 2 (1921), 179—82.
63   C. K. Ogden, *Basic English versus the artificial languages.* London: Kegan Paul, 1935, p. 49.
64   Forster, *The Esperanto movement*, pp. 292—3.
65   Alexander Gode, The case for Interlingua, *The scientific monthly* 77 (1953), 85—6.
66   J. C. Flugel, Esperanto and the international language movement. In his

Men and their motives: psycho-analytical studies. London: Kegan Paul, Trench, Trubner, 1934, pp. 162—6, 179—82.

67 Quoted in *The British Esperantist* 6, no. 71 (Nov. 1910), 202.
68 *The Guardian*, 11 October 1984, p. 2.
69 Forster, *The Esperanto movement*, pp. 257—8.

CHAPTER 6   THE CHALLENGERS TO ESPERANTO

1   H. Jacob, *On language making: a paper read to the Philological Society, King's College, London, February 6, 1948.* London: Dobson, 1949, p. 2.
2   Quoted in Marjorie Boulton, *Zamenhof, creator of Esperanto.* London: Routledge & Kegan Paul, 1960, p. 126.
3   Peter G. Forster, *The Esperanto movement.* The Hague: Mouton, 1982, p. 133.
4   Luther H. Dyer, *The problem of an international auxiliary language and its solution in Ido.* London: Pitman, 1923, p. 58.
5   Forster, *The Esperanto movement.* p. 135.
6   M. Monnerot-Dumaine, *Précis d'interlinguistique générale et spéciale.* Paris: Librairie Maloine, 1960, p. 107.
7   Ibid., p. 105.
8   Otto Jespersen, *An international language.* London: Allen & Unwin, 1928, p. 44.
9   Dyer, *The problem of an international auxiliary language,* p. 137.
10   Monnerot-Dumaine, *Précis d'interlinguistique générale et spéciale,* p. 102.
11   Ibid., p. 108.
12   William Gilbert, *Problems of languages planned for international use.* Bloomington: Charters, 1971, p. 8.
13   F. L. Sack, *The problem of an international language.* Edinburgh: World Organisation of the Teaching Profession, 1951, p. 25.
14   H. Jacob, *A planned auxiliary language.* London: Dobson, 1947, pp. 72—3.
15   Jespersen, *An international language,* p. 89.
16   Henry Jacob, *Otto Jespersen: his work for an international auxiliary language.* Loughton: International Language (Ido) Society of Great Britain, 1943, p. 13.
17   The following discussion of Latino sine flexione draws heavily upon Hubert C. Kennedy, *Peano: life and works of Giuseppe Peano.* Dordrecht: Reidel, 1980.

18 Ibid., p. 108.
19 Ibid., p. 122.
20 Ibid., p. 120.
21 Ibid., p. 134.
22 Jespersen, *An international language*, p. 45.
23 Kennedy, *Peano*, p. 175.
24 Sack, *The problem of an international language*, p. 27.
25 Jacob, *A planned auxiliary language*, p. 144.
26 Quoted in Sack, *The problem of an international language*, p. 28.
27 Ibid., p. 27.
28 Alexander Gode and Hugh E. Blair, *Interlingua: a grammar of the international language*, 2nd edn. New York: Storm, 1951.
29 Alexander Gode, Interlingua: tool of international communication, *Journal of dental medicine* 11 (1956), 111.
30 Alexander Gode, The case for Interlingua, *The scientific monthly* 77 (1953), p. 90.
31 Gode, *Journal of dental medicine* (1956), 112.
32 Ibid., p. 115.
33 *Lingua e vita* 54 (1984), 8.
34 Gode, *Journal of dental medicine* (1956), 116.
35 See, for example, Frank Esterhill, Interlinguistics: some further comparative aspects, *Eco-logos* 22 (1976), 3—4; B. C. Sexton, Esperanto and Interlingua: interlanguages in perspective, *Eco-logos* 22 (1976), 3—6; W. A. Verloren Van Themaat, Relative merits of Esperanto and Interlingua, *Eco-logos* 21 (1975), 7—11.
36 Leslie Jones, *Eurolengo, the language for Europe: a practical manual for business and tourism.* Newcastle-upon-Tyne: Oriel Press, 1972, p. 1.
37 W. Ashby and R. Clark, *Glosa newsletter*, 1982.
38 Wendy Ashby and Ronald Clark, *Glosa 1000.* Richmond: Glosa, 1984, p. 5.
39 Lancelot Hogben, *Interglossa: a draft of an auxiliary for a democratic world order, being an attempt to apply semantic principles to language design.* Harmondsworth: Penguin, 1943, p. 7.
40 W. Ashby and R. Clark, *New internationalist* Jan. 1983, 29.
41 Ibid.
42 Mario Pei, *One language for the world.* New York: Devin-Adair, 1958, p. 121.
43 C. K. Ogden, *Basic English: a general introduction with rules and grammar,* 6th edn. London: Kegan Paul, Trench, Trubner, 1937, p. 11.
44 C. K. Ogden, *Basic for science.* London: Kegan Paul, Trench, Trubner, 1942, pp. 23, 27—8.

45 Ogden, *Basic English: a general introduction,* p. 88.

46 C. K. Ogden, *Basic English applied (science).* London: Kegan Paul, Trench, Trubner, 1931, p. 17.

47 Sack, *The problem of an international language,* pp. 12—16.

48 Ogden, *Basic English applied,* pp. 25—7.

49 Quoted in E. A. Peers, *'New' tongues or modern language teaching of the future.* London: Pitman, 1945, p. 132.

50 H. G. Wells, *The shape of things to come.* London: Hutchinson, 1933, pp. 418—19.

51 Otto Neurath, *International picture language: a facsimile reprint of the [1936] English edition.* Reading: Department of Typography and Graphic Communication, University of Reading, 1980, Editorial introduction, p. 6.

52 Ibid., p. 18.

53 Pei, *One language for the world,* pp. 145—50.

54 Monnerot-Dumaine, *Précis d'interlinguistique générale et spéciale,* p. 79.

CHAPTER 7   PROSPECTS FOR AN INTERNATIONAL LANGUAGE

1 Louis Couturat, *A plea for an international language.* London: Henderson, 1903, p. 3.

2 Peter G. Forster, Esperanto as a social and linguistic movement. *Thought and language in operation* 2 (1971), 201—15.

3 J. C. Flugel, Esperanto and the international language movement. In J. C. Flugel *Men and their motives: psycho-analytical studies.* London: Kegan Paul, Trench, Trubner, 1934, p. 161.

4 W. A. Verloren van Themaat, On the construction of a new artificial language, Eco-logos 18 (1972), 4.

5 H. W. Harrison, *Exit Babel.* London: Allen [1943], p. 63.

6 Albert Guérard, *Europe free and united.* Stanford: Stanford University Press, 1945, p. 165.

7 Mario Pei, *One language for the world.* New York: Devin-Adair, 1958, p. 60.

8 Flugel, *Men and their motives,* pp. 187—99.

9 Eugene Garfield, Let's erect a new tower of Babel, *Current contents* 45 (6 Nov. 1974). Reprinted in his *Essays of an information scientist,* vol. 2. Philadelphia: ISI Press, 1977, pp. 172—4.

10 Edward Sapir and others, Memorandum on the problem of an international auxiliary language, *Romanic review* 16 (1925), 244—56.

11 Edward Sapir, The function of an international auxiliary language. In Edward Sapir, *Culture, language and personality: selected essays*, edited by David G. Mandelbaum. Berkeley: University of California Press, 1966, p. 45.

12 Couturat, *A plea for an international language*, pp. 13—14.

13 Alexander Gode, Interlingua in chemical writing, *Journal of chemical education* 32 (1955), 132—6.

14 Benjamin Lee Whorf, Language, mind and reality. In Benjamin Lee Whorf, *Language, thought and reality: selected writings;* edited by J. B. Carroll. New York: Wiley, 1956, p. 252.

15 Alexander Gode, Interlingua: tool of international communication, *Journal of dental medicine* 11 (1956), 110.

16 Benjamin Lee Whorf, Science and linguistics. In Benjamin Lee Whorf, *Language, thought and reality: selected writings*, p. 214.

17 Michael Cole and Sylvia Scribner, *Culture and thought: a psychological introduction.* New York: Wiley, 1974, pp. 41—2.

18 T. C. Macaulay, Interlanguage. In Elizabeth Daryush (ed.), *The possibility of a universal language.* Oxford: Clarendon Press, 1930, pp. 457—66.

19 J. A. Large, *The foreign-language barrier: problems in scientific communication.* London: Deutsch, 1983.

20 J. E. Holmstrom, The foreign-language barrier, *Aslib proceedings* 14 (1962), 414.

21 Mario Pei, *The story of language*, 2nd edn. London: Allen & Unwin, 1966, pp. 435—41; Pei, *One language for the world*, pp. 206—19.

22 George Steiner, *After Babel: aspects of language and translation.* Oxford: Oxford University Press, 1975, p. 468.

23 S. Frederick Starr, English dethroned, *Change* (May 1978), 27—8.

24 Hiroshi Ohta, Language barriers in Japan: an economist's view, *International social science journal* 31 (1979), 84.

25 Larry E. Smith. English as an International Auxiliary Language, *RELC journal* 7 (1976), 38—42.

26 Steiner, *After Babel*, p. 468.

27 M. I. Isayev, *National languages in the USSR: problems and solutions.* Moscow: Progress, 1977, p. 395.

28 Tamiko Matsumura, Some recent developments in information activities in Japan, *Information services and use* 1 (1981), 144.

29 G. A. Connor and others, *Esperanto: the world interlanguage,* rev. edn. New York: Yoseloff, 1959, p. 8.

30 Joan K. Swinburne, The use of English as the international language of science: a study of the publications and views of a group of French scientists, *The incorporated linguist* 22 (1983), 129—32.

31 Quoted in E. D. Durrant, *The language problem: its history and solution.* Rickmansworth: Esperanto Publishing, 1943, p. 16.

32 Richard E. Wood, A voluntary non-ethnic, non-territorial speech community. In William Francis Mackey and Jacob Ornstein, eds, *Sociolinguistic studies in language contact: methods and cases.* The Hague: Mouton, 1979, pp. 441—2.

33 Connor, *Esperanto*, pp. 5—6.

34 Alexander Gode, The case for Interlingua, *The scientific monthly* 77 (1953), 87.

35 Forster, *Thought and language in operation* 2 (1971), 202.

36 Ibid., p. 213.

37 Bernard Cavanagh, *Esperanto: a first language for all mankind.* London: British Esperanto Association [1971], pp. 22—4.

38 British Esperanto Association, *Newsletter* No. 1 (1977), 4.

39 *British Esperantist* 6 (1910), 202.

40 Ben Patterson, Multilingualism in the European Community, *Multilingua* 1 (1982), 9.

41 I. A. Richards, *Basic English and its uses.* London: Kegan Paul, Trench, Trubner, 1943, p. 11.

42 Karl Vossler, *The spirit of language in civilisation.* London: Kegan Paul, Trench, Trubner, 1932, p. 167.

43 Verloren van Themaat, *Eco-logos* 18 (1972), 3.

Select Bibliography

Acton, H. B., The philosophy of language in Revolutionary France, *Proceedings of the British Academy* 45 (1959), 199—219.

Alston, R. C., *A bibliography of the English language from the invention of printing to the year 1800, 7: Logic, philosophy, epistemology, universal language.* Bradford: Printed for the author by Earnest Cummins, 1967.

Anderson, F. H., *The philosophy of Francis Bacon.* Chicago: University of Chicago Press, 1948.

Anderson, M. S., *The ascendancy of Europe: aspects of European history, 1815—1914.* London: Longman, 1972.

—— *Europe in the eighteenth century, 1713—1783.* Harlow: Longman, 1970.

- Andrade, E. N. Da C., The real character of Bishop Wilkins, *Annals of science* 1 (1936), 4—12.

Appleton, W. A., *A cycle of Cathay: the Chinese vogue in England during the seventeenth and early eighteenth centuries.* New York: Columbia University Press, 1951.

Ashby, Wendy and Clark, Ronald, *Glosa 1000.* Richmond: Glosa, 1984.

Atkinson, Geoffroy, *The extraordinary voyage in French literature, vol. 1: Before 1700.* New York: Franklin, 1920.

—— *The extraordinary voyage in French literature from 1700 to 1720.* Paris: Librairie Ancienne Honoré Champion, 1922.

Aubrey, John, *Aubrey's brief lives:* edited from the original manuscripts and with an introduction by Oliver Lawson Dick, 3rd edn. London: Secker & Warburg, 1960.

Bacon, Francis, *The philosophical works of Francis Bacon*; edited by J. M. Robertson. London: Routledge, 1905.

Baker, Keith Michael, *Condorcet: from natural philosophy to social mathematics.* Chicago: University of Chicago Press, 1975.

Balbin, Julius, Is Esperanto an artificial language?, *Geolinguistics* 8 (1982), 11—27.

Barmine, Alexander, *One who survived.* New York: Putnam, 1945.

Barry, M. D., St. Hildegarde, *New Catholic encyclopedia*, vol. 6. New York: McGraw-Hill, 1967, p. 1117.

Beck, Cave, *The universal character.* London: William Weekley, 1657.

Blackall, Eric A., *The emergence of German as a literary language, 1700—1775.* Cambridge: Cambridge University Press, 1959.

Bloch, Marc, *Feudal society.* London: Routledge & Kegan Paul, 1961.

Boulton, Marjorie, *Zamenhof, creator of Esperanto.* London: Routledge & Kegan Paul, 1960.

The British Esperantist, vol. 1— 1905—.

British Esperanto Association, *Esperanto in the school.* London, 1937.

_____ *Esperanto: the international auxiliary language.* London, 1904.

_____ *Newsletter*, 1972—4.

Bruford, W. H., *Germany in the eighteenth century: the social background of the literary revival.* Cambridge: Cambridge University Press, 1935.

Burnet, James, *Of the origin and progress of language*, vol. 2. Edinburgh: J. Balfour, 1774.

Burney, Pierre, *Les langues internationales.* Paris: Presses Universitaires de France, 1962.

Cavanagh, Bernard, *Esperanto: a first foreign language for all mankind.* London: British Esperanto Association [1971].

Celt, Sandra, The Encyclopaedists on the origin of language: an idiosyncratic synthesis, *The incorporated linguist* 22 (1983), 123—8.

Centre for Research and Documentation on the Language Problem, Basic facts about the international language (Esperanto), *La monda lingvo-problemo* 3 (1971), 164—73.

Christensen, Francis, John Wilkins and the Royal Society's reform of prose style, *Modern language quarterly* 7 (1946), 179—87, 279—90.

Clark, W. J., *International language: past, present and future with specimens of Esperanto and Grammar.* London: Dent, 1907.

Cohen, Jonathan, On the project of a universal character, *Mind* 63 (1954), 49—63.

Cohen, Murray, *Sensible words: linguistic practice in England, 1640—1785.* Baltimore: Johns Hopkins University Press, 1977.

Cole, Michael and Scribner, Sylvia, *Culture and thought: a psychological introduction.* New York: Wiley, 1974.

Comenius, John Amos, *The way of light.* London: Hodder & Stoughton, 1938.

Connor, G. A. et al (eds), *Esperanto: the world interlanguage,* rev. edn. New York: Yoseloff, 1959.

Cooper, J. P. (ed.), *The new Cambridge modern history*, vol. 4. Cambridge: Cambridge University Press, 1970.

Cornelius, Paul, *Languages in seventeenth- and early eighteenth-century imaginary voyages.* Geneva: Librairie Droz, 1965.

Couturat, Louis, D'une application de la logique au problème de la langue internationale. *Revue de métaphysique et de morale* (1908) 761—769.

_____ and Leau, L., *Histoire de la langue universelle.* Paris: Librairie Hachette, 1903.

_____ and others, *International language and science: considerations on the introduction of an international language into science.* London: Constable, 1910.

_____ *La logique de Leibniz: d'après des documents inédits.* Paris: Alcan, 1901.

_____ *A plea for an international language.* London: Henderson, 1903.

Cram, David F., George Dalgarno on *Ars signorum* and Wilkins' *Essay.* In Konrad Koerner, ed. *Progress in linguistic historiography* (Studies in the history of linguistics, vol. 20). Amsterdam: Benjamins, 1980, pp. 113—21.

Cresswell, John and Hartley, John, *Esperanto,* 2nd edn. London: Hodder & Stoughton, 1968.

Dalgarno, George, *Ars signorum, vulgo character universalis et lingua philosophica.* London: J. Hayes, 1661.

Davies, H. Neville, Bishop Godwin's 'Lunatique language', *Journal of the Warburg and Courtauld Institutes* 30 (1967), 296—316.

De Beaufront, Louis, *Complete manual of the auxiliary language Ido,* 3rd edn. London: Pitman, 1919.

DeMott, Benjamin, Comenius and the real character in England, *Publications of the Modern Language Association of America* 70 (1955), 1068—81.

_____ Science versus mnemonics: notes on John Ray and on John Wilkins' *Essay towards a real character, and a philosophical language, Isis* 48 (1957), 3—12.

_____ The sources and development of John Wilkins' philosophical language, *Journal of English and Germanic philology* 57 (1958), 1—13.

Descartes, René, *The philosophical works of Descartes;* rendered into English by E. S. Haldane and G. R. T. Ross, vol. 1. Cambridge: Cambridge University Press, 1911.

Drezen, E., *Osnovy yazykoznaniya: teorii i istorii mezhdunarodnogo yazyka,* 3 vols. Moscow: Ts.K.SESR, 1929.

Durrant, E. D., *The language problem: its history and solution.* Rickmansworth: Esperanto Publishing, 1943.

Dyer, Luther, H., *The problem of an international auxiliary language and its solution in Ido.* London: Pitman, 1923.

Elliott, Ralph W. V., Isaac Newton's 'Of an universall language', *The modern language review* 52 (1957), 1—18.

Emery, Clark, John Wilkins and Noah's Ark, *Modern language quarterly* 9 (1948), 286—91.

Esperanto news, 1975—.

Espinasse, Margaret, *Robert Hooke*. London: Heinemann, 1956.

Esterhill, Frank, Interlinguistics: some further comparative aspects, *Ecologos* 22 (1976), 3—4.

Faiguet de Villeneuve, Joachim, Langue nouvelle. In *Encyclopédie, ou dictionnaire raisonné des sciences, des arts et des métiers,* vol. 9. Paris: A. Neufchastel, 1765, pp. 268—71.

Firth, J. R., *The tongues of men.* London: Watts, 1937.

Fisher, A., Modern languages by way of Esperanto, *Modern languages* 2 (1921), 179—82.

Fishman, Joshua A., *Language and nationalism: two integrative essays.* Rowley, Mass.: Newbury House, 1972.

Flugel, J. C., Esperanto and the international language movement. In J. C. Flugel, *Men and their motives: psycho-analytical studies.* London: Kegan Paul, Trench, Trubner, 1934, pp. 159—213.

Formigari, Lia, *Linguistica ed empirismo nel seicento inglese.* Bari: Editori Laterza, 1970.

Forster, Peter G., Esperanto as a social and linguistic movement, *Thought and language in operation* 2 (1971), 201—15.

―――― *The Esperanto movement.* The Hague: Mouton, 1982.

Funke, Otto, On the sources of John Wilkins' philosophical language (1668), *English studies* 40 (1959), 208—14.

Garfield, Eugene, Let's erect a new Tower of Babel. In E. Garfield, *Essays of an information scientist,* vol. 2. Philadelphia: ISI Press, 1977, pp. 172—4.

Gay, Peter, *The Enlightenment: an interpretation,* 2 vols. London: Weidenfeld & Nicolson, 1967—70.

Gilbert, William, *Problems of languages planned for international use.* Bloomington: Charters, 1971.

Gode, Alexander, The case for Interlingua, *The scientific monthly* 77 (1953), 80—90.

―――― and Blair, Hugh E., *Interlingua: a grammar of the international language,* 2nd edn. New York: Storm, 1951.

―――― Interlingua in chemical writing, *Journal of chemical education* 32 (1955), 132—6.

―――― Interlingua: tool of international communication, *Journal of dental medicine* 11 (1956), 108—17.

Gold, David L., What kind of language is Esperanto?, *Language problems and language planning* 6 (1982), 340—1.

Goodman, Thomas H., Esperanto: threat or ally?, *Foreign language annals* 11 (1978), 201—3.

Gregor, D. B., The cultural value of Esperanto, *Modern languages* 46 (1965), 146—50.

Guérard, A. L., *Europe free and united.* Stanford: Stanford University Press, 1945.

———— *A short history of the international language movement.* London: Unwin, 1922.

Hagler, Margaret, The Esperanto language as a literary medium: a historical discussion of Esperanto literature, 1887—1970, and a stylistic analysis of translated and original Esperanto poetry. Ph.D. Thesis, Indiana University, 1970.

Halloran, J. H., A four year experiment in Esperanto as an introduction to French, *The British journal of educational psychology* 22 (1952), 200—4.

Hampson, Norman, *The Enlightenment.* Harmondsworth: Penguin, 1968.

Harder, Kelsie B., Sir Thomas Urquhart's universal language, *Notes and queries* 201 (1956), 473—6.

Harrison, H. W., *Exit Babel.* London: Allen [1943].

Hartlib, Samuel, *Samuel Hartlib and the advancement of learning;* edited by Charles Webster. Cambridge: Cambridge University Press, 1970.

Haugen, E., The curse of Babel, *Daedalus* 102 (1973), 47—57.

Henderson, P. A. Wright, *The life and times of John Wilkins.* Edinburgh: Blackwood, 1910.

Hertzler, Joyce O., *A sociology of language.* New York: Random House, 1965.

Hitler, Adolf, *Mein Kampf.* Cambridge, Mass.: Riverside, 1943.

Hogben, Lancelot, *Interglossa: a draft of an auxiliary for a democratic world order, being an attempt to apply semantic principles to language design.* Harmondsworth: Penguin, 1943.

Holmstrom, J. E., The foreign-language barrier, *Aslib proceedings* 14 (1962), 413—25.

Isayev, M. I., *National languages in the USSR: problems and solutions.* Moscow: Progress, 1977.

Jacob, H., *On language making: a paper read to the Philological Society, King's College, London, February 6, 1948.* London: Dobson, 1949.

———— (ed.), *On the choice of a common language.* London: Pitman, 1946.

———— *Otto Jesperson: his work for an international auxiliary language.* Loughton: International Language (Ido) Society of Great Britain, 1943.

———— *A planned auxiliary language.* London: Dobson, 1947.

Janton, Pierre, *L'Espéranto.* 2nd edn. Paris: Presses Universitaires de France, 1977.

Jespersen, Otto, *International communication.* London: Kegan Paul, 1931.

An international language. London: Allen & Unwin, 1928.

Johnsen, Julia E. (ed.), *Basic English.* New York: Wilson, 1944.

Jones, Karen Sparck, Some thesauric history, *Aslib proceedings* 24 (1972), 400 – 11.

Jones, Leslie, *Eurolengo, the language for Europe: a practical manual for business and tourism.* Newcastle-upon-Tyne: Oriel Press, 1972.

Jones, Richard Foster, *Ancients and moderns: a study of the rise of the scientific movement in seventeenth-century England,* 2nd edn. Berkeley: University of California Press, 1965.

_____ Science and language in England of the mid-seventeenth century. In Richard Foster Jones, *The seventeenth century: studies in the history of English thought and literature from Bacon to Pope.* Stanford: Stanford University Press, 1951, pp. 143 – 60.

_____ *The triumph of the English language: a survey of opinions concerning the vernacular from the introduction of printing to the Restoration.* London: Oxford University Press, 1953.

Jones, Rowland, *The circles of Gomer, or an essay towards an investigation and introduction of English as an universal language.* London: S. Crowder, 1771.

_____ *Hieroglyfic: or, a grammatical introduction to an universal hieroglyfic language.* London: John Hughs, 1768.

Juliard, Pierre, *Philosophies of language in eighteenth-century France.* The Hague: Mouton, 1970.

Katz, David S., The language of Adam in seventeenth-century England. In Hugh Lloyd-Jones, Valerie Pearl and Blair Worden (eds), *History and imagination.* London: Duckworth, 1981, pp. 132 – 45.

Kelly, Louis G., *The true interpreter: a history of translation theory and practice in the West.* Oxford: Blackwell, 1979.

Kennedy, Hubert C., *Peano: life and works of Giuseppe Peano.* Dordrecht: Reidel, 1980.

Knight, William, *Lord Monboddo and some of his contemporaries.* London: Murray, 1900.

Knowlson, James R., The idea of gesture as a universal language in the XVIIth and XVIIIth centuries, *Journal of the history of ideas* 26 (1965), 495 – 508.

_____ *Universal language schemes in England and France 1600 – 1800.* Toronto: University of Toronto Press, 1975.

Kolakowski, Leszek, *Main currents of Marxism: the rise, growth and dissolution,* vol. 1. Oxford: Clarendon Press, 1978.

Kuehner, Paul, Theories on the origin and formation of language in the eighteenth century in France. Ph.D. Thesis, University of Philadelphia, 1944.

Lach, Donald F., *China in the eyes of Europe: the sixteenth century.* Chicago: University of Chicago Press, 1968.

—— Leibniz and China, *Journal of the history of ideas* 6 (1945), 436—55.

Langer, Susanne K., *Philosophy in a new key: a study in the symbolism of reason, rite and art.* Cambridge, Mass.: Harvard University Press, 1967.

Lapenna, Ivo, The common language question before international organisations. *La monda lingvo-problemo* 2 (1970), 83—100.

—— *Esperanto en perspektivo: faktoj kaj analizoj pri la internacia lingvo.* London: Universala Esperanto-Asocio, 1974.

—— Reply to Mr Macmillan's report: the case for Esperanto, *La monda lingvo-problemo* 3 (1971), 149—61.

Large, J. A., *The foreign-language barrier: problems in scientific communication.* London: Deutsch, 1983.

—— 'Of one language, and of one speech': artificial languages and international communication, *Multilingua* 3 (1984), 11—17.

—— A real character: seventeenth-century universal language schemes, *Multilingua* 2 (1983), 3—8.

Laurat, Lucien, *Staline: la linguistique et l'impérialisme russe.* Paris: Les Isles d'Or, 1951.

League of Nations, *Esperanto as an International Auxiliary Language: Report of the General Secretariat of the League of Nations adopted by the Third Assembly, 1922.* Paris, 1922.

Lieberman, E. James, Esperanto and trans-national identity: the case of Dr Zamenhof, *International journal of the sociology of language* 20 (1979), 89—107.

Lillie, Richard G., Asia and the world language, *Eco-logos* 20 (1974), 2.

Lodwick, Francis, A common writing. In Vivian Salmon, *The works of Francis Lodwick: a study of his writings in the intellectual context of the seventeenth century.* London: Longman, 1972.

—— The ground-work. In Vivian Salmon, *The works of Francis Lodwick: a study of his writings in the intellectual context of the seventeenth century.* London: Longman, 1972.

Long, Bernard, *Esperanto: aims and claims: a discussion of the language problem and its solution.* London: Esperanto Publishing, 1930.

Macaulay, T. C., Interlanguage. In Elizabeth Daryush (ed.), *The possibility of a universal language.* Oxford: Clarendon Press, 1930, pp. 456—68.

McColley, Grant, John Wilkins — a precursor of Locke, *Philosophical review* 47 (1938), 642—3.

McCracken, George, Athanasius Kircher's Universal Polygraphy, *Isis* 39 (1948), 215—28.

McIntosh, Margaret M. C., The phonetic and lingusitic theory of the Royal Society school, from Wallis to Cooper. B.Litt. Thesis, Oxford University, 1956.

Matsumura, Tamiko, Some recent developments in information activities in Japan, *Information services and use* 1 (1981), 139—46.

Miškovská, V. T., La 'Langue nouvelle' de l'Encyclopédie française, *Philologica Pragensia* 4 (1961), 123—5.

Monnerot-Dumaine, M., *Précis d'interlinguistique générale et spéciale.* Paris: Librairie Maloine, 1960.

Müller, Max, *Lectures on the science of language delivered at the Royal Institution of Great Britain in February, March, Apr, and May, 1863.* London: Longman, Green, Longman, Roberts & Green, 1864.

Neurath, Otto, *International picture language: a facsimile reprint of the [1936] English edition.* Reading: Department of Typography and Graphic Communication, University of Reading, 1980.

Nisbet, Stanley, *Esperanto's time has come.* London: Esperanto-Asocio de Brituju, n.d.

Nolting, Louvan E., The deficiency of Esperanto as a world language, *Federal linguist* 5 (1973), 18—22.

Ogden, C. K., *Basic English: a general introduction with rules and grammar,* 6th edn. London: Kegan Paul, Trench, Trubner, 1937.

_____ *Basic English applied (science).* London: Kegan Paul, Trench, Trubner, 1931.

_____ *Basic English versus the artificial languages.* London: Kegan Paul, 1935.

_____ *Basic for science.* London: Kegan Paul, Trench, Trubner, 1942.

_____ *The Basic words: a detailed account of their uses*, 11th edn. London: The Orthological Institute, 1964.

_____ *Brighter Basic: examples of Basic English for young persons of taste and feeling.* London: Kegan Paul, Trench, Trubner, 1931.

_____ *Debabelisation.* London: Kegan Paul, Trench, Trubner, 1931.

_____ *Opposition: a linguistic and psychological analysis.* Bloomington: Indiana University Press, 1967.

_____ *A short guide to Basic English.* Cambridge: The Orthological Institute, n.d.

Ohta, Hirosha, Language barriers in Japan: an economist's views, *International social science journal* 31 (1979), 79—85.

Oldfather, W. A., Latin as an international language, *The classical journal* 16 (1921), 195—206.

Ornstein, Martha, *The role of scientific societies in the seventeenth century.* Hamden: Archon, 1963.

Pankhurst, E. Sylvia, *Delphos: the future of international language.* London: Kegan Paul, Trench, Trubner [1927].

Patterson, Ben, Multilingualism in the European Community, *Multilingua* 1 (1982), 9—15.

Peers, E. A., *'New' tongues or modern-language teaching of the future.* London: Pitman, 1945.

Pei, Mario, *One language for the world.* New York: Devin-Adair, 1958.

―― *The story of language,* 2nd edn. London: Allen & Unwin, 1966.

―― Wanted ― a world language, *Public affairs pamphlets* 434 (1969).

Plot, R., *The natural history of Oxford-shire.* Oxford: At the theater, 1677.

Privat, Edmond, *The life of Zamenhof.* London: Allen & Unwin, 1931.

Pulgram, Ernst, An international language ― when?, *Modern language journal* 32 (1948), 50―68.

Raven, Charles E., *John Ray, naturalist: his life and works.* Cambridge: Cambridge University Press, 1942.

Ray, John, *Further correspondence of John Ray*; edited by R. W. Gunther. London: Printed for the Ray Society, 1928.

―― *Philosophical letters between the late learned Mr. Ray and several of his ingenious correspondents, natives and foreigners.* London: William and John Innys, 1718.

Ricci, Matthew, *China in the sixteenth century: the Journals of Matthew Ricci, 1583―1610*; translated by Louis J. Gallagher. New York: Random House, 1953.

Richards, I. A., *Basic English and its uses.* London: Kegan Paul, Trench, Trubner, 1943.

Roget, Peter Mark, *Roget's thesaurus of English words and phrases*; new edition by Robert A. Dutch. London: Longman, 1962.

Rossi, Paolo, *Francis Bacon: from magic to science.* London: Routledge & Kegan Paul, 1968.

Rundle Stanley, *Language as a social and political factor in Europe.* London: Faber & Faber, 1946.

Russell, Bertrand, *The autobiography of Bertrand Russell.* London: Unwin Paperbacks, 1975.

Sack, F. L., *The problem of an international language.* Edinburgh: World Organisation of the Teaching Profession, 1951.

Sadler, Victor and Lins, Ulrich, Regardless of frontiers: a case study in linguistic persecution. In Samir K. Ghosh (ed.), *Man, language and society.* The Hague: Mouton, 1972, pp. 206―15.

Salmon, Vivian, *The study of language in 17th-century England.* Amsterdam: Benjamins, 1979.

―― *The works of Francis Lodwick: a study of his writings in the intellectual context of the seventeenth century.* London: Longman, 1972.

Sapir, Edward, The function of an international auxiliary language. In E. Sapir, *Culture, language and personality: selected essays;* edited by David G. Mandelbaum. Berkeley: University of California Press, 1966, pp. 45―64.

_____ and others, Memorandum on the problem of an international auxiliary language, *Romanic review* 16 (1925), 244—56.

Schlauch, Margaret, *The gift of tongues.* London: Allen & Unwin, 1943.

Seigel, Jules Paul, The Enlightenment and the evolution of a language of signs in France and England, *Journal of the history of ideas* 30 (1969), 96—115.

Sexton, B. C., Esperanto and Interlingua: interlanguages in perspective. *Ecologos* 22 (1976), 3—6.

Shapiro, Barbara J., *John Wilkins 1614—1672: an intellectual biography.* Berkeley: University of California Press, 1969.

_____ Latitudinarianism and science in seventeenth-century England, *Past and present* 40 (1968), 16—41.

Shenton, Herbert N., Sapir, Edward and Jespersen, Otto, *International communication: a symposium on the language problem.* London: Kegan Paul, Trench, Trubner, 1931.

Sherwood, Bruce Arne and Cheng, Chin-Chuan, A linguistics course on international communication and constructed languages, *Studies in the linguistic sciences* 10 (1980), 189—201.

Slaughter, M. M., *Universal languages and scientific taxonomy in the seventeenth century.* Cambridge: Cambridge University Press, 1982.

Smith, Larry E., English as an International Auxiliary Language, *RELC journal* 7 (1976), 38—42.

Solzhenitsyn, Alexander, *The Gulag archipelago, 1918—1956.* Glasgow: Collins, 1974.

Spinka, Matthew, *John Amos Comenius: that incomparable Moravian.* Chicago: University of Chicago Press, 1943.

Sprague, Charles E., *Handbook of Volapük.* London: Trubner, 1888.

Springer, George P., *Early Soviet theories in communication.* Cambridge, Mass.: MIT Press, 1956.

Starr, S. Frederick, English dethroned, *Change* (May 1978), 26—31.

Steiner, George, *After Babel: aspects of language and translation.* Oxford: Oxford University Press, 1975.

Stimson, Dorothy, Comenius and the Invisible College, *Isis* 23 (1935), 373—88.

_____ Dr Wilkins and the Royal Society, *Journal of modern history* 3 (1931), 539—63.

_____ *Scientists and amateurs: a history of the Royal Society.* New York: Greenwood Press, 1968.

Stojan, P. E., *Bibliografio de internacia lingvo.* Geneva: Bibliografia Servo de Universala Esperanto-Asocio, 1929.

Swinburne, Joan K., The use of English as the international language of science: a study of the publications and views of a group of French scientists, *The incorporated linguist* 22 (1983), 129—32.

Talmey, Max, *Ido: exhaustive text book of the International Language of the Delegation.* New York: Ido Press, 1919.

Tonkin, Humphrey, Equalising language, *Journal of communication* 29 (1979), 124—33.

—— *Esperanto and international language problems: a research bibliography,* 4th edn. Washington: Esperantic Studies Foundation, 1977.

—— and Hoeksema, Thomas, *Esperanto and literary translation.* Rotterdam: Universal Esperanto Association, 1982 (Esperanto Documents No. 29A).

—— An introduction to Esperanto studies, *Esperanto documents,* new series, 6A (1976).

Turnbull, G. H., *Samuel Hartlib: a sketch of his life and his relations to J. A. Comenius.* London: Oxford University Press, 1920.

—— Samuel Hartlib's influence on the early history of the Royal Society, *Notes and records of the Royal Society of London* 10 (1953), 101—30.

Turner, A. J., Andrew Paschall's tables of plants for the universal language, *Bodleian Library record* 9 (1978), 346—50.

Urquhart, Thomas, *The admirable Urquhart: selected writings;* edited by Richard Boston. London: Fraser, 1975.

Vallon, D., Teaching the universal language, *California Teachers Association journal* (May 1968), pp. 21—4.

Verloren van Themaat, W. A., Literature in a constructed language, *La monda lingvo-problemo* 4 (1972), 153—8.

—— On the construction of a new artificial language, *Eco-logos* 18 (1972), 3—5.

—— Relative merits of Esperanto and Interlingua, *Eco-logos* 21 (1975), 7—11.

—— Whorfian linguistic relativism and constructed languages, *International language reporter* No. 3, 15 (1969), 19—24.

Vickery, B. C., The significance of John Wilkins in the history of bibliographical classification, *Libri* 2 (1953), 326—43.

Vives, Juan Luis, *On education;* translated and with an introduction by Foster Watson. Cambridge: Cambridge University Press, 1913.

Vossler, Karl, *The spirit of language in civilisation.* London: Kegan Paul, Trench, Trubner, 1932.

Wallis, John, *A defence of the Royal Society and the Philosophical transactions in answer to the cavils of Dr. William Holder.* London: by T. S. for Thomas Moore, 1678.

Ward, Seth, *Vindiciae academiarum.* Oxford: by Leonard Lichfield for Thomas Robinson, 1654.

Waringhien, Gaston, Le problème d'une langue auxiliaire mondiale, *Norsk Tidsskrift for Sprogvidenskap* 19 (1960), 591—4.

Wells, H. G., *The shape of things to come*. London: Hutchinson, 1933.

Whitmore, Charles E., The problem of a universal language, *Scientific monthly* 71 (1950), 337—42.

Whitrow, Magda, An eighteenth-century faceted classification system, *Journal of documentation* 39 (1983), 88—94.

Whorf, Benjamin Lee, *Language, thought and reality: selected writings*; edited by J. B. Carroll. New York: Wiley, 1956.

—— Languages and logic, *Technology review* (April 1941), 250—72.

Wilkins, John, *The discovery of a new world in the moone*. London: Michael Sparl and Edward Forrest, 1638.

—— *An essay towards a real character, and a philosophical language*. London: Sa. Gellibrand and John Martin, 1668.

—— *Mercury, or the secret and swift messenger*. 2nd edn., London: Rich. Baldwin, 1694.

Williams, Norman, A plea for Esperanto, *Head teachers' review* (October 1952), pp. 136—8.

Wood, Richard E., Current work in the linguistics of Esperanto, *Geolingusitics* 7 (1981), 81—125.

—— Proceedings of the Symposium on the Teaching of Esperanto at United States Universities and Colleges, *La monda lingvo-problemo* 4 (1972), 159—74.

—— A voluntary non-ethnic, non-territorial speech community. In William Francis Mackey and Jacob Ornstein, eds, *Sociolinguistic studies in language contact: methods and cases*. The Hague: Mouton, 1979, pp. 433—50.

Yates, Frances A., *The art of memory*. London: Routledge & Kegan Paul, 1966.

Yost, R. M., *Leibniz and philosophical analysis*. Berkeley: University of California Press, 1954.

Young, Robert Fitzgibbon, *Comenius in England*. London: Oxford University Press, 1932.

Zamenhof, L. L. (Dr Esperanto), *An attempt towards an international language*. New York: Holt, 1889.

Index